ESSENTIALS

COLLEGE ONLINE KEYBOARDING

Keyboarding & Formatting

LESSONS 1-60

Microsoft® Word 2007

2e

Enter

Susie H. VanHuss, Ph.D.
Distinguished Professor Emeritus
University of South Carolina

Connie M. Forde, Ph. D.
Department of Instructional
Systems, Leadership, and
Workforce Development
Mississippi State University

Donna L. Woo
Department Chair
Computer Information Systems
Cypress College
Cypress, California

THOMSON
*
SOUTH-WESTERN

D0146958

Australia Brazil Canada Mexico Singapore Spain United Kingdom United States

THOMSON

SOUTH-WESTERN

Keyboarding & Formatting Essentials, Lessons 1–60, Second Edition
Susie VanHuss, Connie Forde, Donna Woo

VP/Editorial Director:
Jack W. Calhoun

VP/Editor-in-Chief:
Karen Schmohe

Acquisitions Editor:
Jane Phelan

Sr. Developmental Editor:
Dave Lafferty

Consulting Editor:
Mary Todd
Todd Publishing Services

Marketing Manager:
Valerie Lauer

Marketing Coordinator:
Kelley Gilreath

Sr. Content Project Manager:
Martha Conway

Manager of Technology, Editorial:
Liz Prigge

Sr. Technology Project Editor:
Mike Jackson

Sr. Manufacturing Coordinator:
Charlene Taylor

Production House:
GGS Book Services

Printer:
Quebecor World – Eusey Press
Leominster, MA

Copyeditor:
Gary Morris

Art Director:
Bethany Casey

Cover and Internal Designer:
Grannan Graphic Design, Ltd.

Cover Images:
Grannan Graphic Design, Ltd.

Photography Manager:
Deanna Ettinger

Photo Researcher:
Terri Miller

COPYRIGHT © 2008, 2005
Thomson South-Western, a part of The
Thomson Corporation. Thomson, the
Star logo, and South-Western are
trademarks used herein under license.

Printed in the United States of America
1 2 3 4 5 10 09 08 07

Student Edition ISBN 13:
978-0-538-97468-4
Student Edition ISBN 10: 0-538-97468-0

Data CD ISBN 13: 978-0-538-97467-7
Data CD ISBN 10: 0-538-97467-2

Student Edition with CD ISBN 13:
978-0-538-72976-5
Student Edition with CD ISBN 10:
0-538-72976-7

ALL RIGHTS RESERVED.
No part of this work covered by the
copyright hereon may be reproduced
or used in any form or by any means—
graphic, electronic, or mechanical,
including photocopying, recording,
taping, Web distribution or information
storage and retrieval systems, or in any
other manner—without the written
permission of the publisher.

For permission to use material from this
text or product, submit a request online
at http://www.thomsonrights.com.

For more information about our products,
contact us at:

Thomson Higher Education
5191 Natorp Boulevard
Mason, Ohio 45040
USA

Microsoft is a registered trademark of Microsoft Corporation in the U.S. and/or other countries.

The names of all products mentioned herein are used for identification purposes only and may be trademarks or registered trademarks of their respective owners. Thomson South-Western disclaims any affiliation, association, connection with, sponsorship, or endorsement by such owners.

CONTENTS

LEVEL 1
Developing Keyboarding Skill
LESSONS 1–25

LEVEL 2
Formatting Essentials
LESSONS 26–60

SUMMARY OF FUNCTIONS

Lesson	Functions	Lesson	Functions
Module 3 Word Processing Basics		**Module 5 Simple Reports**	
26	Text Formats: Font, Font Size, Grow Font, Shrink Font, Bold, Italic, Underline, Text Highlight Color, and Font Color	38	Styles
	Save and Save As	39	Cover Page
	Close Document	40	Page Numbers
	Open New Document		Remove Page Numbers
	Open Existing Document		Line and Page Breaks
	Quick Print, Print, and Print Preview		Insert File
	Exit Word	42	Hanging Indent
27	Paragraph Formats: Show/Hide	43	Footnotes
	Alignment—Align Text Left, Center, Align Text Right, and Justify	**Module 6 Create Tables**	
	Bullets and Numbering	46	Insert Table
	Line Spacing		Table Tools
	Remove Space Before Paragraph	47	Adjust Column Width
	Clipboard Group: Cut, Copy, and Paste		Center Table Horizontally
	Format Painter		Table Styles
	Quick Access Toolbar	48	Change Table Structure
	Mini Toolbar		Merge and Split Cells
28	Date and Time	49	Shading in Tables
	Margins		Change Row Height and Center Text
	Indent		Remove Table Borders
	View Ruler		Decimal Tab in Table
	Tabs	**Module 7 Edit Business Documents**	
29	Views	52	Symbols
	Slider: Zoom in or out		Special Characters
	Spelling and Grammar		Clipboard
	Help		Paste Options Button
Module 4 Business Correspondence			Find and Replace
31	Vertical Page Position		Customize Quick Access Toolbar
32	Automatic Current Date		Thesaurus
	Center Page	**Module 8 Graphic Essentials**	
33	Envelopes	58	Clip Art
35	Normal Style (default)		Paragraph Borders and Shading
	Change Styles		Page Borders
			Shapes
		59	Columns
			Wrap Text Around Graphic

FOCUS ON THE ESSENTIALS

Building a skill takes practice, and that's what you'll get with the *Keyboarding Essentials 2E* series. More timed writings, five supplemental keyboarding lessons using the keyboarding software, and technique drills throughout.

This versatile skill development program combines keying from the text and computer screen to provide well-rounded practice.

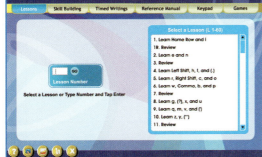

EASY-TO-USE, INTERACTIVE SOFTWARE

Keyboarding Pro DELUXE teaches keyboarding skills in the first 25 lessons and then checks the speed and accuracy of timed writings, drills, and formatting and accuracy in documents for lessons 26–60.

Keyboarding Pro 5 is also available for a keyboarding short course (Lessons 1–25).

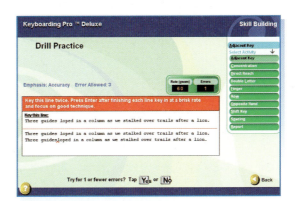

Skill Builders provide numerous Technique Builders and Timed Writings to strengthen skill.

What's more, *Keyboarding Pro* includes 20 additional lessons with both speed and accuracy emphasis that challenge you at every level to improve. Five new assessments help place you at the right level of instruction.

FORMATTING USING MICROSOFT® WORD 2007

Keyboarding Essentials 2E teaches document formatting using the commands of *Microsoft Word 2007*. Defaults have changed with this new version of *Word* and so have the rules for formatting business documents. You'll also learn to create business documents using traditional *Word 2003* formats so you'll be prepared for any workplace situation.

Keyboarding Pro DELUXE software checks documents for accuracy of keystrokes and commands.

Text includes instructions to support *Microsoft Word 2007* and offers many tips for a smooth transition into the new software.

UP-TO-DATE FORMATS

New formats are explained and illustrated with callouts for proper placement.

Model documents make learning easy.

INTERACTIVE REFERENCE MANUAL

Multimedia Presentations reinforce *Word* commands, communication skills, and document formats. Pretests, posttests, and visual learning are all at your fingertips with *Keyboarding Pro DELUXE*.

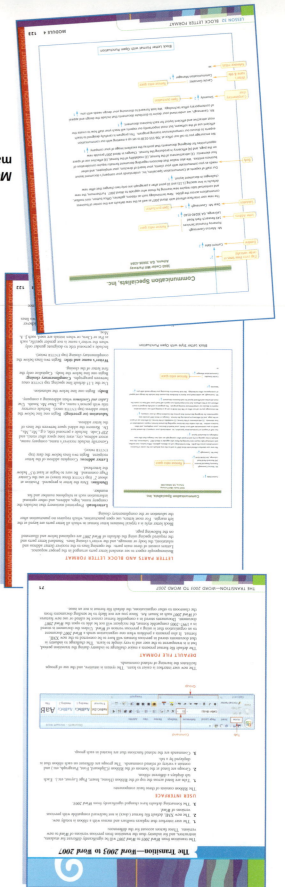

Communication Skills reinforce language arts skills such as proofreading, capitalization, and composition.

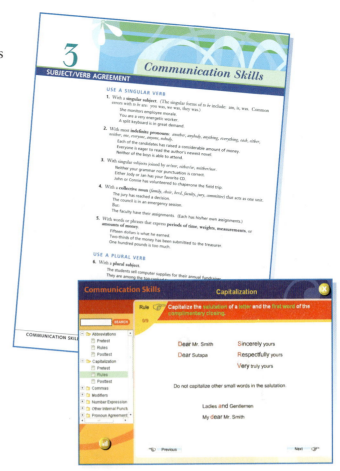

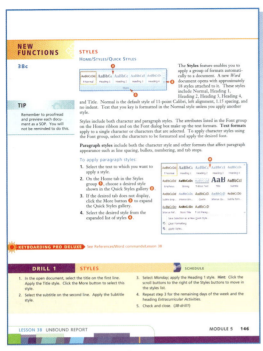

Drills reinforce new functions.

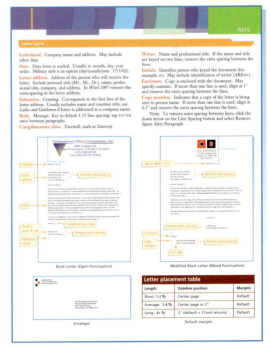

Convenient *file transfer options*—from the Internet or a portable device to another workstation—makes learning on-the-go easy!

KEYBOARDING PRO DELUXE SOFTWARE

The enhanced *Web Reporter* for distance learning allows instructors to manage classes, create a grade book, and add comments to student reports. Students can view these comments online.

The *Reference Manual* provides easy access to model documents.

KEYBOARDING ESSENTIALS 2E

This comprehensive series offers 120 lessons in three different texts: Lessons 1–60 focus on basic keyboarding and formatting; Lessons 61–120 moves onto more advanced formatting and document processing; and the complete course offers all lessons in one convenient text.

REVIEWERS

Debbie Franklin
Bryant & Stratton College
Orchard Park, NY

Jane E. McDowell
Columbus State Community College
Columbus, OH

Teresa Moore
Volunteer State Community College
Gallatin, TN

Vicki R. Robertson
Southwest Tennessee Community College
Memphis, TN

Alice Smith
Indiana Business College
West Lafayette, IN

Karen Van Dyke
St. Louis Community College
St. Louis, MO

Penny Mize Uphaus
Sullivan University
Fort Knox, KY

A WORD FROM THE AUTHORS

Thank you for your support of our keyboarding texts over the past many years. We have designed this text especially for those who need an essentials keyboarding and document formatting approach. We hope our series meets your needs.

Susie VanHuss
Connie Forde
Donna Woo

FORMATTING & DOCUMENT PROCESSING, LESSONS 61–120
(0-538-72979-1)
Document processing is the focus of this text. Five modules focus on designing specialized documents for today's business world: Forms and Financial Documents, Graphic Enhancements, Mass Mailings, Meeting Management, and Legal, Medical, and Employment Documents. A software training manual reviews functions learned in Lessons 1–60.

KEYBOARDING ESSENTIALS COMPLETE, LESSONS 1–120
(0-538-72980-5)
The complete course offers all lessons in one convenient text.

KEYBOARDING PRO DELUXE
(0-538-73006-4)
This all-in-one interactive software combines new key learning and skill building lessons with document production software for *Microsoft Word 2007*. It includes error diagnostics, error checking of both keystrokes and common commands, and multimedia presentations of *Word* functions, communication skills, and document formats.

NEW! SKILL BUILDING PRO
(0-538-72991-0)
Developing speed and accuracy has never been easier or more fun. This fully integrated text and software program includes 60 lessons of instruction as well as self-paced writings, drill practices, timed writings with error diagnostics, games for building skill, and a word processor.

WELCOME TO KEYBOARDING PRO DELUXE

Keyboarding Pro DELUXE is an all-in-one Keyboarding and Document Processing software that builds on the popular *Keyboarding Pro 5*. This interactive software combines new key learning, skill building, and document processing using *Microsoft Word 2007*.

Keyboarding Pro DELUXE includes features such as new key learning; error diagnostics with related drill practice; engaging games; error checking of both keystroke accuracy and common *Word* commands; multimedia presentations on *Word 2007* commands, communication skills, and document formats. It includes 120 lessons. You may be using *Keyboarding Pro 5*, which includes the first 25 lessons of *Keyboarding Pro DELUXE* as well as skill building lessons for speed and accuracy, timed writings, and the numeric keypad lessons and drills.

HOW DO I GET STARTED?

Detailed information is given in the Student's User Guide packaged with your software.

Step 1: Begin by installing the software on your home computer.

Step 2: From the Start menu, select Programs, then South-Western Keyboarding, and click *Keyboarding Pro DELUXE* or *Keyboarding Pro 5*. The Log In dialog box appears. Select the New User button.

Step 3: The first time you use *Keyboarding Pro*, key your user information in the New Student dialog box to create a student record. Do this only once so that all lessons are stored in one file.

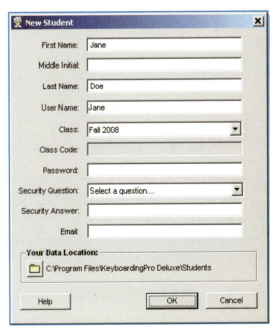

- To select the class in which you are enrolled, click the down arrow on the Class field.
- If your class will be online and you will be using the Web Reporter for managing files, enter a Class Code to easily send your files to your instructor using your browser. When your instructor provides you with the Class Code, copy and paste it into this field. To *copy* the Class Code, hold down the CTRL key and tap *C*; then paste it (CTRL + V) into the Class Code field. (**Note:** If this is an online course, the Class Code field will be active.)
- Notice that by default your student record is saved to C:\Program Files\ KeyboardingPro Deluxe\Students. If you will be saving to a network drive, click the Folder button and browse to identify the path. Click OK.

Step 4: The first time you enter *Keyboarding Pro*, you may be required to key a Skill Analysis to evaluate your current skill level.

The software and the textbook work together. In Lessons 1–25, the software will show you the new key locations and automatically provide a variety of drills. You'll key Textbook Keying exercises and Timed Writings from the book. In Lessons 26–120, you'll key all timings, documents, and tests from your textbook and use multimedia features to review related skills.

Each time you enter *Keyboarding Pro* after the first time, the Log In dialog box displays your name. Select your name and key your password. If you do not see your name, click the Folder button and locate the drive where your student record is located.

To transfer your student record from a portable device such as a flash drive, diskette, or other media, browse to identify the path. If you have sent your student record to the Web Reporter previously, you can update your current file from the Web.

Main Menu

The Main menu provides the primary navigation. It includes tabs for selecting a lesson, a timed writing, and many other options. The first time you enter *Keyboarding Pro*, you may be required to key a Skill Analysis to evaluate your current skill level.

Lessons: The number of lessons available to you depends on the length of your course; typically you will see L1–25, Lessons 1–60, or Lessons 1–120. Results are reported in the Summary Report.

Skill Building: After you know the alphabetic keys (Lesson 10), use these 20 lessons to boost your keyboarding skill. Optional exercises are available for building your skill, including Technique Builders that correlate with supplementary skill building pages in the textbook and Drill Practices that recommend error-diagnostic drills to correct accuracy problems. Results are reported in the Skill Building Report.

Timed Writings: Most timed writings in the textbook are available for additional practice or measurement purposes. Error diagnostics tracks specific accuracy problems and then suggests drills by row, by finger, or by type to improve your accuracy (Lesson 26 and beyond). Your results are reported in the Timed Writing Report.

References: Multimedia presentations reinforce the commonly used *Word 2007* commands. Communication Skills review topics such as proofreading and word usage; a pretest and posttest will help you evaluate your progress. Document Formats illustrate and review common business document formats.

Keypad: You will learn the numeric keypad by touch and build your skill.

NAVIGATION

The buttons at the bottom of the *Keyboarding Pro* main screen will help you execute common functions.

Help answers questions about the screen you are on.

Word Processor enables you to create documents or take timings; it does not launch *Word 2007*.

Send File transmits your student record to your instructor. If you have enrolled in an online course (see step 2 on page ix), your student record will automatically be attached; you can select other files to send as well. You must be logged onto the Internet in order to send files.

Web Reports enables you to view reports online or view comments your instructor may have posted for you. When you get to the link, key your user information from step 2 on page ix.

Log In allows you to transfer your student files to another location such as a portable device (flash drive or to the server) or to the Web Reporter.

Exit quits the program.

HOW DO I COMPLETE DOCUMENTS IN *WORD 2007*?

Beginning in Lesson 26, you will create business documents in *Word 2007*. When you choose a document that is created in *Word 2007*, the Document Options dialog box displays. The first time you key each document, the option *Begin new document* displays, which automatically launches *Word 2007*.

The Document toolbar displays in the upper-right corner. Click the Back button and the document saves automatically without checking it. Click the Check button when you have proofread the document for mistakes and previewed for placement.

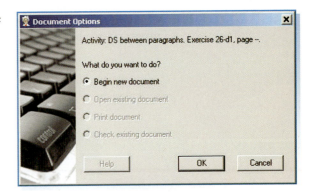

Back   Help

Check

The Document toolbar changes when the checked document is displayed. Click Display Error List to identify the types of mistakes you have made. The error number correlates to the numbered errors on the document. Use the Print command of *Word* if you wish to print the document. Close the document to return to the Lesson menu and continue with the rest of the lesson.

Help   Display Error List   Close the Document

To complete *Word* documents, follow these standard procedures:

1. Key and format the document as directed in the textbook.

2. Proofread for keying or formatting errors. Verify your document against the exercise in the textbook. Preview for placement.

3. Check the document when you are completely satisfied. The software will check the accuracy and display a checked version on screen. Mistakes will be counted above each paragraph and errors will be highlighted.

4. Select Display Error List for an explanation of each error.

5. Scroll to the bottom of the screen to view the report of errors, *gwam*, number of errors, etc.

6. Print the document using the *Word* Print command if desired.

7. Close the document from the *Keyboarding Pro DELUXE* toolbar.

If you wish to edit the document (make corrections), select it again from the Lesson menu. From the Document Options dialog box, choose *Open existing document*. Revise the document as desired and again proofread, preview, check, and close it.

WHAT ELSE SHOULD I KNOW?

Reports. Numerous reports are available by selecting Reports from the menu bar. The Summary Report includes a brief summary of each lesson completed. You can link to a specific lesson report from the Summary Report. The Skill Building Report includes the results of your progress on the Accuracy and Speed Lessons, Drill Practice, and more. The Timed Writing Report tracks the result of your last 20 timings and the best timings at each length. The Document and Production Test Report summarizes the results and grades on those completed.

Web Reports. If you are enrolled in a course that is using the Web Reporter, click the Send File button to send your student report to your instructor. Select any specific document files that you wish to attach. These files are attached automatically when you click Send.

WINDOWS VISTA

When you turn on your computer using *Windows Vista*, it may open to the *Welcome Center*, depending on whether the checkbox for *Run at startup* has been left selected. If the checkbox is de-selected, the "Logon screen" or the "Sign-on screen" immediately appears after booting. This screen lists any users who have been signed up to use the computer. Once a user is selected, you are prompted to enter your password. Enter the password, and the *desktop* appears, displaying an attractive picture. Like the top of a desk, this screen serves as a surface for your work. Your computer manufacturer may have chosen the picture, or you may have selected one during installation.

While the *Windows Vista* desktop looks relatively simple, it contains many sophisticated tools. We will be learning about some of the most important tasks that can be performed from this screen.

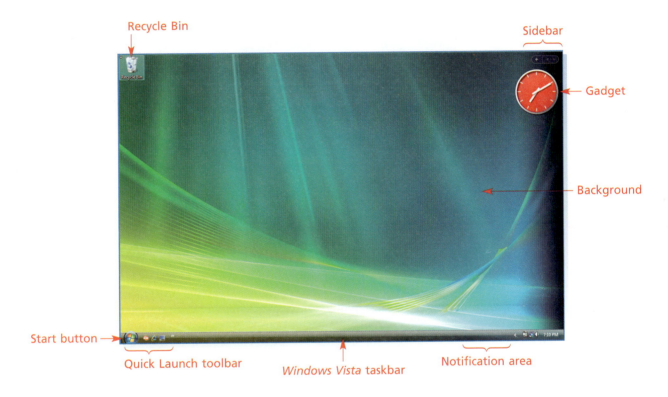

Recycle Bin · Sidebar · Gadget · Background · Start button · Quick Launch toolbar · *Windows Vista* taskbar · Notification area

The *taskbar* is located at the bottom of your screen. It shows which programs are running and allows you to switch to a different program. *Vista* shows a thumbnail sketch of running programs when you hold your mouse over a running program in the taskbar.

Thumbnail of *Microsoft Word*

Install updates

Lock computer

Switch users, log off, sleep, restart, hibernate, shut down

Help

All Programs

Selected list of most frequently used programs

Commonly used folders

Pinned programs

Current user's name and picture

On the right side of the screen, *Sidebar* contains small programs called *gadgets*. *Vista* ships with several interesting gadgets including a clock, currency converter, calculator, and news headlines. You can add or remove gadgets from the *Sidebar*, and additional gadgets are available online.

The Start button is located at the bottom, left-hand corner of the screen. The Start button opens the Start menu, which acts as a gateway to your computer's programs, folders, and settings. Click it to open the Start menu. It is called a menu because it provides a list of choices.

The left pane of the Start menu contains the *pinned program list* and the Search results box. Pinned programs are programs that you use regularly, so *Vista* creates a shortcut to them. You can pin or unpin a program icon to the Start menu by right-clicking it and then choosing Pin to Start Menu or Remove from this list.

The right side of the Start menu contains shortcuts to many of *Vista*'s predefined folders. Quick access to features such as Search, Control Panel, and Help are also available here. You can install updates, lock your computer, put it to sleep, restart it, shut it off, or switch users from here as well.

GET HELP

The Help function in *Windows Vista* is quite extensive. You can also set an option in Help so that *Vista* connects to the Internet any time you search for help.

To access Help, click the Start button; then choose Help and Support. The fastest way to get help is to type a word or phrase in the Search box. You can also click the Browse Help button and then click an item in the index listing of subject headings that appears. Some subject headings contain Help topics within a subject heading. Click the Help topic to open it, and click the subheading to narrow your search.

If you don't find what you need using the Search box or the Browse Help button, you can access Windows Online Help and Support. If all else fails, you can contact a technical support professional via phone, e-mail, or live chat.

Tip: You can also tap F1 to access Help.

CUSTOMIZE THE DESKTOP

Once you begin using *Vista* on a regular basis, you may want to customize your desktop. One of the easiest ways to personalize *Vista* is to change the *desktop background* (formerly called the wallpaper). Change the desktop background if you have a favorite picture you have taken with your camera and want to use it as the background. *Windows Vista* also includes several sample desktop backgrounds that you may choose.

To change the background:

1. Right-click on an empty part of the desktop and choose Personalize. The Vista Personalize appearance and sounds dialog box appears (providing options to).
2. Click the Desktop Background link. The Choose a Desktop Background dialog box appears.
3. Click the down arrow to choose from different groups of pictures, or browse to locate the picture saved in another area. Click the desired picture to use as the desktop background.
4. Choose how you would like to position the picture (*Fit to screen*, *Tile*, or *Center*). Fit to screen covers the entire desktop; Tile repeats a small version of the picture over and over until it fills the entire desktop; Center places the picture in the middle of the desktop and a colored border fills any gaps.
5. Click OK.

Windows Vista allows you to customize your desktop in many other ways including adding a new gadget, controlling icons, changing the mouse pointer, or selecting a screen saver. You may wish to access the *Vista Help* feature to learn about these methods to personalize your desktop.

FILE MANAGEMENT

File management includes the process of creating and managing the electronic files on your computer. Using *Windows Vista*, you can perform many common file-related tasks, such as renaming, deleting files, or compressing files.

In this section, you will also learn to work with auxiliary drives, including CD/DVD and universal serial bus (USB) flash drives. USB flash drives vary in size and shape and can hold gigabytes of information. They are also called thumb drives, key chain drives, and memory keys. Data that needs to be used again in the future must be saved on a storage device such as a USB flash drive, CD/DVD, or hard drive.

UNDERSTAND THE FILE SYSTEM

As with paper files, it is important to establish a logical and easy-to-use computer file management procedure to organize files efficiently so that you can find them quickly and easily. The *Windows Vista* operating system provides a file management program, *Windows Explorer*, which helps you keep track of your files and folders.

USB flash drive

USE WINDOWS EXPLORER

From the desktop, *Windows Explorer* is used to perform many common file management tasks. *Windows Explorer* displays locations such as hard disk drives, CD or DVD drives, removable storage media, or network locations that are connected to your computer. You can also access an external device that might be connected to your computer, such as a digital camera. The figure below displays parts of the *Explorer* window.

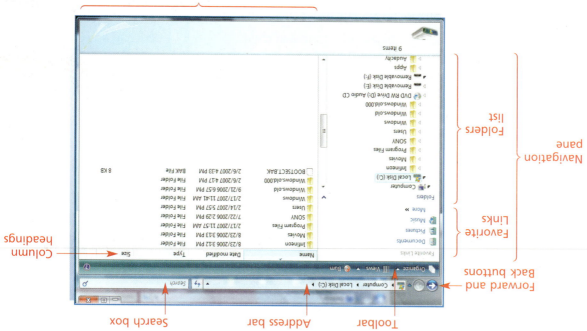

- Files and Folders pane
- Folders list
- Navigation pane
- Favorite Links
- Column headings
- Back buttons
- Forward and Back buttons
- Toolbar
- Address bar
- Search box

At the top of the *Explorer* window, the Address bar displays the currently viewed location as well as a series of links separated by arrows. It shows the path, including folders to arrive at the location displayed. You can click links within the Address bar to navigate to a different folder without closing the current folder window.

Use the Back and Forward buttons on the Address bar to navigate to other folders you have already opened without closing the current window. After you use the Address bar to change folders, for example, you can use the Back button to return to the original folder.

The Navigation pane is located on the left, and it displays the drives and the folders stored on each computer drive. View the files within a folder by clicking the folder.

The Search box searches for a file or subfolder stored in the current folder. The search begins as soon as you begin typing, so as you type *L*, for example, all the files that start with the letter *L* will appear in the folder's file list. Column headings change how the files in the file list are organized. You can sort or group files in the current view.

The toolbar performs common tasks, such as changing the appearance of your files and folders, copying files to a CD, or starting a digital picture slide show. The toolbar's buttons change to show only the commands that are useful. For example, if you click a picture file, the toolbar shows different buttons than it would if you clicked a music file.

The files display in the right pane, called the *Files and Folders pane*. The *Navigation pane* (displayed on the right) contains two parts: the *Favorite Links* (top part) and the *Folders* (the bottom part). The *Favorite Links* area lists places to which you want quick access. The *Folders* list shows a hierarchy of your computer. It displays the drives and folders on your computer.

To access *Windows Explorer*:

1. Right-click on the Start button and select Explore.
2. In the left Folders list, scroll down until you see the desired storage device drive or folder and click.

CHANGE VIEWS OF FILES AND FOLDERS

Clicking the Views button on the toolbar changes the way the file and folder icons are displayed. Each time you click the Views button, the folder window alternates from *List*, *Details*, *Tiles*, and *Large Icons*. Click the arrow next to the Views button and move the slider up or down to view and select one of the other view selections.

WORK WITH FILES AND FOLDERS

Folders are extremely important in organizing files. You will create and manage folders and the files within them so that you can easily locate them. A folder can store files; or in some cases, a folder is used to store additional folders where files are stored. This folder-in-a-folder organization helps to reduce clutter so you can find, navigate, and manage your files, folders, and disks with greater speed. Folders within folders are called subfolders.

All files and folders are represented by an icon. You will know that a folder contains another folder when it has the right-pointing arrow to the left of the folder icon. To "expand" or show the contents of a folder with a right-pointing open arrow, click the arrow icon to the left of the folder name. The triangle changes to a down-pointing solid triangle. Double-click a folder in the Files and Folders pane to open the folder.

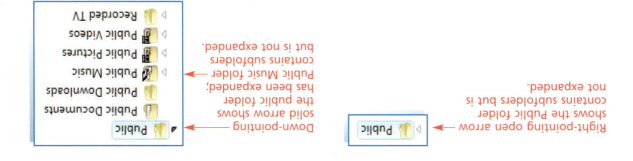

Right-pointing open arrow shows the Public folder contains subfolders but is not expanded.

Down-pointing solid arrow shows the public folder has been expanded; Public Music folder contains subfolders but is not expanded.

To create a folder:

1. Access an *Explorer window* and display the contents of the desired storage device. Click the Organize drop-down arrow and choose New Folder.
2. A new folder displays with the name *New Folder*. The insertion point is blinking next to the highlighted words *New Folder*. Key the desired folder name and tap ENTER.

1. Access *Windows Explorer* and display the contents of your removable storage drive (or the location where you have been instructed to save your document files).
2. Create a folder named *Assignments*.
3. Open the *Assignments* folder, and create a subfolder named *Keyboarding*.
4. Access the contents of your storage drive in the Folders list. Expand the *Assignments* folder located on your storage drive and view its contents.
5. Open the *Assignments* folder. Within it, create a subfolder named *Accounting*.
6. Access Help and Support and use search to get help on *Create folder*. When the search results appear, choose *Create a new folder*. Read the information. Close Help.
7. The *Assignments* folder should be open. Create a subfolder called *Term Papers*.
8. Close *Windows Explorer*.

NAMING FILES

Good file organization begins with giving your folders and files names that are logical and easy to understand. In Drill 1, you created a folder named *Assignments*. You created a new folder within *Assignments* to separate Keyboarding assignments from your Accounting assignments.

In a later lesson, you will be creating a folder named *Module 3* to hold all work that you key in Module 3. You will save the files by the exercise name, such as *26-d1* (Lesson 26, document 1) or *26-d2*. A system like this makes finding files simple.

Filenames can be up to 260 characters long, but in practice you won't use filenames that long. In addition, *Vista* doesn't let you use any of these symbols in a filename: \ / : * ? " < > |

Rename Files or Folders

Occasionally, you may want to rename a file or folder.

To rename a file or folder:

1. Access an *Explorer* window and display the contents of your removable storage drive (or the location where you have been instructed to save your document files or folders).
2. Click the file or folder icon to be renamed.
3. Choose Organize on the toolbar.
4. Select Rename.
5. Key the new name and tap ENTER.

Tip: You can also right-click a file or folder icon, and then left-click Rename from the Shortcut menu. Key the new name, and tap ENTER.

Copy, Move, or Delete Files or Folders

 Copy   Cut   Paste   Delete

Copy a file to leave it in its current location and make a duplicate of it in another location. The new location can be a network location, disk, CD, the desktop, or other storage location. *Cut* a file when you want to move a file. You actually paste the copy to a new location and automatically remove it from the original location. The pasted copy may be placed on the original disk or network location or on a separate location. *Delete* a file to remove a file from the location where it is stored. If the storage location is your hard disk, the file is moved to the *Recycle Bin*. If the storage location is a disk, CD, or network location, the file is permanently removed.

To copy a file or folder, highlight the file or folder icon in an *Explorer* window and choose Organize from the toolbar; then select Copy. Navigate to the desired location, choose Organize from the toolbar, and select Paste. Moving a file or folder is similar to copying, except once you highlight the file or folder icon in the *Explorer* window, you choose Organize from the toolbar and select Cut. View the desired location, choose Organize, and select Paste.

To delete a file or folder, highlight the file icon in the *Explorer* window, choose Organize from the toolbar, and then select Delete. A dialog box will display asking you to confirm the deletion. Choose Yes, and the file is deleted. When you delete a file or folder, it is not removed from storage immediately. It moves to the Recycle Bin until the Recycle Bin is emptied. This step gives you the opportunity to restore the file to its original location if you discover that it should not have been deleted.

To empty the Recycle Bin:

1. Access *Windows Explorer* and click the Recycle Bin icon.

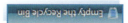

2. Choose Empty Recycle Bin from the toolbar.

3. Click Yes to confirm that you want to permanently delete the item(s).

Tip: To permanently delete a file or folder from your computer without first sending it to the Recycle Bin, click the filename and press SHIFT + DELETE.

DRILL 2 **COPY FOLDER FROM CD TO STORAGE DRIVE**

1. Insert your data CD in the CD drive and insert your USB drive or other storage device.
2. Access *Windows Explorer* and display drives on your computer.
3. Click the CD drive icon.
4. Click the *File Management* folder.
5. Click Organize in the toolbar and select Copy.
6. Click the drive and folder in which you want to copy the *File Management* folder (in this case, Removable Disk E or wherever your USB drive resides).
7. Choose Organize on the toolbar and then select Paste. The folder contents remain on the CD and have also been copied to the new location. You should see the *File Management* folder on your USB drive.
8. Leave *Windows Explorer* open if you are continuing with Drill 3.

1. *Windows Explorer* should be open and displaying drives on your computer.

2. Navigate to the USB drive.

3. Expand the *File Management* folder.

4. Click once in the Files and Folders pane (right side) to select the file named *john doe*. Click Organize on the toolbar and choose Rename. Key **new john doe** and tap ENTER.

5. In the Files and Folders pane, click the *new john doe* file icon once. Choose Organize from the toolbar, and then select Delete. Confirm the deletion of this file from your storage device.

6. Expand the *File Management* folder. Highlight the *Assignment 1* file icon. Choose Organize from the toolbar, and select Cut. Access the *Assignments* folder on your storage drive. Choose Organize and then select Paste.

7. Use the procedures just described to move the file *term paper 1* to the *Term Papers* folder on your storage drive.

8. Use the procedures just described to move the file *keyboarding homework* to the *Keyboarding* folder on your storage drive.

9. Rename the *File Management* folder *Practice*.

10. Delete the *Assignments* folder and all its contents.

11. Close *Windows Explorer*.

Tip: You can also drag and drop files or folders to a new location when you are copying or moving.

It is very important to understand the file management capabilities of the *Vista Windows* operating system when using a computer for any task. Continue to learn about file management in *Vista* as you work through the drills and exercises in this book. Use Help when necessary.

KNOW YOUR COMPUTER

The numbered parts are found on most computers. The location of some parts will vary.

1. **CPU (Central Processing Unit):** Internal operating unit or "brain" of computer.

2. **CD-ROM drive:** Reads data from and writes data to a CD.

3. **Monitor:** Displays text and graphics on a screen.

4. **Mouse:** Used to input commands.

5. **Keyboard:** An arrangement of letter, figure, symbol, control, function, and editing keys and a numeric keypad.

© FRANKSITEMAN.COM 2007

KEYBOARD ARRANGEMENT

© FRANKSITEMAN.COM 2007

1. **Alphanumeric keys:** Letters, numbers, and symbols.

2. **Numeric keypad:** Keys at the right side of the keyboard used to enter numeric copy and perform calculations.

3. **Function (F) keys:** Used to execute commands, sometimes with other keys. Commands vary with software.

4. **Arrow keys:** Move insertion point up, down, left, or right.

5. **ESC (Escape):** Closes a software menu or dialog box.

6. **TAB:** Moves the insertion point to a preset position.

7. **CAPS LOCK:** Used to make all capital letters.

8. **SHIFT:** Makes capital letters and symbols shown at tops of number keys.

9. **CTRL (Control):** With other key(s), executes commands. Commands may vary with software.

10. **ALT (Alternate):** With other key(s), executes commands. Commands may vary with software.

11. **Space Bar:** Inserts a space in text.

12. **ENTER (return):** Moves insertion point to margin and down to next line. Also used to execute commands.

13. **DELETE:** Removes text to the right of insertion point.

14. **NUM LOCK:** Activates/deactivates numeric keypad.

15. **INSERT:** Activates insert or typeover.

16. **BACKSPACE:** Deletes text to the left of insertion point.

Level

1

DEVELOPING KEYBOARDING SKILL

LEARNING OUTCOMES

Keyboarding

- To key the alphabetic and numeric keys by touch.
- To develop good keyboarding techniques.
- To key fluently—at least 25 words per minute.
- To develop reasonable accuracy.

Communication Skills

- To develop proofreading skills.
- To apply proofreaders' marks and revise text.

Activity 5

SEARCH SAVVY

Ready to sharpen your searching skills? Here are some tips:

- Choose search terms carefully. Use the most specific words, and put the most important and unique terms first.
- Use phrases when possible (in most search engines, anything inside quotation marks).
- When a word must appear in the search results, tag it as mandatory (in many search engines, a + before the word).
- Use Boolean logic in search engines to reduce off-target hits.
- Explore the Help feature of your search engine.
- If your top 25 to 50 hits aren't on point, rephrase your search or try a different search engine.

DRILL

Test the tips listed above and your searching savvy by searching on three topics that interest you. For example, you might want to search for major league baseball statistics. You could start your search using *baseball* as a search term. You also could search using *baseball statistics* to narrow the results. But to quickly get exactly what you want, you could search using *major league baseball statistics*.

Activity 6

HOMEWORK HELPER

The Internet is a wonderful tool to help you do your homework. At your fingertips are dictionaries, encyclopedias, tutors, museums, laboratories, magazines, newspapers, books, and many other resources.

DRILL

Visit these websites to complete the following tasks.

1. http://www.m-w.com — Find the definition of piscine.
2. http://www.howstuffworks.com — Print an article on how batteries work.
3. http://www.vote-smart.org — Examine the voting record of one of your state senators. Print information showing how the senator voted on two bills that interest you.
4. http://www.ajr.org — Print a story from a newspaper in another state.
5. http://memory.loc.gov — Print a primary source for an American history topic.
6. http://www.consumerworld.org — Search for recalls. Then do a further search for automobile recalls. Determine whether anyone you know has one of these vehicles.

Keyboarding Assessment/Placement

WARMUP

1. Open *Keyboarding Pro*.
2. Go to the Word Processor by clicking the WP.
3. Key each line twice. Tap ENTER after each group of lines.
4. Close the document by clicking **X** in the upper-right corner.

alphabet Max quietly promised a very big gift for the jazz club next week. Zack worked on five great projects and quickly became the expert. Jack Meyer analyzed the data by answering five complex questions.

figures The invoice dated 9/28/07 was for $18,493.56; it is due 10/24/07. Our dinner on 6/25/08 cost $432.97 plus 18% tip totaling $510.90. The 3 invoices (#49875, #52604, and #137986) totaled $379,912.46.

easy Pam may go with me to town to work for the auditor if he is busy. Jan and six girls may go to the lake to sit on the dock and fish. My neighbor may tutor the eight girls on the theory and problems.

Timed Writing

1. From the main screen, click the Timed Writing tab.

2. Choose 3' as the length. Choose *pretest* from the list of writings.
3. Tap TAB to begin. Key from the textbook.
4. Repeat the timing for 3'.
5. Your results will be displayed in the Timed Writing Report, which is available on the menu bar.

LA
all letters

	gwam	1'	3'
Most businesses want to be seen as good citizens. Working with		13	4
the arts is one way in which they can give back to the community		26	9
in which they operate. It is easy to support the arts because most		39	13
people believe that a vibrant arts program is key to the quality of		53	18
life for local citizens. Quality of life is a major factor in recruiting		68	23
new employees.		71	24
Most art groups are nonprofits that provide tax benefits to those		13	28
who give to them. A business may give money, services, or products,		27	33
or it may sponsor an event. Sponsoring an event is not the same		40	37
as making a gift. The business receives a public relations benefit		54	42
by having its name linked with the event, whereas a gift may have		67	46
no obvious benefit. Both forms help the arts.		76	49
A business may also support the arts by buying and displaying		13	53
art in its facilities. Some choose to use the art of local artists, while		27	58
others buy high-quality art from well-known artists. The former		40	63
helps to build a good local art community. The latter may bring		53	67
recognition to the business for the quality of its artwork.		66	71

1' | 1 | 2 | 3 | 4 | 5 | 6 | 7 | 8 | 9 | 10 | 11 | 12 |
3' | 1 | 2 | 3 | 4 |

2   *Internet Activities*

Activity 3

EXPLORE SEARCH ENGINES

To find information on the World Wide Web (WWW), the best place to start is often a search engine. Search engines are used to locate specific information. Just a few examples of search engines are AltaVista, Excite, Google, Ask, Lycos, and Yahoo.

 To go to a search engine, click the Search button on your Web browser. (Browsers vary.)

DRILL

1. Go to the search engines on your browser. Click on the first search engine. Browse the hyperlinks available such as Maps, People Finder, News, Weather, Stock Quotes, Sports, Games, etc. Click each search engine and explore the hyperlinks.

2. Conduct the following search using Dogpile, a multithreaded search engine that searches multiple databases;

   a. Open the website for Dogpile (http://www.dogpile.com).

   b. In the Search entry box, key the keywords **American Psychological Association** publications; click Go Fetch.

3. Pick two of the following topics and search for each using more than one search engine. Look over the first ten results you get from each search. Which search engine gave you the greatest number of promising results for each topic?

aerobics	antivirus software	interview techniques
career change	college financing	dress for success

4. Key your findings in a report.

5. Check and close. (*ia2-a3-drill*)

Activity 4

SEARCH YELLOW PAGES

Searching the Yellow Pages for information on businesses and services is commonplace, both in business and at home. Let your computer do the searching for you the next time.

DRILL

1. Open the search engine dogpile.com. Click Yellow Pages.

2. Determine a city that you would like to visit. Assume you will need overnight accommodations. Use the Yellow Pages to find a listing of hotels in this city.

3. Your best friend lives in (*you provide the city*); you want to send him/her flowers. Find a listing of florists in this city.

4. You create a third scenario and find listings.

5. Key your findings in a report.

6. Check and close. (*ia2-a4-drill*)

Alphabetic Keys

MODULE 1

LEARNING OUTCOMES

- Key the alphabetic keys by touch.
- Key using proper techniques.
- Key at a rate of 14 *gwam* or more.

LESSON 1 | Home Row, Space Bar, Enter, I

1a
WP

Home Row Position and Space Bar

1. Open *Keyboarding Pro* and create your student record.
2. Go to the Word Processor. (The **WP** will appear next to exercises keyed in the Word Processor in Lessons 1–25.)
3. Practice the steps at the right until you can place your hands in home-row position without watching.
4. Key the drills at the bottom of the page several times.
5. Continue to the next page; keep the document on your screen.

HOME ROW POSITION

1. Drop your hands to your side. Allow your fingers to curve naturally. Maintain this curve as you key.
2. Lightly place your left fingers over the **a s d f** and the right fingers over the **j k l ;**. You will feel a raised element on the *f* and *j* keys, which will help you keep your fingers on the home position. You are now in **home-row position**.

SPACE BAR AND ENTER

Tap the Space Bar, located at the bottom of the keyboard, with a down-and-in motion of the right thumb to space between words.

Enter Reach with the fourth (little) finger of the right hand to ENTER. Tap it to return the insertion point to the left margin. This action creates a **hard return**. Use a hard return at the end of all drill lines. Quickly return to home position (over ;).

Key these lines

```
a s d f SPACE j k l ; ENTER
a s d f SPACE j k l ; ENTER
```

Document 5

Newsletter

LATIN STREET DANCE

1. In the open document, add the main title, **Eighth Annual Folk Festival**. Format the title in 14-point center and bold.
2. Format the main body of the newsletter for two columns. Balance the columns.
3. Search for a clip art related to "Hispanic" and insert it flush left in the first paragraph. Search for a clip art related to "guitar" and insert it flush right in the last paragraph of the newsletter. Set the position of the first clip art to Middle Left. Set the position of the second clip art to Top Right. Change the wrapping style for each of the clip art images to Tight.
4. Check and close. (*mod9-d5*)

Document 6

Unbound Report

GLOBALIZATION

1. In the open document, key the title **GLOBALIZATION** and position the title at approximately 2 inches. Apply the Title style.
2. Add page numbers in the upper-right hand corner on all pages except the first. Choose Plain Number 3 style.
3. Add bullets for the items below paragraph 5 (beginning with Political and ending with Recreational).
4. Apply Heading 1 style to the side headings.
5. Insert the following footnote in paragraph 4 at the end of the sentence where you see [1].

   [1]Makayla Record, "The Blue Riband of the North Atlantic: Westbound and Eastbound Crossings," *The GreatShips Journal*, April 3, 2009, http://www.greatships.org/globalization.htm (accessed May 2, 2009).

6. Check and close. (*mod9-d6*)

Document 7

Cover Page

1. Create a title page for the report prepared in Document 6. Use the Cover Page feature.
2. Key the following information:
   Document title: **Globalization**
   Document subtitle: **In the 21st Century**
   Author name: **Student's Name**
3. Check and close. (*mod9-doc7*)

NEW KEYS

1b
Procedures for Learning New Keys

Apply these steps each time you learn a new key.

1. Find the new key on the illustrated keyboard. Then find it on your keyboard.
2. Watch your finger make the reach to the new key a few times. Keep other fingers curved in home position. For an upward reach, straighten the finger slightly; for a downward reach, curve the finger a bit more.
3. Repeat the drill until you can key it fluently.

1c Home Row

1. The Word Processor should be open.
2. Key lines 1-9 once. Tap ENTER once at the end of each line and twice to double-space (DS) between 2-line groups.
3. Keep the document on your screen.

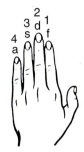

Tap Space Bar once.

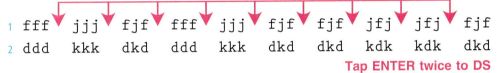

```
1  fff  jjj  fjf  fff  jjj  fjf  fjf  jfj  jfj  fjf
2  ddd  kkk  dkd  ddd  kkk  dkd  dkd  kdk  kdk  dkd
```
Tap ENTER twice to DS
```
3  sss  lll  sls  sss  lll  sls  sls  lsl  lsl  sls
4  aaa  ;;;  a;a  aaa  ;;;  a;s  a;a  ;a;  ;a;  a;a
```
DS
```
5  ff  jj  ff  jj  fj  fj  fj  dd  kk  dd  kk  dk  dk  dk
6  ss  ll  ss  ll  sl  sl  sl  aa  ;;  aa  ;;  a;  a;  a;
```
DS
```
7  f  j  d  k  s  l  a  ;
8  ff  jj  dd  kk  ss  ll  aa  ;;
9  fff  jjj  ddd  kkk  sss  lll  aaa  jjj  ;;;
```

1d i

1. Apply the standard plan for learning the letter *i*.
2. Key lines 10–12 in the Word Processor. Keep fingers curved. Repeat until you can key it fluently.
3. Click X in the upper right corner of your screen to exit the Word Processor. You will be at the Main menu of *Keyboarding Pro*.

```
10  i  ik ik ik  is is  id id  if if  ill i  ail  did kid lid
11  i  ik  aid  ail  did  kid  lid  lids  kids  ill  aid  did  ilk
12  id  aid  aids  laid  said  ids  lid  skids  kiss  disk  dial
```

1. Key the letter using the block letter style and open punctuation.
2. Check and close. (*mod9-d4*)

Current Date | Grupo Azteca | Mr. Jorge Bustos | Chairman of the Board | Hamburgo 195 | Col Juarez | 03100 Reforma | Mexico City | Distrito Federal | MEXICO

Dear Mr. Bustos

Under the direction of Vice President Marita Norales, the marketing division of Grupo Azteca has just concluded a survey of 1200 consumers of Spanish-language music. Consumers in major metropolitan areas throughout the United States were contacted both in person and over the phone.

Results showed that the majority of music purchasers were between 15 and 24 years of age, and that among this group thirty percent of consumers made seventy percent of purchases. This closely mirrors results of polls of non-Spanish-language music consumers. Consumers in this age group indicated preference for the Latin Pop (62%) and Latin Hip-Hop (22%) subgenres above all other choices. As Ms. Norales predicted, this detailed marketing survey has provided Grupo Azteca with a focus for growth over the coming years.

Our survey results showed a major disparity in response to the question, "Are you satisfied with the Spanish-language music selection available?" Over eighty percent of respondents who mostly purchased their Spanish-language music at smaller retailers answered "Very Satisfied" or "Mostly Satisfied." Among consumers who mostly purchased their Spanish-language music at larger chain retailers, this number dropped to only thirty-one percent. We therefore suggest a strategy of aggressively placing Grupo Azteca products in large chain retailers.

Total sales of Spanish-language music have grown at least fifteen percent in each of the last four years. With the detailed customer preference data we have compiled, Grupo Azteca is well positioned to become a leader in this exploding market.

Sincerely | Your Name | Administrative Assistant

1e
Lesson 1 from Software

1. Read the information at the right. Then do Lesson 1 from *Keyboarding Pro*.

STANDARD PLAN for Using Keyboarding Pro

1. Select the Lessons tab. Select a lesson from the drop-down list or key the lesson number (Figure 1-1).

2. The first activity is displayed automatically. Follow the directions on screen. Key from the screen. The software will move automatically to the next activity.

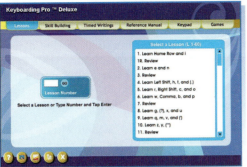

Figure 1-1 Lesson Menu

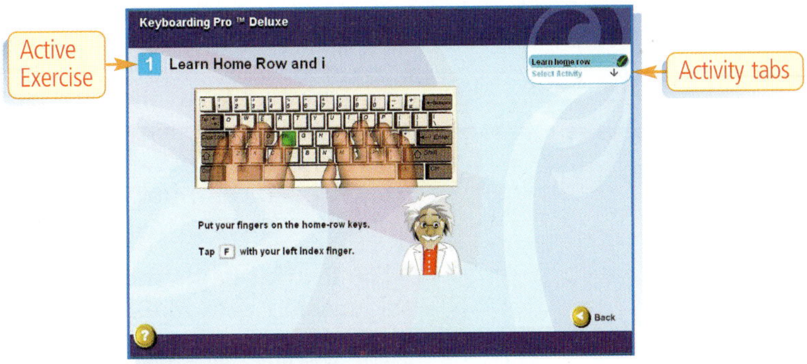

Figure 1-2 Lesson 1: Learn Home Row and i

3. Key the Textbook Keying activity from the textbook (lines 13–18 below). Tap ESC or click the Stop button to end the activity.

4. Figure 1-3 shows the Lesson Report. A check mark next to the exercise indicates that it is completed.

5. To end the lesson, check with your instructor. You may do the following:

- Print your Lesson Report, view the Performance Graph or send your student record to the Web Reporter.

6. From the Main menu, select the Exit button to quit the program. You may choose to transfer your file to another location.

Textbook Keying

1. Key each line once; do not key the numbers. Tap ENTER at the end of each line. Keep your eyes on the book.
2. Tap ESC or click the Stop button to end the activity.

```
13 a  a;  al  ak  aj  s  s;  sl  sk  sj  d  d;  dl  dk  dj
14 j  ja  js  jd  jf  k  ka  ks  kd  kf  l  la  ls  ld  lf
15 a;  sl  a;sl  dkfj  a;sl  dkfj  a;sldkfj  asdf  jk
16 a;  sl  a;sl  dk  fj  dkfj  a;sl  dkfj  fkds;a;  fj
17 f  ff  j  jj  d  dd  k  kk  s  ss  l  ll  a  aa  ;  ;;  fj
18 afj;  a  s  d  f  j  k  l  ;  asdf  jkl;  fdsa  jkl;
```

1f End the lesson

1. Follow steps 5 and 6 above to print the Lesson Report, send your files to the Web Reporter, and exit the software.
2. Clean up your work area.

Figure 1-3 Lesson Report Screen

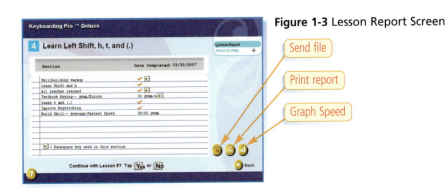

Document 2

Invitation

1. Key and format this document attractively.
2. Use a 20-point font for the title and add a special text effect.
3. Use a different font size for the subtitle. Use a fancy bullet for the bulleted list.
4. Check and close. (*mod9-d2*)

Grupo Azteca Presents
A Festival of Spanish Music

This festival is an unprecedented journey into the musical glories of Seville's Golden Age. Leading exponents of Spanish early music—from Spain, Britain and Morocco—perform in a variety of beautiful historic buildings. Carefully planned with regard to pace, balance, musical type and architecture, the experience is enhanced with talks, dinners, optional visits and the company of like-minded fellow participants.

The festival is planned and administered by Martín Randall Music Management, and admission is available exclusively through Grupo Azteca.

The festival package includes the following:

- Admission to seven concerts, all of which are private.
- Accommodations for five nights. You choose from a range of six carefully selected city-centre hotels. The choice of hotel determines the price you pay.
- Flights between the United States and Spain with British Airways and Iberia. *(There is a price reduction if you make your own arrangements for getting to Seville.)*
- Three dinners (with wine), all breakfasts, and interval drinks.
- Coach travel between the airport and your hotel, and on a few occasions within Seville.
- Lectures on the music and short talks on other aspects of Sevillian history and culture.
- All tips and taxes.
- The assistance in Spain of a team of Spanish-speaking festival staff.
- Practical and cultural information and a detailed program booklet.

Contact Alberto Gonzalez at +52 555 351 5500.

Bosque de Duraznos
No. 61, 4° Piso
Bosques de las Lomas
11700, D.F.
Mexico

Document 3

Table

1. Search the Internet for "Billboard top Latin albums."
2. Once the top ten albums are located, listen to some of them if possible to expose yourself to some of these songs with which you might not be familiar.
3. Create a table similar to the one below.
4. Format the table attractively.
5. Check and close. (*mod9-d3*)

Top Latin Albums			
Artist Name	**Album Name**	**Position This Week**	**Position Last Week**

WARMUP

Getting Started
1. Start *Keyboarding Pro*.
2. Select your name and key your password. Click OK.
3. Select Lesson 1R.
4. Key each exercise as directed in the software.

Fingers curved and upright

1Ra Textbook Keying

1. Key each line once. Tap ENTER twice to double space (DS) between 2-line groups.
2. Try to keep your eyes on the book the entire time you key.
3. Tap ESC or click Stop to end the exercise.

```
1  f  j  fjf  jj  fj  fj  jf  dd  kk  dd  kk  dk  dk  dk
2  s  ;  s;s  ;;  s;  s;  s;  aa  ;;  aa  ;;  a;  a;  a;
```
Tap ENTER twice to DS.
```
3  fj  dk  sl  a;  fjdksla;  jfkdls;a  ;a  ;s  kd  j
4  f  j  fjf  d  k  dkd  s  l  sls  a  ;  fj  dk  sl  a;a
```
DS
```
5  a;  al  ak  aj  s  s;  sl  sk  sj  d  d;  dl  dk  djd
6  ja  js  jd  jf  k  ka  ks  kd  kf  l  la  ls  ld  lfl
```

SKILL BUILDING

1Rb Keyboard Review
Key these lines from the software screen as directed.

```
7   f  fa  fad  s  sa  sad  f  fa  fall  fall  l  la  lad  s  sa  sad
8   a  as  ask  a  ad  add  j  ja  jak  f  fa  fall;  ask;  add  jak

9   ik  ki  ki  ik  is  if  id  il  ij  ia  ij  ik  is  if  ji  id  ia
10  is  il  ill  sill  dill  fill  sid  lid  ail  lid  slid  jail

11  if  is  il  kid  kids  ill  kid  if  kids;  if  a  kid  is  ill
12  is  id  if  ai  aid  jaks  lid  sid  sis  did  ail;  if  lids;

13  a  lass;  ask  dad;  lads  ask  dad;  a  fall;  fall  salads
14  as  a  fad;  ask  a  lad;  a  lass;  all  add;  a  kid;  skids

15  as  asks  did  disk  ail  fail  sail  ails  jail  sill  silk
16  ask  dad;  dads  said;  is  disk;  kiss  a  lad;  salad  lid

17  aid  a  lad;  if  a  kid  is;  a  salad  lid;  kiss  sad  dads
18  as  ad  all  ask  jak  lad  fad  kids  ill  kill  fall  disks
```

1Rc End the Lesson
1. Print the Lesson Report if directed by your instructor.
2. If necessary, transfer your student record to another location.
3. If instructed, select Send File to send your record to the Web Reporter.
4. Exit the software; clean up your work area.

Grupo Azteca

LEARNING OUTCOMES

- Apply keying, formatting, and word processing skills.
- Work independently and with few specific instructions.

GRUPO AZTECA

Grupo Azteca is a Latino music conglomerate located in Mexico City. As an administrative assistant, you will prepare a number of documents using many of the formatting and word processing skills you have learned throughout Lessons 26 to 60.

Document 1

Memo

TIP

Remember to proofread and preview each document as a SOP. You will not be reminded to do this.

1. Prepare this memo.
2. Search for Hispanic; replace with Latino.
3. Check and close. (*mod9-d1*)

TO:	Ricardo Sanchez	**FROM:**	Student's Name
SUBJECT:	Telephone Interviews	**DATE:**	Current date

With the Hispanic population of the United States surging recently and the growth projected to continue for many years to come, Grupo Azteca has positioned itself to become a major player in the Spanish-language music market. A detailed consumer survey to be concluded by the Grupo Azteca marketing team will show specific areas of focus that will be important to Grupo Azteca.

"It is essential for Grupo Azteca to identify our best customers and most important genres if we want to break into this exploding music market," stated Vice President of Marketing Marita Norales. "What we will learn from this research will drive our business plan over the coming years." The understanding of customer preferences and buying patterns has been a major factor in Grupo Azteca's success in traditional genres, and is judged to be even more important as Grupo Azteca begins to focus on Spanish-language music.

Norales and her marketing team plan to survey 1200 purchasers of Spanish-language music. Five hundred will be contacted by phone after making purchases at large chain stores, while the remainder will be surveyed in person in smaller music stores and at Spanish-language concerts. Respondents will come from major metropolitan areas in the Southwest, southern Florida, as well as New York City and Chicago. All interviewers will be Spanish-English bilingual to ensure all consumers' replies are correctly understood and recorded.

E and N

1. Open *Keyboarding Pro.*
2. Locate your student record.
3. Select Lesson 2.

1 ff dd ss aa ff dd ss aa jj kk ll ;; fj dk sl a; a;

2 fj dk sl a; fjdksla; a;sldkfj fj dk sl a; fjdksla;

3 aa ss dd ff jj kk ll ;; aa ss dd ff jj kk ll ;; a;

4 if a; as is; kids did; ask a sad lad; if a lass is

NEW KEYS

2b E and N
Key each line once; DS between groups.

e Reach *up* with *left second* finger.

n Reach *down* with *right first* finger.

e

5 e ed ed led led lea lea ale ale elf elf eke eke ed

6 e el el eel els elk elk lea leak ale kale led jell

7 e ale kale lea leak fee feel lea lead elf self eke

n

8 n nj nj an an and and fan fan and kin din fin land

9 n an fan in fin and land sand din fans sank an sin

10 n in ink sink inn kin skin an and land in din dink

all reaches learned

11 den end fen ken dean dens ales fend fens keen knee

12 if in need; feel ill; as an end; a lad and a lass;

13 and sand; a keen idea; as a sail sank; is in jail;

14 an idea; an end; a lake; a nail; a jade; a dean is

2c Textbook Keying
Key each line once; DS between groups.

TECHNIQUE TIP

Keep your eyes on the text-book copy.

15 if a lad;

16 is a sad fall

17 if a lass did ask

18 ask a lass; ask a lad

19 a;sldkfj a;sldkfj a;sldkfj

20 a; sl dk fj fj dk sl a; a;sldkfj

21 i ik ik if if is is kid skid did lid aid laid said

22 ik kid ail die fie did lie ill ilk silk skill skid

> Reach with little finger; tap Enter key quickly; return finger to home key.

In addition, DataNet recognizes the international opportunity that exists in China. Yet major competitive threats exist, and DataNet must closely examine its competition before entering a new international market.

Formulation of a strategy to achieve DataNet's goals involves concentrating its efforts on major affluent coastal cities like Shanghai. Recently, DataNet executives visited with top Chinese Communist Party officials in Huainan and discussed investing in that city, including building a factory there.

Competition for business remains intense with Chinese technology companies as well as other international conglomerate vendors. Yet DataNet has reformulated its strategy and is doubling its efforts to achieve its goals. Successful implementation of its strategy within the next two years will improve DataNet's market share both domestically as well as internationally.

CHECKPOINT

Congratulations! You have successfully completed the lessons in Module 8. To check your understanding and for more practice, complete the objective assessment and performance assessment located on the textbook website at www.collegekeyboarding.com.

2d Reinforcement

Key each line once; concentrate on what you are keying.

i

23 ik ik ik if is il ik id is if kid did lid aid ails
24 did lid aid; add a line; aid kids; ill kids; id is

n

25 nj nj nj an an and and end den ken in ink sin skin
26 jn din sand land nail sank and dank skin sans sink

e

27 el els elf elk lea lead fee feel sea seal ell jell
28 el eke ale jak lake elf els jaks kale eke els lake

all reaches

29 dine in an inn; fake jade; lend fans; as sand sank
30 in nine inns; if an end; need an idea; seek a fee;
31 if a lad; a jail; is silk; is ill; a dais; did aid
32 adds a line; and safe; asks a lass; sail in a lake

2e End the lesson

1. Print the Lesson Report.
2. If appropriate, send your student record to the Web Reporter.
3. Exit the software; clean up your work area.

WORKPLACE SUCCESS

Keyboarding: The Survival Skill

© CREATAS IMAGES/JUPITERIMAGES

Keyboarding is a valuable and necessary skill for everyone in this technological world. It is an expected tool for effective communication throughout one's life.

Students who resort to "hunting and pecking" to key their school assignments are constantly searching for the correct letter on the keyboard. Frustration abounds for students who wish to enter their research report into the computer, but do not have the touch keyboarding skills required to accomplish the task quickly and proficiently. Students who can key by touch are much more relaxed because they can keep their eyes on the screen and concentrate on text editing and composing.

Some people claim that voice-activated computers will replace the need for keyboarding. Voice activation currently works best in conjunction with keyboarding. The first draft of a document can be inputted using voice; the draft is then edited using the keyboard. Together, this process can greatly speed work performance.

1. Key the newsletter below.

2. Format the document using two equal columns.

3. Create a heading using Comic Sans MS font, 18 point, and blue text color.

4. Create a paragraph border around the last paragraph. Choose White, Background 1, Darker 15% shading, 3-point solid dark red shadow border.

5. Create a triple-line box page border that is dark red and ½ point.

6. Insert an appropriate clip art in the second column.

7. Insert the rectangle and arrow shapes as shown below. Fill and group the shapes. Move the shapes below the columns.

8. Preview and proofread the document.

9. Check the test and close. (*60-d1*)

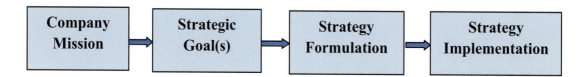

Strategic Planning Review

The last Board meeting involved reviewing the strategic planning for DataNet, Inc. The meeting began with an examination of the current mission statement, "Delivering the best-in-class integrated mobile and Internet solutions specifically tailored to meet our customers' business needs." To achieve this mission, DataNet has established a strategic goal of expanding and developing its international operations. More specifically, DataNet has the strategic goal of developing its business in the world's most populous country with more than 1 billion people, China.

DataNet conducted an extensive environmental analysis and organizational scan during the past year. This scanning inside the firm helped DataNet document its strengths and weaknesses. The external examination of the environment identified threats and opportunities DataNet faces. For example, DataNet's mission statement focuses on its strength of delivering a superior product as well as service. New leadership at many ranks in the company may be viewed as a potential weakness.

continued

LESSON 3 — Review

WARMUP 3a

Key each line at a steady pace; tap and release each key quickly. Key each line again at a faster pace.

home 1	ad ads lad fad dad as ask fa la lass jak jaks alas
n 2	an fan and land fan flan sans sand sank flank dank
i 3	is id ill dill if aid ail fail did kid ski lid ilk
all 4	ade alas nine else fife ken; jell ink jak inns if;

SKILL BUILDING

3b Rhythm Builder
Key each line twice.

Lines 5–8: Think and key words. Make the space part of the word.

Lines 9–12: Think and key phrases. Do not key the vertical rules separating the phrases.

easy words

5 if is as an ad el and did die eel fin fan elf lens
6 as ask and id kid and ade aid eel feel ilk skis an
7 ail fail aid did ken ale led an flan inn inns alas
8 eel eke nee kneel did kids kale sees lake elf fled

easy phrases

9 el el|id id|is is|eke eke|lee lee|ale ale|jill jill
10 is if|is a|is a|a disk|a disk|did ski|did ski|is a
11 sell a|sell a|sell a sled|fall fad|fall fad|did die
12 sees a lake|sees a lake|as a deal|sell a sled|all a a

3c Technique Practice
Key each 2-line group twice.

TECHNIQUE TIP

Reach with the little finger; tap Enter key quickly; return finger to home key.

home row: fingers curved and upright

13 jak lad as lass dad sad lads fad fall la ask ad as
14 asks add jaks dads a lass ads flak adds sad as lad

upward reaches: straighten fingers slightly; return quickly to home position

15 fed die led ail kea lei did ale fife silk leak lie
16 sea lid deal sine desk lie ale like life idea jail

double letters: don't hurry when stroking double letters

17 fee jell less add inn seek fall alee lass keel all
18 dill dell see fell eel less all add kiss seen sell

WARMUP 60a

Key each line, striving for control. Repeat if desired.

alphabet 1 Jayne Cox puzzled over workbooks that were required for geometry.

figures 2 Edit pages 308 and 415 in Book A; pages 17, 29, and 60 in Book B.

one hand 3 Plum trees on a hilly acre, in my opinion, create no vast estate.

easy 4 If they sign an entitlement, the town land is to go to the girls.

| 1 | 2 | 3 | 4 | 5 | 6 | 7 | 8 | 9 | 10 | 11 | 12 | 13 |

SKILL BUILDING

60b Timed Writing

1. Key two 3' timed writings. Strive for control.

all letters

gwam 3' | 5'

What is a college education worth today? If you asked that question to a random sample of people, you would get a wide range of responses. Many would respond that you cannot quantify the worth of a bachelor's degree. They quickly stress that many factors other than wages enhance the quality of life. They tend to focus on the benefits of sciences and liberal arts and the appreciation they develop for things that they would never have been exposed to if they had not attended college.

Data show, though, that you can place a value on a college education—at least in respect to wages earned. Less than twenty years ago, a high school graduate earned only about fifty percent of what a college graduate earned. Today, that number is quite different. The gap between the wages of a college graduate and the wages of a high school graduate has more than doubled in the last twenty years.

The key factor in economic success is education. The new jobs that pay high wages require more skills and a college degree. Fortunately, many high school students do recognize the value of getting a degree. Far more high school graduates are going to college than ever before. They know that the best jobs are jobs for knowledge workers and those jobs require a high level of skill.

gwam 3'	5'
4	2
9	5
13	8
18	11
22	13
26	16
31	18
33	20
37	22
41	25
45	27
50	30
54	32
58	35
59	36
63	38
68	41
72	43
76	46
81	48
85	51

3' | 1 | 2 | 3 | 4 |
5' | 1 | 2 | 3 |

APPLICATIONS

60c

Assessment

 Continue

 Check

With *Keyboarding Pro DELUXE*: When you complete a document, proofread it, check the spelling, and preview for placement. When you are completely satisfied, click the Continue button to move to the next document. Click the Check button when you are ready to error-check the test. Review and/or print the document analysis results.

Without *Keyboarding Pro DELUXE*: Key the documents in sequence. When time has been called, proofread all documents again and identify errors.

3d Textbook Keying

Key each line once; DS between groups of two lines.

TECHNIQUE TIP

Tap keys quickly.
Tap the Space Bar with down-and-in motion.
Tap Enter with a quick flick of the little finger.

reach review

19 ea sea lea seas deal leaf leak lead leas fleas keas
20 as ask lass ease as asks ask ask sass as alas seas

DS

21 sa sad sane sake sail sale sans safe sad said sand
22 le sled lead flee fled ale flea lei dale kale leaf

DS

23 jn jn nj nj in fan fin an; din ink sin and inn an;
24 de den end fen an an and and ken knee nee dean dee

phrases (think and key phrases)

25 and and land land el el elf elf self self ail nail
26 as as ask ask ad ad lad lad id id lid lid kid kids

27 if if|is is|jak jak|all all|did did|nan nan|elf elf
28 as a lad| ask dad| fed a jak| as all ask| sales fad

29 sell a lead|seal a deal|feel a leaf|if a jade sale
30 is a|is as if|a disk|aid all kids|did ski|is a silk

3e Timed Writing

1. Key lines 35–38 for 1'. If you finish before time is up, repeat the lines.
2. Practice the remaining lines in the game.
3. End your lesson.
4. Clean up your work area.

d/e
31 den end fen ken dean dens ales fend fens keen knee
32 a deed; a desk; a jade; an eel; a jade eel; a dean

n/a
33 an an in in and and en end end sane sane sand sand
34 a land; a dean; a fan; a fin; a sane end; end land

e/n
35 el eel eld elf sell self el dell fell elk els jell
36 in fin inn inks dine sink fine fins kind line lain

all reaches
37 an and fan dean elan flan land lane lean sand sane
38 sell a lead; sell a jade; seal a deal; feel a leaf

1. Key the text below.
2. Create two columns of equal width; balance the columns so that both end at about the same point.
3. At the right of two of the numbered items, insert an appropriate graphic. Wrap text around the graphics using square wrapping and right alignment; size the graphics appropriately.
4. Check and close. (*59-d2*)

TIPS ON CULTURE AND CUSTOMS

North American business executives need knowledge of customs and practices of their international business partners. The following suggestions provide an important starting point for understanding other cultures.

1. Know the requirement of handshaking. Taking the extra moment to shake hands at every meeting and again on departure will reap benefits.
2. Establish friendship first if important for that culture. Being a friend may be important first; conducting business is secondary. Establish a friendship; show interest in the individual and the family. Learn people's names and pronounce them correctly in conversation.
3. Understand the meaning of time. Some cultures place more importance on family, personal, and church-related activities than on business activities. Accordingly, they have longer lunches and more holidays. Therefore, they place less importance on adherence to schedules and appointment times.
4. Understand rank. Protocol with regard to who takes precedence is important; i.e., seating at meetings, speaking, and walking through doorways. Do not interrupt anyone.
5. Know the attitudes of space. Some cultures consider 18 inches a comfortable distance between people; however, others prefer much less. Adjust to their space preferences. Do not move away, back up, or put up a barrier, such as standing behind a desk.
6. Understand the attitude of hospitality. Some cultures are generous with hospitality and expect the same in return. For example, when hosting a party, prepare a generous menu; finger foods may be considered "ungenerous."
7. Share their language appropriately. Although the business meeting may be conducted in English, speak the other language in social parts of the conversation. This courteous effort will be noted.

LESSON 4 | Left Shift, H, T, Period

WARMUP 4a

Key each line twice. Keep eyes on copy.

home row	1	al as ads lad dad fad jak fall lass asks fads all;
e/i/n	2	ed ik jn in knee end nine line sine lien dies leis
all reaches	3	see a ski; add ink; fed a jak; is an inn; as a lad
easy	4	an dial id is an la lake did el ale fake is land a

NEW KEYS

4b Left [Shift] and [h]

Key each line once.

Follow the "Standard procedures for learning new keyreaches" on p. 4 for all remaining reaches.

left shift Reach *down* with *left fourth* (little) finger; shift, tap, release.

h Reach to *left* with *right first* finger.

4c Textbook Keying
Key the drill once: Strive for good control.

left shift

5 J Ja Ja Jan Jan Jane Jana Ken Kass Lee Len Nan Ned
6 and Ken and Lena and Jake and Lida and Nan and Ida
7 Inn is; Jill Ina is; Nels is; Jen is; Ken Lin is a

h

8 h hj hj he he she she hen aha ash had has hid shed
9 h hj ha hie his half hand hike dash head sash shad
10 aha hi hash heal hill hind lash hash hake dish ash

all reaches learned

11 Nels Kane and Jake Jenn; she asked Hi and Ina Linn
12 Lend Lana and Jed a dish; I fed Lane and Jess Kane
13 I see Jake Kish and Lash Hess; Isla and Helen hike

14 he she held a lead; she sells jade; she has a sale
15 Ha Ja Ka La Ha Hal Ja Jake Ka Kahn La Ladd Ha Hall
16 Hal leads; Jeff led all fall; Hal has a safe lead
17 Hal Hall heads all sales; Jake Hess asks less fee;

59-d1

Newsletter

1. Key the newsletter below. Use .5" left and right margins.

2. Key the title, **Arena Update**, using Arial, 48 point, bold. Use 18-point Arial type for the internal headings.

3. Insert clip art files, as shown in the newsletter. You may substitute any appropriate clip art you find if you cannot find the same images. Wrap the text around the graphics.

4. Balance columns so they all end at about the same place.

5. Create a double-line page border that is dark red and 1¹/₂ point.

6. Check and close. (*59-d1*)

Arena Update

Get your shovels ready!

The architects have put the final touches on the arena plans, and the groundbreaking has been scheduled for March 18. Put the date on your calendar and plan to be a part of this exciting time. The Groundbreaking Ceremony will begin at 5:00 at the new arena site. After the ceremony, you will join the architects in the practice facility for refreshments and an exciting visual presentation of the new arena. The party ends when we all join the Western Cougars as they take on the Central Lions for the final conference game.

Cornerstone Club Named

Robbie Holiday of the Cougars Club submitted the winning name for the new premium seating and club area of the new arena. Thanks to all of you who submitted suggestions for naming the new club. For his suggestion, which was selected from over 300 names submitted, Robbie has won season tickets for next year and the opportunity to make his seat selection first. The Cornerstone Club name was selected because members of our premium club play a crucial role in making our new arena a reality. Without the financial support of this group, we could not lay the first cornerstone of the arena.

Cornerstone Club members have first priority in selecting their seats for both basketball and hockey in a specially designated section of the new arena. This section provides outstanding seats for both basketball games and hockey matches. Club members also have access to the Cornerstone Club before the game, during halftime, and after the game. They also receive a parking pass for the lot immediately adjacent to the arena. If you would like more information about the Cornerstone Club and how you can become a charter member, call the Cougars Club office during regular business hours.

What View Would You Like?

Most of us would like to sit in our seats and try them out before we select them rather than look at a diagram of the seating in the new arena. Former Cougar players make it easy for you to select the perfect angle to watch the ball go in the basket. Mark McKay and Jeff Dunlap, using their patented Real View visualization software, make it possible for you to experience the exact view you will have from the seats you select. In fact, they encourage you to try several different views. Most of the early testers of the new seat selection software reported that they came in with their minds completely made up about the best seats in the house. However, after experiencing several different views with the Real View software, they changed their original seat location request.

4d t and . (period)

Key each line once.

Period: Space once after a period that follows an initial or an abbreviation. To increase readability, space twice after a period that ends a sentence.

t Reach *up* with *left first* finger.

. (period) Reach *down* with *right third* finger.

t

18 t tf tf aft aft left fit fat fete tiff tie the tin
19 tf at at aft lit hit tide tilt tint sits skit this
20 hat kit let lit ate sit flat tilt thin tale tan at

. (period)

21 .l .l l.l fl. fl. L. L. Neal and J. N. List hiked.
22 Hand J. H. Kass a fan. Jess did. I need an idea.
23 Jane said she has a tan dish; Jae and Lee need it.

all reaches learned

24 I did tell J. K. that Lt. Li had left. He is ill.
25 tie tan kit sit fit hit hat; the jet left at nine.
26 I see Lila and Ilene at tea. Jan Kane ate at ten.

SKILL BUILDING

4e Reinforcement

Key with control; concentrate as you practice the new reaches.

reach review
27 tf .l hj ft ki de jh tf ik ed hj de ft ki l. tf ik
28 elf eel left is sis fit till dens ink has delt ink

h/e
29 he he heed heed she she shelf shelf shed shed she
30 he has; he had; he led; he sleds; she fell; he is

i/t
31 it is if id did lit tide tide tile tile list list
32 it is; he hit it; he is ill; she is still; she is

shift
33 Hal and Nel; Jade dishes; Kale has half; Jed hides
34 Hi Ken; Helen and Jen hike; Jan has a jade; Ken is

enter
35 Nan had a sale.
36 He did see Hal.
37 Lee has a desk.
38 Ina hid a dish.

TECHNIQUE TIP

Tap Enter without pausing or looking up from the copy.

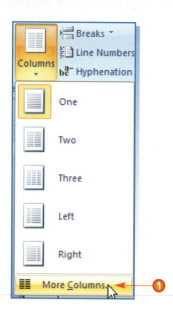

If you are creating multiple-column pages, you may want to add a vertical line between columns. Vertical lines help create order, move the eye up and down the page, and separate unrelated stories.

To insert a line between columns:
PAGE LAYOUT/PAGE SETUP/COLUMNS

1. On the Page Layout tab, in the Page Setup group, click Columns.
2. Choose More Columns .
3. In the Columns dialog box, click Line between and click OK.

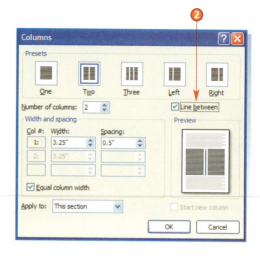

DRILL 2   **WRAP TEXT AROUND GRAPHIC**   PRODUCTIVITY

1. In the open document, balance the columns.
2. Change the Wrapping style of the graphic. If the graphic moves to the left column, drag it back so it is positioned above the *Integration* paragraph.
3. Check to see that the graphic is center-aligned.
4. Preview, check, and close the document when you are satisfied. (*59-drill2*)

INTERNET ACTIVITY

59e Search for Books

Search the Internet and locate at least five top-selling books about virtual teams. You will use these books in the next activity.

COMMUNICATION

59f
Composing and Editing

Use proper bibliography style to list each book you found in *59e*. After each citation, use your own words to compose a short summary (1-2 sentences) for each book. A sample is provided below. Alphabetize the list by author. (*59f*)

Gladwell, Malcolm. *Blink: The Power of Thinking Without Thinking.* New York: Little Brown and Company, 2005.

This book discusses how individuals process information on a subconscious level in the blink of an instant. Gladwell states that most people can make better instant judgments by training their mind and senses to focus on the most relevant facts and that less input (as long as it is the right input) is better than more.

LESSON 5 ▷ R, Right Shift, C, O

WARMUP 5a

Key each line twice.

home keys	1	a; ad add al all lad fad jak ask lass fall jak lad
t/h/i/n	2	the hit tin nit then this kith dint tine hint thin
left shift/.	3	I need ink. Li has an idea. Hit it. I see Kate.
all reaches	4	Jeff ate at ten; he left a salad dish in the sink.

NEW KEYS

5b r and Right Shift

Key each line once.

r Reach *up* with *left first* finger.

right shift Reach *down* with *right fourth* finger; shift, tap, release.

r

5 r rf rf riff riff fir fir rid ire jar air sir lair
6 rf rid ark ran rat are hare art rant tire dirt jar
7 rare dirk ajar lark rain kirk share hart rail tart

right shift

8 D D Dan Dan Dale Ti Sal Ted Ann Ed Alf Ada Sid Fan
9 and Sid and Dina and Allen and Eli and Dean and Ed
10 Ed Dana; Dee Falk; Tina Finn; Sal Alan; Anna Deeds

all reaches learned

11 Jane and Ann hiked in the sand; Asa set the tents.
12 a rake; a jar; a tree; a red fire; a fare; a rain;
13 Fred Derr and Rai Tira dined at the Tree Art Fair.

5c Textbook Keying

Key each line once; DS between groups of two lines.

14 ir ir ire fir first air fair fire tire rid sir
15 fir jar tar fir flit rill till list stir dirt fire

DS

16 Feral is ill. Dan reads. Dee and Ed Finn see Dere.
17 All is still as Sarah and I fish here in the rain.

DS

18 I still see a red ash tree that fell in the field.
19 Lana said she did sail her skiff in the dark lake.

TIP

Shortcut: To create a new column, press CTRL + SHIFT + ENTER.

At times, you will want to start a new column instead of letting the text flow naturally from one column to the next.

To force the starting of a new column:

1. Position the insertion point where the new column is to start.
2. On the Page Layout tab, in the Breaks group, click Column.

 KEYBOARDING PRO DELUXE > See References/Word commands/Lesson 59

DRILL 1   **SIMPLE COLUMNS**   TRAINING

1. In the open file, on the Page Layout tab, in the Page Setup group, click Columns.

   a. Format the document in three equal-width columns. Preview the document.

   b. Change the columns to two balanced columns. Preview the document.

   c. Select *Productivity Enhancement Program*, click Columns and click One. Tap ENTER after the heading.

   d. Apply 20-point Arial Black font. Center-align the banner heading.

2. Add an appropriate clip art image related to "training" within the last paragraph. Change the text wrapping to Square, and align the graphic to the margin.

3. Check and close. (*59-drill1*)

WRAP TEXT AROUND GRAPHICS

When graphic elements are included in documents such as newsletters or reports, text usually wraps around the graphic.

TIP

You can also place the insertion point over the graphic and right-click to access the Format Picture dialog box. Click the Layout tab to access text wrapping.

To wrap text around graphics:

1. Select the graphic.
2. Under Drawing Tools, on the Format tab, in the Arrange group, choose Text Wrapping ❶.
3. Select the desired wrapping style ❷ (Square).
4. Click the desired alignment ❸ (Right), and then click OK.

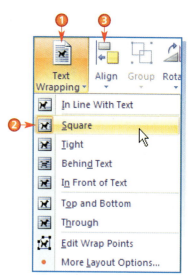

5d c and o

Key each line once.

c Reach *down* with *left second* finger.

o Reach *up* with right *third* finger.

c

20 c c cd cd cad cad can can tic ice sac cake cat sic
21 clad chic cite cheek clef sick lick kick dice rice
22 call acid hack jack lack lick cask crack clan cane

o

23 o ol ol old old of off odd ode or ore oar soar one
24 ol sol sold told dole do doe lo doll sol solo odor
25 onto door toil lotto soak fort hods foal roan load

all reaches learned

26 Carlo Rand can call Rocco; Cole can call Doc Cost.
27 Trina can ask Dina if Nick Corl has left; Joe did.
28 Case sent Carole a nice skirt; it fits Lorna Rich.

SKILL BUILDING

5e Keyboard Reinforcement
Key each line once; key at a steady pace. Strive for control.

TECHNIQUE TIP

Reach up without moving hands away from your body. Use quick keystrokes.

o/r
29 or or for for nor nor ore ore oar oar roe roe sore
30 a rose|her or|he or|he rode|or for|a door|her doll

i/t
31 is is tis tis it it fit fit tie tie this this lits
32 it is|it is|it is this|it is this|it sits|tie fits

e/n
33 en en end end ne ne need need ken ken kneel kneels
34 lend the|lend the|at the end|at the end|need their

c/o
35 ch ch check check ck ck hack lack jack co co cones
36 the cot|the cot|a dock|a dock|a jack|a jack|a cone

all reaches
37 Jack and Rona did frost nine of the cakes at last.
38 Jo can ice her drink if Tess can find her a flask.
39 Ask Jean to call Fisk at noon; he needs her notes.

COLUMNS

PAGE LAYOUT/PAGE SETUP/COLUMNS

Text may be formatted in multiple columns on a page to make it easier to read. A newsletter, for example, is usually formatted in columns. Typically, newsletters are written in an informal, conversational style and are formatted with **banners** (text that spans multiple columns), newspaper columns, graphic elements, and other text enhancements. In newspaper columns, text flows down one column and then to the top of the next column. A simple, uncluttered design with a significant amount of white space is recommended to enhance the readability of newsletters.

To create columns of equal width:

1. On the Page Layout tab, in the Page Setup group, click Columns ❶.

2. Click to choose the desired number of columns ❷.

Column format may be applied before or after keying text. Generally, column formats are easier to apply after text has been keyed.

Occasionally, you may want certain text (such as a banner or headline) to span more than one column.

To format a banner:

1. Select the text to be included in the banner.

2. On the Page Layout tab, in the Page Setup group, click Columns.

3. Drag the number of columns to one and format the banner appropriately.

Balanced columns end at the same point on the page.

To balance columns:

1. Position the insertion point at the end of the text to be balanced.

2. Insert a Continuous section break (on the Page Layout tab, in the Page Setup group, click Breaks and click Continuous).

W, Comma, B, P

WARMUP 6a

Key each line twice; avoid pauses.

home row 1 ask a lad; a fall fad; had a salad; ask a sad jak;
o/t 2 to do it; to toil; as a tot; do a lot; he told her
c/r 3 cots are; has rocks; roll cot; is rich; has an arc
all reaches 4 Holt can see Dane at ten; Jill sees Frank at nine.

NEW KEYS

6b w and , (comma)

Key each line once.

Comma: Space once after a comma.

w Reach *up* with *left third* finger.

, (comma) Reach *down* with *right second* finger.

w

5 w ws ws was was wan wit low win jaw wilt wink wolf
6 sw sw ws ow ow now now row row own own wow wow owe
7 to sew; to own; was rich; was in; is how; will now

, (comma)

8 k, k, k, irk, ilk, ask, oak, ark, lark, jak, rock,
9 skis, a dock, a fork, a lock, a fee, a tie, a fan,
10 Jo, Ed, Ted, and Dan saw Nan in a car lift; a kit

all reaches learned

11 Win, Lew, Drew, and Walt will walk to West Willow.
12 Ask Ho, Al, and Jared to read the code; it is new.
13 The window, we think, was closed; we felt no wind.

6c Textbook Keying

Key each line once.

14 walk wide sown wild town went jowl wait white down
15 a dock, a kit, a wick, a lock, a row, a cow, a fee
16 Joe lost to Ron; Fiji lost to Cara; Don lost to Al
17 Kane will win; Nan will win; Rio will win; Di wins
18 Walter is in Reno; Tia is in Tahoe; then to Hawaii

LESSON 59

Documents with Columns

WARMUP 59a

Key each line, striving for control. Repeat if desired.

alphabet	1	Jimmy Favorita realized that we must quit playing by six o'clock.
figure	2	Joell, in her 2001 truck, put 19 boxes in an annex at 3460 Marks.
double letters	3	Merriann was puzzled by a letter that followed a free book offer.
easy	4	Ana's sorority works with vigor for the goals of the civic corps.

| 1 | 2 | 3 | 4 | 5 | 6 | 7 | 8 | 9 | 10 | 11 | 12 | 13 |

SKILL BUILDING

59b Textbook Keying

1. Key the drill, concentrating on good keying techniques. Tap ENTER twice after each 2-line group.
2. Repeat the drill if time permits.

adjacent reaches	5	Is assessing potential important in a traditional career program?
	6	I saw her at an airport at a tropical resort leaving on a cruise.
direct reaches	7	Fred kicked a goal in every college soccer game in June and July.
	8	Ned used their sled on cold days and my kite on warm summer days.
double letters	9	Bobby Lott feels that the meeting at noon will be cancelled soon.
	10	Pattie and Tripp meet at the swimming pool after football drills.

59c Timed Writing

1. Key a 1' timing on each paragraph; work to increase speed.
2. Key a 3' timing on all paragraphs.

all letters

	gwam	1'	3'
Surrogate grandparents and pet therapy might not be the types	12	4	62
of terms that you expect to find in a medical journal, but they are	26	9	66
concepts that are quite popular with senior citizens. Two of the	39	13	71
most common problems experienced by senior citizens who do not live	53	18	75
with or near a family member are loneliness and the craving to feel	66	22	80
needed and loved.	70	23	81
Senior citizens who are healthy and who are stable mentally	12	27	85
often can have a high-quality relationship with deprived children	25	32	89
who do not have grandparents of their own. They often have time to	39	36	94
spare and the desire to give these needy children extra attention	52	41	98
and help with their schoolwork and other needs. At first, it may	65	45	103
seem that children gain the most from relationships with seniors.	79	50	107
However, it soon becomes evident that the surrogate grandparents	92	54	112
tend to benefit as much or even more than the children.	103	58	115

| 1' | 1 | 2 | 3 | 4 | 5 | 6 | 7 | 8 | 9 | 10 | 11 | 12 | 13 | 14 |
| 3' | | 1 | | | 2 | | | 3 | | | 4 | | |

6d b and p

Key each line once.

b Reach *down* with *left first* finger.

p Reach *up* with *right fourth* (little) finger.

b

19 bf bf bf biff fib fib bib bib boa boa fib fibs rob
20 bf bf bf ban ban bon bon bow bow be be rib rib sob
21 a dob, a cob, a crib, a lab, a slab, a bid, a bath

p

22 p; p; pa pa; pal pal pan pan pad par pen pep paper
23 pa pa; lap lap; nap nap; hep ape spa asp leap clap
24 a park, a pan, a pal, a pad, apt to pop, a pair of

all reaches learned

25 Barb and Bob wrapped a pepper in paper and ribbon.
26 Rip, Joann, and Dick were all closer to the flash.
27 Bo will be pleased to see Japan; he works in Oslo.

SKILL BUILDING

6e Keyboard Reinforcement

Key each line once; key at a steady pace.

reach review

28 ki kid did aid lie hj has has had sw saw wits will
29 de dell led sled jn an en end ant hand k, end, kin

s/w

30 ws ws lows now we shown win cow wow wire jowl when
31 Wes saw an owl in the willow tree in the old lane.

b/p

32 bf bf fib rob bid ;p p; pal pen pot nap hop cap bp
33 Rob has both pans in a bin at the back of the pen.

6f Speed Builder

Key each line twice. Work for fluency.

34 to do|can do|to bow|ask her|to nap|to work|is born
35 for this|if she|is now|did all|to see|or not|or if

all reaches

36 Dick owns a dock at this lake; he paid Ken for it.
37 Jane also kept a pair of owls, a hen, and a snake.

38 Blair soaks a bit of the corn, as he did in Japan.
39 I blend the cocoa in the bowl when I work for Leo.

58-d2

Continued

Market Analysis

- The population in the metropolitan area is growing both in the college's service area and in the demographic segments that represent the greatest market enrollment.

- The metropolitan area continues to add employment opportunities at a growth rate of 22 percent, but the area economy suffers from some of the same insecurities about the future as do other areas.

- Information technology is creating more customer potential and new demands for the delivery of coursework as well as generating new opportunities for competitors to enter this educational market.

- The pace of change is forcing people at all levels of the economy to learn new skills at the same time people are being asked to work harder—and sometimes hold more than one job.

- The new school improvement plan has not taken shape as quickly as anticipated, but a move toward mastering skills and testing for proficiencies—not rote knowledge—is gaining momentum.

WORKPLACE SUCCESS

Let's Do Lunch—Business Etiquette Around the World

© PURESTOCK/JUPITERIMAGES

Each culture has its own customs when it comes to social and business relations. While business lunches and dinners are common around the globe, they are handled differently in most countries. It is important to understand cultural etiquette when dining in order to avoid embarrassment to maximize your chances of business success.

In the U.S., it is customary to get down to business immediately. Yet this attitude may turn off clients from another country. Most Latin Americans, for example, prefer to be social over lunch before discussing business. You might be asked about your family, and you should reciprocate. Business lunches may last two or more hours. In Britain, a business lunch might occur at a local pub. Usually, there is less talk of family or personal life. The British are more formal, and so the talk is usually centered on business, economics, or politics. For the Japanese, lunch is traditionally the main meal of the day. Many Japanese enjoy slurping their noodles in order to make them cooler. Guests will never see a host paying the bill since it is always done discretely beforehand or after the lunch.

These examples provide a few tips when business is conducted at the international dining table. Take the time and learn the customs of other countries in order to build relationships and be an effective businessperson.

WARMUP 7a

Key each line twice; begin new lines promptly.

© FRANKSITEMAN.COM 2007

LEFT FINGERS   4 \ 3 \ 2 \ 1 \ 1 \ 2 \ 3 \ 4   RIGHT FINGERS

all   1 We often can take the older jet to Paris and back.
home   2 a; sl dk fj a;sl dkfj ad as all ask fads adds asks
1st row 3 Ann Bascan and Cabal Naban nabbed a cab in Canada.
3rd row 4 Rip went to a water show with either Pippa or Pia.

SKILL BUILDING

7b Textbook Keying
Key each line once; DS between groups of three lines.

 5 ws ws was was wan wan wit wit pew paw nap pop bawl
 6 bf bf fb fb fob fob rib rib be be job job bat back
 7 p; p; asp asp pan pan ap ap ca cap pa nap pop prow

DS

 8 Barb and Bret took an old black robe and the boot.
 9 Walt saw a wisp of white water renew ripe peppers.
10 Pat picked a black pepper for the picnic at Parks.

7c Textbook Keying
Key each line once; DS between groups of three lines

words   11 a an pan so sot la lap ah own do doe el elf to tot
phrases   12 if it|to do|it is|do so|for the|he works|if he bid
sentences 13 Jess ate all of the peas in the salad in the bowl.

DS

TECHNIQUE TIP

words: key as a single unit rather than letter by letter;

phrases: say and key fluently;

sentences: work for fluency.

words   14 bow bowl pin pint for fork forks hen hens jak jaks
phrases   15 is for|did it|is the|we did a|and so|to see|or not
sentences 16 I hid the ace in a jar as a joke; I do not see it.

DS

words   17 chap chaps flak flake flakes prow prowl work works
phrases   18 as for the|as for the|and to the|to see it|and did
sentences 19 As far as I know, he did not read all of the book.

PAGE BORDERS

Attractive page borders can also be added to pages using various line styles, weights, and colors.

To apply a page border:
PAGE LAYOUT/PAGE BACKGROUND/PAGE BORDERS

1. On the Page Layout tab, in the Page Background group, click Page Borders.
2. Make sure the Page Border tab is active on the Borders and Shading dialog box.
3. Choose the desired border setting, line style, line color, and line width; click OK.

DRILL 4 — PAGE BORDERS

1. Open *58-drill3*.
2. Add a page border that is dark red and ½ point.

3. Check and close. (*58-drill4*)

APPLICATIONS

58-d1

Multiple-Page Manual with Picture and Page Border

CLEANING MANUAL

CLEAN.JPG

1. In the open document, format both lines of the title in 28-point Cambria, bold, red.
2. Insert the picture *clean.jpg* from the data files between the title lines and the text at the bottom of page one.
3. Add the page border that looks like a house.
   (**Hint:** This is a custom border. On the Page Borders tab, in the Borders and Shading dialog box, click Custom and then click Art. Select the border that looks like houses.)
4. Check and close. (*58-d1*)

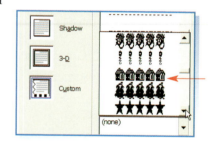

58-d2

One-Page Report with Clip Art and Shape

1. Key and format the title on the next page, **Trend Analysis Report**, using 36-point Arial font, bold, and Light Blue text color.
2. Create a subheading below the title by keying **Market Trends** using Arial Black 20-point font and adding Light Blue shading to the paragraph.
3. Key the bulleted list. Click the Decrease Indent button to align the bullets at the left margin.
4. Search for clip art using the keyword **academic**, and add an appropriate piece of clip art centered below the five paragraphs.
5. Insert an Explosion 2 shape to the right of the clip art. Inside the shape, key **Key Market Trends** in 16-point Times New Roman font. Add a complementary fill color to the shape. If necessary, adjust the size of the shape so that the text fits properly.
6. At the bottom of the page, key **Understanding our community to prepare for our future!** in 18-point Brush Script MT font.
7. Check and close. (*58-d2*)

7d Technique Practice

Key each set of lines once.

▼ Space once after a period following an abbreviation.

spacing: space *immediately* after each word

```
20  ad la as in if it lo no of oh he or so ok pi be we
21  an ace ads ale aha a fit oil a jak nor a bit a pew
22  ice ades born is fake to jail than it and the cows
```

spacing/shifting

```
           ▼                              ▼
23  Ask Jed.  Dr. Han left at ten; Dr. Crowe, at nine.
24  I asked Jin if she had ice in a bowl; it can help.
25  Freda, not Jack, went to Spain.  Joan likes Spain.
```

7e

Using the Word Processor Timer

Exercises to be keyed in the Word Processor are identified with the Word Processor icon. Follow the instructions in the textbook and key from the textbook.

STANDARD PLAN for Using the Word Processor Timer

You can check your speed in the Word Processor using the Timer.

1. In the Word Processor, click the Timer button on the status bar.
2. The Timer begins once you start to key and stops automatically. Do not tap ENTER at the end of a line. Wordwrap will cause the text to flow to the next line automatically.
3. To save the timing, click the File menu and Save as. Use your initals (*xx*), the exercise number, and number of the timing as the filename. Example: *xx-7f-t1* (your initials, exercise 7f, timing1).
4. Click the Timer button again to start a new timing.
5. Each new timing must be saved with its own name.

7f Timed Writing

1. Take two 1' writings. If you finish before time is up, begin again.
2. Do not tap ENTER at the ends of the lines.

Goal: 12 *gwam*.

```
                                                        gwam
It is hard to fake a confident spirit.  We will do      10
better work if we approach and finish a job and         20
know that we will do the best work we can and then      30
not fret.                                               32
|  1  |  2  |  3  |  4  |  5  |  6  |  7  |  8  |  9  | 10 |
```

7g Word Processor

1. In the Word Processor, key each line once for fluency. Do not save your work.
2. Set the Timer in the Word Processor for 30". Take two 30" writings on each line. Do not save the timings.

Goal: to reach the end of the line before time is up.

```
                                                        gwam
26  Dan took her to the show.                            12
27  Jan lent the bowl to the pros.                       14
28  Hold the wrists low for this drill.                  16
29  Jessie fit the black panel to the shelf.            18
30  Jake held a bit of cocoa and an apricot for Diane.  20
31  Dick and I fish for cod on the docks at Fish Lake.  20
32  Kent still held the dish and the cork in his hand.  20
|  1  |  2  |  3  |  4  |  5  |  6  |  7  |  8  |  9  | 10 |
```

PARAGRAPH BORDERS AND SHADING

PAGE LAYOUT/PAGE BACKGROUND/PAGE BORDERS

Borders and shading can be applied to paragraphs, pages, or selected text. Various line styles, weights, and colors can be applied to borders. Shading can be applied in a variety of colors and patterns.

> This paragraph illustrates a 3-D border with a 3-point purple line. The shading for the paragraph is Purple, Accent 4, 60%.

To apply a paragraph border:

PAGE LAYOUT/PAGE BACKGROUND/PAGE BORDERS/BORDERS

1. Click in the paragraph or select the text to be formatted with a border.
2. On the Page Layout tab, in the Page Background group, click Page Borders to display the Borders and Shading dialog box.
3. In the Borders and Shading dialog box, click the Borders tab.
4. Select the border setting, line style, color, and width; then click OK.

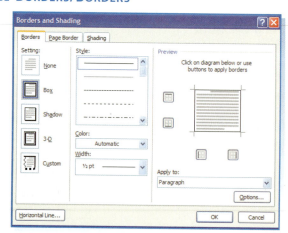

To apply shading:

PAGE LAYOUT/PAGE BACKGROUND/PAGE BORDERS/SHADING

1. Click in the paragraph or select the text to be formatted with a border.
2. On the Page Layout tab, in the Page Background group, click Page Borders.
3. Click the Shading tab.
4. Select the fill and pattern, and then click OK.

DRILL 3   BORDERS AND SHADING

1. Key the paragraph at the right.
2. Then apply a ½-point red, double-line box border and Dark Blue, Text 2, Lighter 60% shading.
3. Check and close. (58-drill3)

> This paragraph is formatted with a ½-point red, double-line box border and Dark Blue, Text 2, Lighter 60% shading.

G, Question Mark, X, U

Key each line twice. Keep eyes on copy.

all 1 Dick will see Job at nine if Rach sees Pat at one.
w/b 2 As the wind blew, Bob Webber saw the window break.
p/, 3 Pat, Pippa, or Cap has prepared the proper papers.
all 4 Bo, Jose, and Will fed Lin; Jack had not paid her.

NEW KEYS

8b g and ?

Key each line once; repeat.

Question mark: The question mark is usually followed by two spaces.

g Reach to *right* with *left first* finger.

? Left SHIFT; reach *down* with *right fourth* finger.

g

5 g g gf gaff gag grog fog frog drag cog dig fig gig
6 gf go gall flag gels slag gala gale glad glee gals
7 golf flog gorge glen high logs gore ogle page grow

?

8 ? ?; ?; ? ? Who? When? Where? Who is? Who was?
9 Who is here? Was it he? Was it she? Did she go?
10 Did Geena? Did he? What is that? Was Jose here?

all reaches learned

11 Has Ginger lost her job? Was her April bill here?
12 Phil did not want the boats to get here this soon.
13 Loris Shin has been ill; Frank, a doctor, saw her.

8c Textbook Keying

Key each line once; DS between groups.

reach review
14 ws ws hj hj tf tf ol ol rf rf ed ed cd cd bf bf p;
15 wed bid has old hold rid heed heed car bed pot pot

g
16 gf gf gin gin rig ring go gone no nog sign got dog
17 to go|to go|go on|go in|go in|to go in|in the sign

?
18 ?; ?;? who? when? where? how? what? who? It is I?
19 Is she? Is he? Did I lose Jo? Is Gal all right?

TECHNIQUE TIP

Concentrate on correct reaches.

GROUPING SHAPES

Shapes or other objects are often grouped when they are used together. The objects are grouped so they can be moved as one item. They can also be ungrouped if you need to change the formatting of individual objects.

To group shapes or other objects:
DRAWING TOOLS/FORMAT/ARRANGE/GROUP

1. Select the objects you want to group by holding down SHIFT as you click each object.
2. Under Drawing Tools, on the Format tab, in the Arrange group, choose Group.
3. To ungroup an object, select the grouped objects. Under Drawing Tools, from the Format tab, in the Arrange group, click the down arrow on the Group command and select Ungroup.

TIP

You can also right-click the shape and choose Add Text.

To add text to a shape:
DRAWING TOOLS/FORMAT/INSERT SHAPES/EDIT TEXT BUTTON

Under Drawing Tools, from the Format tab, in the Insert Shapes group, click the Edit Text button. This allows you to add text to a shape or to edit text that is already in the shape.

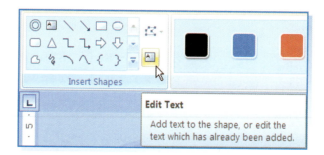

To delete a shape from your document:

Click the shape that you want to delete, and then tap DELETE.

KEYBOARDING PRO DELUXE   See References/Word commands/Lesson 58

DRILL 2   SHAPES

1. In a new document, insert a rounded rectangle, right arrow, triangle, right arrow, and a circle as shown below.
2. Fill each shape with a color.

3. Select all shapes and group them.
4. Add the text as shown. (Hint: Tap ENTER before keying the text on the rounded rectangle and the circle. Use the Remove Space After Paragraph command if necessary to get the text to align properly.)
5. Check and close. (58-drill2)

8d x and u

Key each line once; repeat.

x Reach *down* with *left third* finger.

u Reach *up* with *right first* finger.

x

20 x x xs xs ox ox lox sox fox box ex hex lax hex fax
21 sx six sax sox ax fix cox wax hex box pox sex text
22 flax next flex axel pixel exit oxen taxi axis next

u

23 u uj uj jug jut just dust dud due sue use due duel
24 uj us cud but bun out sun nut gun hut hue put fuel
25 dual laud dusk suds fuss full tuna tutus duds full

all reaches learned

26 Paige Power liked the book; Josh can read it next.
27 Next we picked a bag for Jan; then she, Jan, left.
28 Is her June account due? Has Lou ruined her unit?

SKILL BUILDING

8e Reinforcement
Key each line once; work for control.

29 nut cue hut sun rug us six cut dug axe rag fox run
30 out of the sun|cut the action|a fox den|fun at six
31 That car is not junk; it can run in the next race.

32 etc. tax nick cure lack flex walls uncle clad hurt
33 lack the cash|not just luck|next in line|just once
34 June Dunn can send that next tax case to Rex Knox.

8f Timed Writing
Take two 1' timings. If time permits, continue to paragraph 2. Apply wordwrap.

TECHNIQUE TIP

Wordwrap: Text within a paragraph moves automatically to the next line. Tap ENTER only to begin a new paragraph.

```
          .         4         .         8         .
How a finished job will look often depends on how
     12        .        16        .        20
we feel about our work as we do it.  Attitude has
     .        24        .        28        .
a definite effect on the end result of work we do.
```
Tap ENTER once
```
          .         4         .         8         .
When we are eager to begin a job, we relax and do
     12        .        16        .        20
better work than if we start the job with an idea
     .        24        .        28        .
that there is just nothing we can do to escape it.
```

1. In a new document, search for *computers* in the clip art gallery. Insert a photo of a group of people working together. (If you can't find a photo such as this, insert a *computer* clip art of your choice into the document.)

2. Size the clip art to approximately 5 inches wide. Make sure you maintain its proportion. Use the Horizontal Ruler to guide you.

3. On the Picture Tools Format tab, in the Arrange group, choose Tight from the Text Wrapping command and choose Align Center from the Align command to move the photo to the center of the page near the top margin.

4. Check and close. (*58-drill1*)

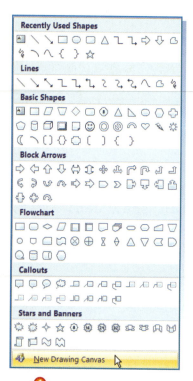

SHAPES

INSERT/ILLUSTRATIONS/SHAPES

You can add one or more shapes to a document. Shapes are often combined to create a more complex drawing object. Available shapes include lines, basic geometric shapes, arrows, equation shapes, flowchart shapes, stars, banners, and callouts.

To add a shape to your document:

INSERT/ILLUSTRATIONS/SHAPES/SELECT SHAPE

1. On the Insert tab in the Illustrations group, click Shapes to display the Shapes gallery .

2. Click the shape you want, click anywhere in the document, and then drag to place the shape.

3. Click anywhere in the document, and then drag to place the shape.

TIP

To create a perfect square or circle (or constrain the dimensions of other shapes), press and hold SHIFT while you drag.

You can change the look of your shape by changing its fill or by adding effects, such as shadows, glows, reflections, soft edges, bevels, and three-dimensional (3-D) rotations to it. A **fill** is the interior of a shape. When you change the fill color of a shape, you can also add a texture, picture, or gradient to the fill. A **gradient** is a gradual progression of colors and shades, usually from one color to another color, or from one shade to another shade of the same color. A **3-D effect** adds depth to a shape. You can add a built-in combination of 3-D effects to your shape, or you can add individual effects.

To add or change a fill color:

DRAWING TOOLS/FORMAT/SHAPE STYLES/SHAPE FILL

1. Click the shape in which you want to add a fill.

2. In the Shape Styles group, click Shape Fill. Choose one of the Theme Colors, one of the Standard Colors, or click More Fill Colors to select the color that you want. To choose no color, click No Fill.

3. Click Shape Outline to change the Outline Weight or Color.

4. Click Shadow Effects or 3-D Effects to add shadow or 3-D effects.

Q, M, V, Apostrophe

WARMUP 9a

Key each line twice.

all letters	1	Lex gripes about cold weather; Fred is not joking.
space bar	2	Is it Di, Jo, or Al? Ask Lt. Coe, Bill; he knows.
easy	3	I did rush a bushel of cut corn to the sick ducks.
easy	4	He is to go to the Tudor Isle of England on a bus.

NEW KEYS

9b q and m

Key each line once; repeat.

q Reach *up* with *left fourth* finger.

m Reach *down* with *right first* finger.

q

5 q qa qa quad quad quaff quant queen quo quit quick
6 qa qu qa quo quit quod quid quip quads quote quiet
7 quite quilts quart quill quakes quail quack quaint

m

8 m mj mj jam man malt mar max maw me mew men hem me
9 m mj ma am make male mane melt meat mist amen lame
10 malt meld hemp mimic tomb foam rams mama mire mind

all reaches learned

11 Quin had some quiet qualms about taming a macaque.
12 Jake Coxe had questions about a new floor program.
13 Max was quick to join the big reception for Lidia.

9c Textbook Keying

Key each line once for control. DS between groups of two lines.

m/x	14	me men ma am jam am lax, mix jam; the hem, six men
	15	Emma Max expressed an aim to make a mammoth model.

DS

q/u	16	qa qu aqua aqua quit quit quip quite pro quo squad
	17	Did Quin make a quick request to take the Qu exam?

DS

g/n	18	fg gn gun gun dig dig nag snag snag sign grab grab
	19	Georgia hung a sign in front of the union for Gib.

PICTURES

INSERT/ILLUSTRATIONS/PICTURES

Pictures can also be inserted into your documents. Pictures are photographs or other images created in a software other than *Word*. They may be located on the user's computer or another storage device.

To insert a picture:

INSERT/ILLUSTRATIONS/PICTURES

1. Click where you want to insert the picture.

2. On the Insert tab, in the Illustrations group, click Picture ❶.

3. Select the desired drive and folder. Click the desired picture to select it, and click Insert ❷.

Although inserted slightly differently, the steps for sizing and moving clip art and pictures are the same.

To size clip art or pictures:

1. Select the clip or picture.

2. Position your insertion point over one of the open circles ❷ around the edge of the image.

3. When the pointer turns to a double-headed arrow ❸, click and drag the image to your desired size. Drag the lower-right handle down and to the right to increase the size; drag it up and to the left to make the clip smaller.

To move a clip art or picture:

PICTURE TOOLS/FORMAT/ARRANGE/TEXT WRAPPING

1. Click to select the clip art to display the Picture Tools.

2. On the Format tab, in the Arrange group ❶, click the Text Wrapping command. Choose Tight (or one of the text-wrapping options) from the drop-down list.

3. Drag the shape to its new location.

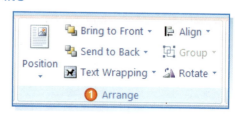

TIP

Remember to proofread and preview each document as a SOP. You will not be reminded to do this.

TIP

You can drag the square handle on the sides of a clip to size the image, but you'll distort its size. Always drag a corner handle to maintain the clip's proportion.

TIP

To move or "nudge" the shape in very small increments, hold down CTRL while you tap the Up Arrow, Down Arrow, Right Arrow, or Left Arrow keys.

9d
v and ' (apostrophe)
Key each line once; repeat.

Apostrophe: The apostrophe shows (1) omission (as Rob't for Robert or it's for it is) or (2) possession when used with nouns (as Joe's hat).

v Reach *down* with *left first* finger.

' Reach to the right with the *right fourth* finger.

v

20 v vf vf vie vie via via vim vat vow vile vale vote
21 vf vf ave vet ova eve vie dive five live have lave
22 cove dove over aver vivas hive volt five java jive

' (apostrophe)

23 '; '; it's it's Rod's; it's Bo's hat; we'll do it.
24 We don't know if it's Lee's pen or Norma's pencil.
25 It's ten o'clock; I won't tell him that he's late.

all reaches learned

26 It's Viv's turn to drive Iva's van to Ava's house.
27 Qua, not Vi, took the jet; so did Cal. Didn't he?
28 Wasn't Fae Baxter a judge at the post garden show?

SKILL BUILDING

9e Reinforcement
Key each line once.

v/?
29 Viola said she has moved six times in five months.
30 Does Dave live on Vine Street? Must he leave now?

q/?
31 Did Viv vote? Can Paque move it? Could Val dive?
32 Didn't Raquel quit Carl Quent after their quarrel?

direct reach
33 Fred told Brice that the junior class must depart.
34 June and Hunt decided to go to that great musical.

double letter
35 Harriette will cook dinner for the swimming teams.
36 Bill's committee meets in an accounting classroom.

TECHNIQUE TIP
Keep your hands still as you reach to the third or bottom rows.

9f Timed Writing
Key the paragraph once for control. Key it again a little faster.

```
          .         4         .         8         .
We must be able to express our thoughts with ease
   12         .        16         .        20
if we desire to find success in the business world.
   .        24         .        28
It is there that sound ideas earn cash.
```

58c Timed Writing

Take two 1' timings on the paragraph; work to increase speed.

all letters

gwam 1'

Good plans typically are required to execute most tasks	11
successfully. If a task is worth doing, it is worth investing the time	25
that is necessary to plan it effectively. Many people are anxious to	39
get started on a task and just begin before they have thought about	53
the best way to organize it. In the long run, they frequently end up	67
wasting time that could be spent more profitably on important	79
projects that they might prefer to tackle.	87

1' | 1 | 2 | 3 | 4 | 5 | 6 | 7 | 8 | 9 | 10 | 11 | 12 | 13 |

NEW FUNCTIONS

58d Graphics Elements

Clip art, pictures, and shapes are graphics elements that enhance documents such as announcements, invitations, reports, and newsletters. In this lesson, you will work with these graphics elements.

CLIP ART

INSERT/ILLUSTRATIONS/CLIP ART

Clip art is a graphics file that includes illustrations (created by hand or by computer software).

Word 2007 (and other applications such as *Excel*, *PowerPoint*, and *Publisher*) provides a collection of pictures, clip art, and sounds that can be added to documents. Additional clips are available online. You can also add your own clips to the collection. The clips are organized into different collections to simplify finding appropriate clip art. The Clip Organizer adds keywords to enable you to search for various types of clip art. You also have the option of selecting the collection and viewing thumbnail sketches (small pictures) of the various clip art available in each category. Once clip art has been inserted into a document, you can size it, copy and paste it, wrap text around it, or drag it to other locations.

TIP

In Microsoft Clip Organizer, select the **clip** you want to add to your open document. Drag the clip into the document.

To insert a clip art:

INSERT/ILLUSTRATIONS/CLIP ART

1. On the Insert tab, in the Illustrations group, click Clip Art.

2. In the Clip Art task pane, key a word or phrase in the Search for text box that describes the clip art that you want to search for, such as *laptop* ❶.

3. In the Search in box ❷ click the down arrow and select Everywhere to search All Collections.

4. Click Go.

5. In the list of results, click the clip art ❸ to insert it in your document.

LESSON 10 — Z, Y, Quotation Mark, Tab

LESSON 10

WARMUP 10a

Key each line twice.

all letters	1	Quill owed those back taxes after moving to Japan.
spacing	2	Didn't Vi, Sue, and Paul go? Someone did; I know.
q/v/m	3	Marv was quite quick to remove that mauve lacquer.
easy	4	Lana is a neighbor; she owns a lake and an island.

NEW KEYS

10b z and y
Key each line once; repeat.

z Reach *down* with *left fourth* finger.

y Reach *up* with *right first* finger.

z

5 za za zap zap zing zig zag zoo zed zip zap zig zed

6 doze zeal zero haze jazz zone zinc zing size ozone

7 ooze maze doze zoom zarf zebus daze gaze faze adze

y

8 y yj yj jay jay hay hay lay nay say days eyes ayes

9 yj ye yet yen yes cry dry you rye sty your fry wry

10 ye yen bye yea coy yew dye yaw lye yap yak yon any

all reaches learned

11 Did you say Liz saw any yaks or zebus at your zoo?

12 Relax; Jake wouldn't acquire any favorable rights.

13 Has Mazie departed? Tex, Lu, and I will go alone.

10c Textbook Keying
Key each line once. DS between groups.

14 Cecilia brings my jumbo umbrella to every concert.

direct reach 15 John and Kim recently brought us an old art piece.

16 I built a gray brick border around my herb garden.

DS

17 sa ui hj gf mn vc ew uy re io as lk rt jk df op yu

adjacent reach 18 In Ms. Lopez' opinion, the opera was really great.

19 Polly and I were joining Walker at the open house.

Graphics Essentials

MODULE 8

LEARNING OUTCOMES

- Apply graphics and pictures to enhance document format.
- Insert and format columns in documents.
- Build keyboarding and production skills.

LESSON 58   ## Basic Graphics

WARMUP 58a

Key each line, striving for control. Repeat if desired.

alphabet 1 Dave Cagney alphabetized items for next week's quarterly journal.

figures 2 Close Rooms 4, 18, and 20 from 3 until 9 on July 7; open Room 56.

easy/figures 3 Toy & Wurt's note for $635 (see our page 78) was paid October 29.

easy 4 The auditor is due by eight, and he may lend a hand to the panel.

| 1 | 2 | 3 | 4 | 5 | 6 | 7 | 8 | 9 | 10 | 11 | 12 | 13 |

SKILL BUILDING

58b **Textbook Keying**
1. Key the drill, concentrating on good keying techniques. Tap ENTER twice after each 4-line group.
2. Repeat the drill if time permits.

5 Sand castles are fun to build but are poor shelter in a downpour.

adjacent reaches 6 The Hoosiers scored three points in the fourth to avoid an upset.

7 Her articles are going to be reported in an edition of the paper.

8 Fewer people attend West Point to play polo than to join a choir.

9 A dazed beggar scattered after a red car swerved on a wet street.

one hand 10 Mimi feasts on milky eggs at noon after I feed Kipp plum dessert.

11 Mo started ragweed tests in a vacated garage after greeting Dave.

12 You debate Phil after I defeat John; rest up, you brave braggart!

13 Handiwork is busy work, but it's also a memento of a rich entity.

balanced hand 14 The hairy ape bit the fish, but the apricot and corn lay dormant.

15 Henry may dismantle an authentic antique auto for Zoe's sorority.

16 An Irish auditor quit work at the city and ambled to the fields.

LESSON 58 BASIC GRAPHICS   **MODULE 8**   244

10d

" (quotation mark) and **TAB**

Key each line once; repeat.

TAB Reach *up* with *left fourth* finger.

" Shift; then reach to the right with the *right fourth* finger.

" (quotation mark)

20 "; "; " " "lingo" "bugs" "tennies" I like "malts."

21 "I am not," she said, "going." I just said, "Oh?"

tab key

22   The tab key is used for indenting paragraphs and aligning columns.

23   Tabs that are set by the software are called default tabs, which are usually a half inch.

SKILL BUILDING

10e Textbook Keying

Key lines 24–30 once. Tap TAB to indent each paragraph. Use wordwrap, tapping ENTER only at the end of each paragraph.

24   The expression "I give you my word," or put another
25 way, "Take my word for it," is just a way I can say, "I
26 prize my name; it clearly stands in back of my words."
27 I offer "honor" as collateral.

tab 28   Tap the tab key and begin the line without a pause to maintain fluency.

29   She said that this is the lot to be sent; I agreed with her.

30   Tap Tab before starting to key a timed writing so that the first line is indented.

10f Timed Writing

Take two 1' timings beginning with paragraph 1. If you finish before time is up, continue with paragraph 2. Use wordwrap.

Goal: 15 *gwam*

TECHNIQUE TIP

Wordwrap: Text within a paragraph moves automatically to the next line. Tap ENTER only to begin a new paragraph.

	gwam	1'
Tab → All of us work for progress, but it is not		8
always easy to analyze "progress." We work hard		18
for it; but, in spite of some really good efforts,		28
we may fail to receive just exactly the response we		39
want.		40
Tab → When this happens, as it does to all of us,		9
it is time to cease whatever we are doing, have		18
a quiet talk with ourselves, and face up to the		28
questions about our limited progress. How can we		38
do better?		40

| 1 | 2 | 3 | 4 | 5 | 6 | 7 | 8 | 9 | 10 |

57-d3

Edit Report

 COMMUNITY PARK

TIP

Use Format Painter to copy heading format to other headings and paragraph formats to other paragraphs.

1. Make the following edits in the report.

2. Change the format from a leftbound report to an unbound report. Position the title at about 2", center it, and apply Arial 14-point bold format; convert to uppercase. Apply Arial 12-point bold format to side headings; ensure that headings are kept with the paragraphs below them. Remove space after the side headings.

3. Apply double spacing and 12-point Times New Roman to the first paragraph and remove extra space after the paragraph; copy format to other paragraphs. Insert page numbers at the top right; do not show on the first page.

4. Use Find and Replace to locate all occurrences of *theme* and replace it with *community* each time it occurs. Use uppercase and lowercase appropriately.

5. Add the following sentence to the end of the first paragraph in the document:

   The planning Commission also asked the Committee to recommend the most desirable location for the park.

6. Two paragraphs in the document need editing. Make the edits shown below:

   All members of the Committee visited the three *potential* sites ~~selected~~—the Westlake site, the Southside site, and the Woodcreek site to determine if $\frac{1}{m}$ the sites were both feasible and desirable for the location of the new theme park. The Committee used the *comprehensive* criteria developed by the planning commission for the *in-depth* review of each site. A *summary* copy of the criteria is attached; A description of each site follows. *The complete document is posted on the Commission's website, www.planningcommission.gov.*

   All three sites met the size criteria and are within the cost projections of the planning commission. The table ~~on the next page shows~~ *shown below details* the comparative costs of the sites when both land and the estimated cost of the infrastructure are considered. *The infrastructure cost estimates for all sites were prepared by J.M. Moore Engineering.*

   (Key the following table after this paragraph and before the heading *Other Factors*. Apply Black Medium Shading 2.)

Site Costs *Center, bold, 14-point type*			
Cost Category	**Westlake** *Center column heads*	**Southside**	**Woodcreek**
Land	$720,000	$630,000	$676,000
Infrastructure	175,000	210,000	180,000
Total	$805,000	$840000	$856,000

Left-align first column

7. Check the test and close. (*57-d3*)

CHECKPOINT ➡

Congratulations! You have successfully completed the lessons in Module 7. To check your understanding and for more practice, complete the objective assessment and performance assessment located on the textbook website at www.collegekeyboarding.com.

LESSON 11

Review

WARMUP 11a

Key each line twice (slowly, then faster).

alphabet 1 Zeb had Jewel quickly give him five or six points.

" (quote) 2 Can you spell "chaos," "bias," "bye," and "their"?

y 3 Ty Clay may envy you for any zany plays you write.

easy 4 Did he bid on the bicycle, or did he bid on a map?

| 1 | 2 | 3 | 4 | 5 | 6 | 7 | 8 | 9 | 10 |

SKILL BUILDING

11b
Keyboard Reinforcement
Key each line once; repeat the drill to increase fluency.

TECHNIQUE TIP

Work for smoothness, not speed.

5 za za zap az az maze zoo zip razz zed zax zoa zone

6 Liz Zahl saw Zoe feed the zebra in an Arizona zoo.

7 yj yj jy jy joy lay yaw say yes any yet my try you

8 Why do you say that today, Thursday, is my payday?

9 xs xs sax ox box fix hex ax lax fox taxi lox sixes

10 Roxy, you may ask Jay to fix any tax sets for you.

11 qa qa aqua quail quit quake quid equal quiet quart

12 Did Enrique quietly but quickly quell the quarrel?

13 fv fv five lives vow ova van eve avid vex vim void

14 Has Vivi, Vada, or Eva visited Vista Valley Farms?

11c Speed Builders
Key each balanced-hand line twice, as quickly as you can.

15 is to for do an may work so it but an with them am

16 am yam map aid zig yams ivy via vie quay cob amend

17 to do is for an may work so it but am an with them

18 for it|for it|to the|to the|do they|do they|do it

19 Pamela may go to the farm with Jan and a neighbor.

20 Rod and Ty may go by the lake if they go downtown.

| 1 | 2 | 3 | 4 | 5 | 6 | 7 | 8 | 9 | 10 |

TIP

Remember to proofread and preview each document before you move to the next one.

1. Key the memo shown below.
2. TO: Planning Commission | FROM: Community Park Site Committee | Current date | SUBJECT: Community Park Site Assessment | Copy to Mayor Charles Morgan
3. Continue to next document. (*57-d1*)

The Community Park Site Committee has completed its assessment of the potential sites for the new park. Our report is enclosed.

The Committee unanimously recommends that the Westlake site be used for the new park. The Woodcreek site was considered acceptable, but it is not as desirable as the Westlake site. The Southside site was the least desirable of the three sites.

Please contact us if you have any questions.

57-d2

Block Letter

1. Key the following letter; use the current date, block letter style, and your name as the signature.
2. Center the page.
3. Continue to next document. (*57-d2*)

Ms. Margaret C. Worthington
4957 Mt. Elon Church Road
Hopkins, SC 29061-9837

Dear Ms. Worthington

The Planning Commission has authorized me to contact you to discuss the possible purchase of the 120-acre site that we discussed with you for the new Community Park. When we spoke with you yesterday, you indicated that you would be available to meet with us any afternoon next week. If it is still convenient, we would like to meet with you on Wednesday afternoon at 2:00 at the site.

Earlier you indicated that you had a recent survey and an appraisal of the property. We would appreciate it if you could have those documents available for the meeting.

If this time is not convenient, please call my office and leave a message so that I may reschedule the meeting. We look forward to working with you.

Sincerely

11d Textbook Keying

Key each line once. Tap ENTER at the end of each line. DS between the groups of lines.

© FRANKSITEMAN.COM 2007

enter: key smoothly without looking at fingers

```
21  Make the return snappily
22  and with assurance; keep
23  your eyes on your source
24  data; maintain a smooth,
25  constant pace as you key.
```
DS

space bar: use down-and-in motion

```
26  us me it of he an by do go to us if or so am ah el
27  Have you a pen?  If so, print "Free to any guest."
```
DS

caps lock: press to toggle it on or off

```
28  Use ALL CAPS for items such as TO, FROM, or SUBJECT.
29  Did Kristin mean Kansas City, MISSOURI, or KANSAS?
```

TECHNIQUE TIP

Tap [CAPS LOCK] to capitalize several letters. Tap it again to toggle [CAPS LOCK] off.

11e Timed Writing

1. Take two 2' timings on all paragraphs. If you finish before time is up, start over with paragraph 1. Use wordwrap. Key fluently but with control.
   Goal: 16 wam
2. End the lesson but do not exit the software.

To determine gross-words-a-minute (gwam) rate for 2':

Follow these steps if you are *not* using the Timer in the Word Processor.

1. Note the figure at the end of the last line completed.

2. For a partial line, note the figure on the scale direcly below the point at which you stopped keying.

3. Add these two figures to determine the total gross words a minute (gwam) you keyed.

```
                                                         gwam  2'

     Have  we  thought  of  communication  as  a  kind    4 | 31
of war that we wage through each day?                      8 | 35
     When  we  think  of  it  that  way,  good  language  12 | 39
would  seem  to  become  our  major  line  of  attack.    17 | 44
     Words  become  muscle;  in  a  normal  exchange or in 22 | 49
a  quarrel,  we  do  well  to  realize  the  power of words. 27 | 54
```

11f Enrichment

1. Click the Skill Building tab from the main menu and choose Technique Builder; select Drill 1a.
2. Key Drill 1a from page 31. Key each line once striving for good accuracy.
3. The results will be listed on the Skill Building Report.

LESSON 57 | Assessment

WARMUP 57a

Key each line, striving for control. Repeat if desired.

alphabet	1	Max Biqua watched jet planes flying in the azure sky over a cove.
figures	2	Send 105 No. 4 nails and 67 No. 8 brads for my home at 329 Annet.
3rd row	3	We two were ready to type a report for our quiet trio of workers.
easy	4	Pamela owns a big bicycle; and, with it, she may visit the docks.

| 1 | 2 | 3 | 4 | 5 | 6 | 7 | 8 | 9 | 10 | 11 | 12 | 13 |

SKILL BUILDING

57b Timed Writing

Key two 3' timed writings. Strive for control.

all letters

gwam 3' | 5'

Voting is a very important part of being a good citizen. However, many young people who are eligible to vote choose not to do so. When asked to explain or justify their decision, many simply shrug their shoulders and reply that they have no particular reason for not voting. The explanation others frequently give is that they just did not get around to going to the voting polls.

A good question to consider concerns ways that we can motivate young people to be good citizens and to go to the polls and to vote. Some people approach this topic by trying to determine how satisfied people who do not vote are with the performance of their elected officials. Unfortunately, those who choose not to vote are just as satisfied with their elected officials as are those who voted.

One interesting phenomenon concerning voting relates to the job market. When the job market is strong, fewer young people vote than when the job market is very bad. They also tend to be less satisfied with their elected officials. Self-interest seems to be a powerful motivator. Unfortunately, those who do not choose to vote miss the point that it is in their best interest to be a good citizen.

	3'	5'
	4	2
	8	5
	12	7
	16	10
	21	13
	25	15
	29	18
	34	21
	39	23
	43	26
	48	29
	52	31
	56	34
	61	36
	65	39
	69	41
	74	44
	78	47
	79	47

3' | 1 | 2 | 3 | 4 |
5' | 1 | 2 | 3 |

APPLICATIONS

57c

Assessment

 Continue

 Check

With *Keyboarding Pro DELUXE*: When you complete a document, proofread it, check the spelling, and preview for placement. When you are completely satisfied, click the Continue button to move to the next document. Click the Check button when you are ready to error-check the test. Review and/or print the document analysis results.

Without *Keyboarding Pro DELUXE*: Key the documents in sequence. When time has been called, proofread all documents again and identify errors.

LESSON 12 — Review

WARMUP 12a

Key each line twice (slowly, then faster).

alphabet	1	Jack won five quiz games; Brad will play him next.
q	2	Quin Racq quickly and quietly quelled the quarrel.
z	3	Zaret zipped along sizzling, zigzag Arizona roads.
easy	4	Did he hang the sign by the big bush at the lake?

| 1 | 2 | 3 | 4 | 5 | 6 | 7 | 8 | 9 | 10 |

SKILL BUILDING

12b New Key Review
Key each line once; DS between groups. Work for smoothness, not speed.

b/f	5	bf bf fab fab ball bib rf rf rib rib fibs bums bee
	6	Did Buffy remember that he is a brass band member?
z/y	7	za za zag zig zip yj yj jay eye day lazy hazy zest
	8	Liz amazed us with the zesty pizza on a lazy trip.
q/u	9	qa qa quo qt. quit quay quad quarm que uj jug quay
	10	Where is Quito? Qatar? Boqueirao? Quebec? Quilmes?
v/m	11	vf vf valve five value mj mj ham mad mull mass vim
	12	Vito, enter the words vim, vivace, and avar; save.
all	13	I faced defeat; only reserves saved my best crews.
	14	In my opinion, I need to rest in my reserved seat.
all	15	Holly created a red poppy and deserves art awards.
	16	My pump averages a faster rate; we get better oil.

12c Textbook Keying
Key each line once; DS between groups. Work for smooth, unhurried keying.

de/ed	17	ed fed led deed dell dead deal sled desk need seed
	18	Dell dealt with the deed before the dire deadline.
ol/lo	19	old tolls doll solo look sole lost love cold stole
	20	Old Ole looked for the long lost olive oil lotion.
op/po	21	pop top post rope pout port stop opal opera report
	22	Stop to read the top opera opinion report to Opal.
we/ew	23	we few wet were went wears weather skews stew blew
	24	Working women wear sweaters when weather dictates.

TECHNIQUE TIP

Keep fingers curved and body aligned properly.

The Marshall Tract *Heading 2*

The Marshall tract consists of over 1,200 acres of environmentally sensitive coastal property. Approximately one-half of the tract consists of wetlands with a conservation and preservation easement on the property. A portion of the remaining property has endangered species, including the red cockaded woodpecker. An eagle nest has also been spotted on the property.

Insert

The master plan calls for the retention of the property because of its potential for research and environmental education. The short-term plans call for the establishment of a system of nature trails and boardwalks and the development of a parking area for visitors. Long-term plans specify the design and construction of a research and learning center.

The Richardson Tract *Heading 2*

The Richardson tract consists of an entire barrier island that is used for research purposes. The property currently has a very basic research and education center. The gift agreement severely restricts development of facilities on the island; therefore, it is not likely to be highly developed at any point in the future.

Midlands Properties *Heading 1*

The Midlands portfolio of property consists of more than sixty individual parcels of land. Approximately 60 percent of the land was purchased and 40 percent was received as gifts. The land is valued at $12,650,000.

The Wheeler Tract *Heading 2*

A decision has been made to sell this property. Currently, the property is being surveyed and a new appraisal has been ordered. The property will be put placed on the market as soon as the survey and appraisal have been completed.

The Blossom Tract *Heading 2*

The Foundation contracted to have infrastructure *work completed before turning the tract over to Midlands University for development.*

12d Textbook Keying

Key each line once; DS between groups of three lines. Concentrate and key with control.

TECHNIQUE TIP

Keep hands quiet; do not bounce. Keep fingers curved and upright.

25 a for we you is that be this will be a to and well
26 as our with I or a to by your form which all would
27 new year no order they so new but now year who may

DS

28 This is Lyn's only date to visit their great city.
29 I can send it to your office at any time you wish.
30 She kept the fox, owls, and fowl down by the lake.

DS

31 Harriette will cook dinner for the swimming teams.
32 Annette will call at noon to give us her comments.
33 Johnny was good at running and passing a football.

| 1 | 2 | 3 | 4 | 5 | 6 | 7 | 8 | 9 | 10 |

12e Timed Writing

Key a 2' timing on both paragraphs. If you finish before time is up, start again with paragraph 1. Key fluently but not rushed. Repeat the timing again for 2'.

all letters

Goal: 16 gwam

Copy Difficulty
What factors determine whether copy is difficult or easy? Research shows that difficulty is influenced by syllables per word, characters per word, and percent of familiar words. Carefully controlling these three factors ensures that speed and accuracy scores are reliable—that is, increased scores reflect increased skill.

In Level 1, all timings are easy. Note "E" inside the triangle at left of the timing. Easy timings contain an average of 1.2 syllables per word, 5.1 characters per word, and 90 percent familiar words. Easy copy is suitable for the beginner who is mastering the keyboard.

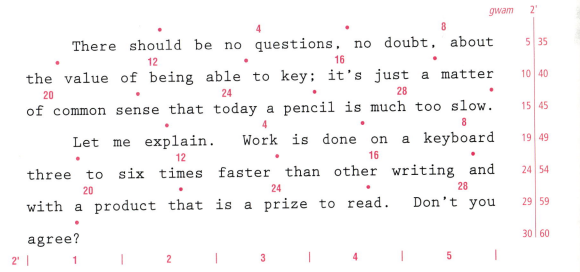

	gwam	2'
There should be no questions, no doubt, about	5	35
the value of being able to key; it's just a matter	10	40
of common sense that today a pencil is much too slow.	15	45
Let me explain. Work is done on a keyboard	19	49
three to six times faster than other writing and	24	54
with a product that is a prize to read. Don't you	29	59
agree?	30	60

2' | 1 | 2 | 3 | 4 | 5 |

1. In the open document, position title about 2" from top of page and apply Title format.

2. Format headings as noted in the copy below and ensure that they are not separated from the paragraphs that follow.

3. Open *55-d1*, copy the *Property Location and Value* table, and paste it after the second paragraph. Apply Medium Grid 3 – Accent 5 table design. Delete extra blank lines if any. Insert the following footnote so that the note reference mark is positioned after the word *Value* in the table title:

   [1]Property values are based on the appraised value at the time of acquisition.

4. Make all edits shown below. Add text shown in script to the document.

5. Prepare a cover page using the design of your choice.

6. Proofread. Ensure that you have made all edits and followed all instructions.

7. Check and close. (*56-d2*)

Master Plan for Properties

The Midlands University Foundation properties are categorized into four classifications: Coastal Property, Midlands Property, other in-state property, and out-of-state property. The Foundation acquires property either by purchasing it or by accepting gifts from donors desiring to support Midlands University.

Insert → *Generally, the Foundation retains coastal properties for research and environmental education purposes and properties in the Midlands area for future development and use by Midlands University. Usually, properties in the other two categories are held only if they are likely to appreciate significantly; otherwise, they are sold and the proceeds are used to support various University needs. Currently, the total value of the out-of-state property is $2,145,000.*

Insert table here.

Coastal Properties   *Heading 1*

                                              seven

Currently the Foundation owns ~~a number of~~ different tracts of land in the Coastal Region valued at $18,325,000. Decisions on the future use of five of the tracts are pending. The master plan contains specific plans for only two of the tracts,the Marshall tract and the Richardson tract.

                    ∧ *em dash*

LESSON 13 | Review

WARMUP 13a

Key each line twice (slowly, then faster).

alphabet	1	Bev quickly hid two Japanese frogs in Mitzi's box.
shift	2	Jay Nadler, a Rotary Club member, wrote Mr. Coles.
, (comma)	3	Jay, Ed, and I paid for plates, knives, and forks.
easy	4	Did the amendment name a city auditor to the firm?

| 1 | 2 | 3 | 4 | 5 | 6 | 7 | 8 | 9 | 10 |

SKILL BUILDING

13b Textbook Keying

Key each line once; DS between groups of lines. Key the text as suggested:

Lines 5–7: Key the words as a single unit.

Lines 8–10: Key the words letter by letter.

Lines 11–13: Vary your keying as your fingers find the right rhythm.

word-level response: key short, familiar words as units

5 is to for do an may work so it but an with them am
6 Did they mend the torn right half of their ensign?
7 Hand me the ivory tusk on the mantle by the bugle.

letter-level response: key more difficult words letter by letter

8 only state jolly zest oil verve join rate mop card
9 After defeat, look up; gaze in joy at a few stars.
10 We gazed at a plump beaver as it waded in my pool.

combination response: use variable speed; your fingers will let you feel the difference

11 it up so at for you may was but him work were they
12 It is up to you to get the best rate; do it right.
13 This is Lyn's only date to visit their great city.

| 1 | 2 | 3 | 4 | 5 | 6 | 7 | 8 | 9 | 10 |

13c Keyboard Reinforcement

Key each line once; fingers well curved, wrists low.

p	14	Pat appears happy to pay for any supper I prepare.
x	15	Knox can relax; Alex gets a box of flax next week.
v	16	Vi, Ava, and Viv move ivy vines, leaves, or stems.
'	17	It's a question of whether they can't or won't go.
?	18	Did Jan go? Did she see Ray? Who paid? Did she?
.	19	Ms. E. K. Nu and Lt. B. A. Walz had the a.m. duty.
"	20	"Who are you?" he asked. "I am," I said, "Marie."
;	21	Find a car; try it; like it; work a price; buy it.

56-d1

Edit Memo

TRAIL DESIGN

1. In the open document, position the first line of the heading correctly. Search for *sights* and replace with *sites* each time it occurs.
2. Add bullets to the list of sites. Use a nonbreaking space with Phase 1 and Phase 2 to avoid the number from being placed on a separate line from Phase.
3. Make other edits shown and add reference initials.
4. Check and close. *(56-d1)*

To: Trail design task force

From: Dianne Gibson

Date: Current

Subject: Trail design

Thanks for participating in the Trail Design meeting last week. We did make a tremendous amount of progress on this exciting project. Specific sights were designated for the components of phase one of the Environmental learning center complex and the first trail loop. Tentative sights were identified for the phase two components including the conference center.

Ken provides us with a new lay out of the property showing the following sights that were designated during the visit.

Main Entrance
Parking area
Environmental Learning Center
General shelter buildings
Outdoor linear classrooms
First trail loop with key interpretative sights designated
Sustainability exhibit sights

Please review the positioning of these sights to make sure that both the layout and documentation interprets the groups decisions properly. Once we recieve feed back from every one, Ken will finalize the design documents.

Our timeframe requires us to have finalized concept documents within two weeks to turn over to the architects. The architects will develop the construction documents needed to obtain the necessary permits.

13d Textbook Keying

Troublesome Pairs: Key each line once; DS between groups.

TECHNIQUE TIP

Keep hands and arms still as you reach up to the third row and down to the first row.

```
t  22  at fat hat sat to tip the that they fast last slat
r  23  or red try ran run air era fair rid ride trip trap
t/r 24 A trainer sprained an arm trying to tame the bear.
                                                       DS
m  25  am me my mine jam man more most dome month minimum
n  26  no an now nine once net knee name ninth know never
m/n 27 Many men and women are important company managers.
                                                       DS
o  28  on or to not now one oil toil over only solo today
i  29  it is in tie did fix his sit like with insist will
o/i 30 Joni will consider obtaining options to buy coins.
                                                       DS
a  31  at an as art has and any case data haze tart smart
s  32  us as so say sat slap lass class just sassy simple
a/s 33 Disaster was averted as the steamer sailed to sea.
                                                       DS
e  34  we he ear the key her hear chef desire where there
i  35  it is in tie did fix his sit like with insist will
e/i 36 An expression of gratitude for service is desired.
```

13e Timed Writing

Key a 2' writing on both paragraphs. If you finish before time is up, start again with paragraph 1. Key fluently but not rushed. Repeat the timing again for 2'.

all letters

Goal: 16 *gwam*

```
                                                       gwam  2'
            •            4            •           8
      The questions of time use are vital ones; we      5
      •           12           •           16
miss so much just because we don't plan.                9
            •            4            •           8
      When we organize our days, we save time for      13
      •           12           •           16
those extra premium things we long to do.              17
2' |     1     |     2     |     3     |     4     |     5     |
```

LESSON 56 Edit Documents

WARMUP 56a

Key each line, striving for control. Repeat if desired.

alphabet	1	Jacki might analyze the data by answering five complex questions.
figures	2	Memo 67 asks if the report on Bill 35-48 is due the 19th or 20th.
double letters	3	Aaron took accounting lessons at a community college last summer.
easy	4	Hand Bob a bit of cocoa, a pan of cod, an apricot, and six clams.

| 1 | 2 | 3 | 4 | 5 | 6 | 7 | 8 | 9 | 10 | 11 | 12 | 13 |

SKILL BUILDING

56b Textbook Keying

1. Key the drill, concentrating on good keying techniques; tap ENTER twice after each 2-line group.
2. Repeat the drill if time permits.

First row

5 Zam name bank man came exam cave band comb six mine vent back van
6 Zack came back excited; Max made a banner for a vacant zinc mine.

Home row

7 sad lass lag had gag laggard fax hulk salad sales flask glass has
8 Dallas Klass had a jello salad; Ada asked for a large salad also.

Third row

9 were pot toy pew wept you quit power quip peer tower or rope wire
10 Terry wrote Troy for help after a power tower guide wire was cut.

56c Timed Writing

Key two 3' timed writings. Strive for control.

all letters

	gwam	3'	5'
For many years, readers who had chosen a particular book had		4	2
just one question to answer: Do you want to purchase a hardcover		8	5
or a paperback book? It was assumed that books would be purchased		13	8
from a retail outlet, such as a bookstore. Currently, books are		17	10
being marketed and sold online. The book itself, however, is still		22	13
printed on paper.		23	14
With the technology that is on the market today, a third		27	16
alternative, the electronic or the so-called e-book, is emerging.		31	19
E-books are sold in digitized form. The book must be read from the		36	21
website on a computer or on a special device designed for reading		40	24
e-books. Many publishers are experimenting with electronic books,		45	27
but only a few well-known ones have moved into the e-book market		49	29
in a major way. Most e-book companies are small organizations that		54	32
are willing to take a risk to make a profit.		56	34
The cost of producing and selling books in digital form is		60	36
far less than it is in paper form. The result is that books		65	39
that appeal to small markets are now feasible in digital form. The		69	41
cost was too great in print form. Many publishers have two key		73	44
concerns about the e-book market. The first is that a large number		78	47
of readers still are not comfortable reading from electronic media		82	49
for long time periods. The second factor is that they worry about		87	52
copyright protection. Many are very aware of the problems the music		91	55
industry experienced in this area.		94	56

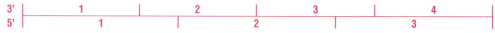

3'	1	2	3	4
5'	1	2	3	

1

Skill Builder

Skill Building   Technique Builder

From the Skill Building tab, select Technique Builder and then the drill. Key each line once at a comfortable rate. Tap ENTER at the end of each line. Single-space the drill. Concentrate and key accurately. Repeat if desired.

DRILL 1

Goal: reinforce key locations

Key each line once at a comfortable, constant rate.

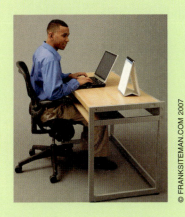

© FRANKSITEMAN.COM 2007

TECHNIQUE TIP

Keep
- your eyes on source copy
- your fingers curved, upright
- your wrists low but not touching
- your elbows hanging loosely
- your feet flat on the floor

Drill 1a

A We saw that Alan had an alabaster vase in Alabama.
B My rubber boat bobbed about in the bubbling brook.
C Ceci gave cups of cold cocoa to Rebecca and Rocco.
D Don's dad added a second deck to his old building.
E Even as Ellen edited her document, she ate dinner.
F Our firm in Buffalo has a staff of forty or fifty.
G Ginger is giving Greg the eggs she got from Helga.
H Hugh has eighty high, harsh lights he might flash.

Drill 1b

I Irik's lack of initiative is irritating his coach.
J Judge J. J. Jore rejected Jeane and Jack's jargon.
K As a lark, Kirk kicked back a rock at Kim's kayak.
L Lucille is silly; she still likes lemon lollipops.
M Milt Mumm hammered a homer in the Miami home game.
N Ken Linn has gone hunting; Stan can begin canning.
O Jon Soto rode off to Otsego in an old Morgan auto.
P Philip helped pay the prize as my puppy hopped up.
Q Quiet Raquel quit quoting at an exquisite marquee.

Drill 1c

R As Mrs. Kerr's motor roared, her red horse reared.
S Sissie lives in Mississippi; Lissa lives in Tulsa.
T Nat told Betty not to tattle on her little sister.
U Ula has a unique but prudish idea on unused units.
V Eva visited every vivid event for twelve evenings.
W We watched as wayworn wasps swarmed by the willow.
X Tex Cox waxed the next box for Xenia and Rex Knox.
Y Ty says you may stay with Fay for only sixty days.
Z Hazel is puzzled about the azure haze; Zack dozes.

55-d2

Report with Table

LEPPARD

1. In the open document, change format to leftbound report.
2. Position title about 2" from the top of the page and apply Title style to both the first page and the Reference Page.
3. Use Heading 1 format for all side headings. Capitalize main words in all side headings.
4. Insert the following table where noted on the first page:

Capacity	Babcock	Leppard
Number of beds	184	385
Hospital utilization average daily census	94	326
Medicare utilization average daily census	53	104
Full-time equivalent	364	1,682

5. Format the title of Table 1 using Heading 2 and center it.
6. Use Table Design, Light List - Accent 1. Center column headings.
7. Insert a column to the left of *Babcock*; use the column heading *Juk*, and insert the following data in the column:

    165

    136

    60

    615

8. Replace each of the citations (example: Miguel, 2008, 6) in the report with the following footnotes:

    Isabella Miguel, *Hospital Growth Analysis* (Atlanta, 2008), p. 6.

    Andrew Glenn, *Metro Analysis Feasibility Study—Leppard Outpatient Center* (Atlanta, 2008), p. 8.

    Mark Gibson, "Outpatient Costs in the Southeast," *Health Care News*, January 2008, p. 36.

9. Use the Keep with Next feature to ensure that headings remain with the text that follows them and that the table is not separated from its title or divided on two pages.
10. Number the pages using a plain number at the top right side. Do not show the number on the first page.
11. Use Spelling and Grammar to check the document.
12. Proofread using Full Screen Reading view.
13. Check and close. (*55-d2*)

DRILL 2

Goal: strengthen up and down reaches

Keep hands and wrists quiet; fingers well curved in home position; stretch fingers up from home or pull them palmward as needed.

home position

1 Hall left for Dallas; he is glad Jake fed his dog.
2 Ada had a glass flask; Jake had a sad jello salad.
3 Lana Hask had a sale; Gala shall add half a glass.

down reaches

4 Did my banker, Mr. Mavann, analyze my tax account?
5 Do they, Mr. Zack, expect a number of brave women?
6 Zach, check the menu; next, beckon the lazy valet.

up reaches

7 Prue truly lost the quote we wrote for our report.
8 Teresa quietly put her whole heart into her words.
9 There were two hilarious jokes in your quiet talk.

DRILL 3

Goal: strengthen individual finger reaches

first finger

1 Bob Mugho hunted for five minutes for your number.
2 Juan hit the bright green turf with his five iron.
3 The frigates and gunboats fought mightily in Java.

second finger

4 Dick said the ice on the creek had surely cracked.
5 Even as we picnicked, I decided we needed to diet.
6 Kim, not Mickey, had rice with chicken for dinner.

third/fourth finger

7 Pam saw Roz wax an aqua auto as Lex sipped a cola.
8 Wally will quickly spell Zeus, Apollo, and Xerxes.
9 Who saw Polly? Zoe Pax saw her; she is quiet now.

DRILL 4

Goal: strengthen special reaches

Emphasize smooth stroking. Avoid pauses, but do not reach for speed.

adjacent reaches

1 Falk knew well that her opinions of art were good.
2 Theresa answered her question; order was restored.
3 We join there and walk north to the western point.

direct reaches

4 Barb Nunn must hunt for my checks; she is in debt.
5 In June and December, Irvin hunts in Bryce Canyon.
6 We decided to carve a number of funny human faces.

double letters

7 Anne stopped off at school to see Bill Wiggs cook.
8 Edd has planned a small cookout for all the troop.
9 Keep adding to my assets all fees that will apply.

| 1 | 2 | 3 | 4 | 5 | 6 | 7 | 8 | 9 | 10 |

1. Key the report double spaced; apply Times New Roman 12-point font. Remove space after paragraphs.

2. Use approximately a 2" top margin; add the title: **FOUNDATION PROPERTY**; apply Arial 14-point bold format. Add side headings; apply Arial 14-point bold format.

3. Number the pages at the top right and suppress the page number on the first page.

4. Make the edits shown in the table. In addition, apply Arial 14-point format to the table title and Arial 12-point format to the column heads; add a row at the bottom of the table. Key in the three columns: **Total**, **$34,815,000**, and **100%**.

5. Proofread carefully and make corrections.

6. Check and close. (*55-d1*)

The Foundation owns both out-of-state and in-state property. However, the bulk of the property is located within South Carolina. Properties are acquired either by gift or purchase.

Insert side heading:
Out-of-State Property

Virtually all of the out-of-state property is acquired by gift. Occasionally, a parcel of undeveloped or developed land will be offered to the Foundation at a bargain price. The Foundation then sells the property as soon as it is feasible to do so and retains the profit. The total value of the out-of-state property is $2,145,000.

Insert side heading:
South Carolina Property

Some of the in-state property is purchased by the Foundation for future use. Other property is donated to the Foundation. Donated property may be retained for future use or sold. In-state property is divided into three regions—Coastal, Midlands, and Other. The following table shows the distribution of the property by region:

Property Location and Value		*Bold*
South Carolina Regions *Bold and Center headings*	Value of Property in ~~Region~~	~~Percentage of~~ Total Property
Coastal Region *Set right*	$18,325,000	53%
Midlands Region *align tab*	12,650,000	*Center* 36%
Other Regions—In-State *at 3.5"*	3,840,000	*align* 11%

The total value of the in-state property is $34,815,000. More than half of the property is located in the Coastal region. The next largest concentration is in the Midlands region. The property values are based on the appraisal price at the time of the acquisition. Most real estate professionals estimate that the current value is more than double the value shown in the table.

DRILL 5

Goal: improve troublesome pairs

Use a controlled rate without pauses.

```
     1  ad add did does dish down body dear dread dabs bad
d/k  2  kid ok kiss tuck wick risk rocks kayaks corks buck
     3  Dirk asked Dick to kid Drake about the baked duck.

     4  deed deal den led heed made needs delay he she her
e/i  5  kit kiss kiln kiwi kick kilt kind six ribs kill it
     6  Abie had neither ice cream nor fried rice in Erie.

     7  fib fob fab rib beg bug rob bad bar bed born table
b/v  8  vat vet gave five ever envy never visit weave ever
     9  Did Harv key jibe or jive, TV or TB, robe or rove?

    10  aft after lift gift sit tot the them tax tutu tyro
t/r 11  for far ere era risk rich rock rosy work were roof
    12  In Toronto, Ruth told the truth about her artwork.

    13  jug just jury judge juice unit hunt bonus quiz bug
u/y 14  jay joy lay you your only envy quay oily whey body
    15  Willy usually does not buy your Yukon art in July.
```

DRILL 6

Goal: fluency

```
1  Dian may make cocoa for the girls when they visit.
2  Focus the lens for the right angle; fix the prism.
3  She may suspend work when she signs the torn form.
4  Augment their auto fuel in the keg by the autobus.
5  As usual, their robot did half turns to the right.
6  Pamela laughs as she signals to the big hairy dog.
7  Pay Vivian to fix the island for the eighty ducks.
```

DRILL 7

Goal: eyes on the copy

Option: In the Word Processor, set the Timer for Variable and then either 20" or 30". Choose a *gwam* goal that is two to three words higher than your best rate. Try to reach your goal.

	words	30"	20"
1 Did she make this turkey dish? **ENTER**		12	18
2 Blake and Laurie may go to Dubuque.		14	21
3 Signal for the oak sleigh to turn right.		16	24
4 I blame Susie; did she quench the only flame?		18	27
5 She turns the panel dials to make this robot work.		20	30

LESSON 55

Edit Tables and Reports

WARMUP 55a

Key each line, striving for control. Repeat if desired.

1 When Jorg moves away, quickly place five dozen gloves in the box.
2 Flight 372 leaves at 10:46 a.m. and arrives in Omaha at 9:58 p.m.
3 I obtain unusual services from a number of celebrated decorators.
4 She may sign an authentic name and title to amend this endowment.

| 1 | 2 | 3 | 4 | 5 | 6 | 7 | 8 | 9 | 10 | 11 | 12 | 13 |

SKILL BUILDING

55b Textbook Keying

1. Key the drill, concentrating on good keying techniques; tap ENTER twice after each 2-line group.
2. Repeat the drill if time permits.

adjacent reaches
5 Teresa's choice is to use a free option that is quite easy to do.
6 Sergio was trying to avoid errors, but he still made quite a few.

direct reaches
7 Frederick lost my large, bright red golf umbrella on a sunny day.
8 Debra bought too much junk, but she found the prices to be great.

first row
9 Zack and Max became exercise advocates, but they ate many pizzas.
10 Max Mizel verbalized his excessive love for throwing curve balls.

home row
11 Ada Hall's class was at a lake in Dallas; Kala Klass had a salad.
12 Sally's glass flask was full of salt; Sal also saw a glass flask.

third row
13 Trey, a poet, wrote the quote for Peter; we were there with Trey.
14 Poppy hurt her eye at their pool; were you, Troy, or Peter there?

55c Timed Writing

Key two 3' timed writings. Strive for control.

all letters

	gwam	3'

Reports are one of the best means by which busy executives ... 4 | 44
at any level of a business can keep well informed. The pertinent ... 8 | 48
data in reports can be used to solve a wide variety of problems ... 13 | 53
that arise, make any changes that may be required, analyze ... 17 | 57
results, and make precise, timely decisions. ... 20 | 60

The quality of the plans and decisions made on the basis of ... 24 | 64
the information found in reports depends in large measure on how ... 28 | 68
well the reports are produced. A good report is a thorough and ... 32 | 72
objective summary of all pertinent facts and figures. If reports ... 37 | 77
are not well produced, the firm will surely suffer. ... 40 | 80

3' | 1 | 2 | 3 | 4 |

Timed Writings

Any timed writing in the book can be completed using the Timed Writing feature.

TO USE THE TIMED WRITING FEATURE:

1. Select the Timed Writing tab from the Main screen.
2. Scroll to select the timed writing.
3. Select the source and the timing length. For example,
   - Select Paragraph 1 and 1'. Key paragraph 1; if you finish before time is up, repeat the same paragraph.
   - Select Paragraph 2 and 1'. Key paragraph 2; repeat the same paragraph if you finish before time is up.
   - Select the Entire Writing and 2'. Try to maintain your 1' rate. If you finish before time is up, start over, beginning with paragraph 1.
4. Timings save automatically.
5. The Timed Writing Report displays the results of the last 20 timed writings and the best three timings at each speed.

Goal: build staying power
1. Key each paragraph as a 1' timing.
2. Key a 2' timing on both paragraphs.

all letters

Writing 1: **18 gwam**	gwam 2'

Why spend weeks with some problem when just a few quiet | 6
minutes can help us to resolve it. | 9
If we don't take time to think through a problem, it will | 15
swiftly begin to expand in size. | 18

Writing 2: 20 gwam

We push very hard in our quest for growth, and we all | 5
think that only excellent growth will pay off. | 10
Believe it or not, one can actually work much too hard, | 16
be much too zealous, and just miss the mark. | 20

Writing 3: 22 gwam

A business friend once explained to me why he was often | 6
quite eager to be given some new project to work with. | 11
My friend said that each new project means he has to | 16
organize and use the best of his knowledge and his skill. | 22

Writing 4: 24 gwam

Don't let new words get away from you. Learn how to spell | 6
and pronounce new words and when and how finally to use them. | 12
A new word is a friend, but frequently more. New words | 18
must be used lavishly to extend the size of your own word power. | 24

2' | 1 | 2 | 3 | 4 | 5 | 6 |

54-d2

Memo

1. Key the memo below. Make all of the corrections noted by proofreaders' marks.
2. Send the memo to **David C. Kline** from **Carolyn M. Pastides**; use the current date and the subject **Economic Development Project**.
3. Search for *Department of Commerce* and replace it with *Board of Economic Development* each time it appears.
4. Check and close. (*54-d2*)

TIP

Remember to insert a nonbreaking hyphen:

Insert tab/Symbol; then click More Symbols, and click the Special Characters tab and select nonbreaking hyphen.

Shortcut: CTRL + SHIFT + -

The meeting with representatives of the department of commerce and the representatives being recruited to move here provided a very interesting perspective on the changing approach of recruiting small, knowledge based companies rather than large manufacturing operations. The company being recruited is a recent spin-off form a research project at a major university. Its stage of development could best be described as developmental.

We signed non-disclosure forms and the Department of Commerce provided us with financials provided by the company's auditor. However, the audit was not signed, and the management letter was not included. I have requested that the CFO bring to the meeting tomorrow a complete copy of the audit and proformas for two years forward. My guess is that the audit will contain a going concern clause. The company currently has a stockholders' deficit of approximately $15,000,000.

Unless financing is obtained, it is unlikely that the company can continue to operate. I requested copies of contracts are agreements that would support the revenue projections in the proformas.

The technology developed by the company is exciting, and the upside potential of the joint venture appears to be very good. Documentation of prototype orders was provided. Because of the risk involved in a company at this early stage of development, it is imperative that we do a lot of due diligence before investing in this company.

Writing 5: **26 *gwam***

gwam 2'

We usually get best results when we know where we are   5
going. Just setting a few goals will help us quietly see what   12
we are doing.   13

Goals can help measure whether we are moving at a good   19
rate or dozing along. You can expect a goal to help you find   25
good results.   26

Writing 6: **28 *gwam***

To win whatever prizes we want from life, we must plan to   6
move carefully from this goal to the next to get the maximum   12
result from our work.   14

If we really want to become skilled in keying, we must   19
come to see that this desire will require of us just a little   26
patience and hard work.   28

Writing 7: **30 *gwam***

Am I an individual person? I'm sure I am; still, in a   5
much, much bigger sense, other people have a major voice in   12
thoughts I think and actions I take.   15

Although we are each a unique person, we all work and   21
play in organized groups of people who do not expect us to   26
dismiss their rules of law and order.   30

2'| 1 | 2 | 3 | 4 | 5 | 6 |

**WORKPLACE
SUCCESS**

1. Use a search engine such as Google to find five articles that would help you as a relatively new employee learn more about building credibility. Use *building credibility* as keywords. Avoid articles that focus on building credibility for a business, brand, or product.

2. Select two articles that you found to be most helpful. Then do the following:

   - Key the name of the first article, the name of the author, and the Web address (URL). Apply left align and bold.

   - Write a paragraph pointing out at least two things in the article that made you believe it was helpful.

   - Write a second paragraph explaining why the article itself had credibility—why it was believable.

3. Follow the same procedure for the second article.

4. Proofread and edit your work carefully.

5. Check and close. (*54d*)

APPLICATIONS

54-d1

Memo

1. Key the memo below.

2. Position the heading at about 2".

3. Move paragraph 2 so that it will be the last paragraph.

4. Search for *NatureDesigns* and replace it with *NatureLink* each time it appears.

5. Use the Thesaurus to find another option for *wide-ranging* in the third sentence; select the first option.

6. Change the date in the memo from *November 10* to two weeks from today.

7. Check and close. (*54-d1*)

To: Richard M. Taylor | From: Dianne Gibson | Date: Current | Subject: Trail Design

Last week, Madilyn signed the contract for the trail design for Phase 1 of our Georgetown property. NatureDesigns was selected as the contractor. This firm was chosen because of its wide-ranging experience in selecting interpretative sites, designing trails, and installing boardwalks to protect wetlands and environmentally sensitive areas.

Please let me know if you plan to participate in the initial meeting with NatureDesigns.

The first onsite meeting is scheduled for November 10. We plan to meet at the main entrance at 10:30 a.m. to tour the property and review the procedures that NatureDesigns plans to use in designing the trails near the red cockaded woodpecker (RCW) habitat. Since RCW is an endangered species, we want to balance the desire of ecotourists to observe these birds and the need to protect them.

xx | c Bruce Diamond

Figure and Symbol Keys

LEARNING OUTCOMES

- Key the numeric keys by touch.
- Use symbol keys correctly.
- Build keying speed and accuracy.
- Apply correct number expression.
- Apply proofreaders' marks.
- Apply basic Internet skills.

LESSON 14   1 and 8

WARMUP 14a

Key each line twice.

Line 2: Space once after a series of brief questions within a sentence.

alphabet	1 Jessie Quick believed the campaign frenzy would be exciting.
space bar	2 Was it Mary? Helen? Pam? It was a woman; I saw one of them.
3rd row	3 We were quietly prepped to write two letters to Portia York.
easy	4 Kale's neighbor works with a tutor when they visit downtown.

| 1 | 2 | 3 | 4 | 5 | 6 | 7 | 8 | 9 | 10 | 11 | 12 |

SKILL BUILDING

14b Textbook Keying

The words at the right are from the 100 most used words.

Key each line once; work for fluency.

Top 100 High-Frequency Words

5 a an it been copy for his this more no office please service

6 our service than the they up was work all any many thank had

7 business from I know made more not me new of some to program

8 such these two with your about and have like department year

9 by at on but do had in letter most now one please you should

10 their order like also appreciate that there gentlemen letter

11 be can each had information letter may make now only so that

12 them time use which am other been send to enclosed have will

Edit Memos and E-mail

WARMUP 54a

Key each line, striving for control. Repeat if desired.

1 Sandra quickly gave the boy a major prize for his excellent work.
2 Invoice #758 for $294 is due 2/14/03 and #315 for $67 is due now.
3 Todd and Ann meet with a committee at noon to discuss all issues.
4 He may sign both of the forms for the amendment to the endowment.

| 1 | 2 | 3 | 4 | 5 | 6 | 7 | 8 | 9 | 10 | 11 | 12 | 13 |

SKILL BUILDING

54b Textbook Keying
1. Key the drill, concentrating on good keying techniques.
2. Repeat the drill if time permits.

5 Lou kicked the gray umbrella Fred gave me and broke it in pieces.
6 Cecilia jumped in the pool, kicked the side, and fractured a toe.
7 Bunny browsed in the library while June served the healthy lunch.

8 Teresa was there to operate the projection equipment on Saturday.
9 Walker sang three hymns, and Louisa taught everyone how to polka.
10 Guy and Teresa were going to buy ice cream after the polo match.

COMMUNICATION

54c
Composing and Editing

1. Use the information below to compose and send an e-mail to your instructor.
2. Use the subject line **Extra Credit Assignment**.
3. Read the second bulleted item carefully. Select one of the three topics, key the title of the topic on the first line of a new document, and apply Title style. Check and close. (*54c-attach*)
4. Proofread and edit the e-mail carefully before sending it.
5. Print a copy of your e-mail.

- Thank your instructor for providing the opportunity to complete an extra-credit assignment.

- Indicate which of the three topics available (E-Mail Etiquette, First Impressions Count, and Developing a Professional Attitude) you selected. Add a sentence indicating why you selected that topic for the three-page paper.

- Indicate that an electronic copy of your paper is attached to this e-mail and that a printed version has been placed in the appropriate assignment folder. Attach the file *54c-attach* to your e-mail.

NEW KEYS

14c 1 and 8

Key each line once.

Note: The digit "1" and the letter "I" have separate values on a computer keyboard. Do not interchange these characters.

1 Reach *up* with *left fourth* finger.

8 Reach *up* with *right second* finger.

Abbreviations: Do not space after a period within an abbreviation, as in Ph.D., U.S., C.O.D., a.m.

1

13 1 1a a1 1 1; 1 and a 1; 1 add 1; 1 aunt; 1 ace; 1 arm; 1 aye

14 1 and 11 and 111; 11 eggs; 11 vats; Set 11A; May 11; Item 11

15 The 11 aces of the 111th Corps each rated a salute at 1 p.m.

8

16 8 8k k8 8 8; 8 kits; ask 8; 8 kites; kick 8; 8 keys; spark 8

17 OK 88; 8 bags; 8 or 88; the 88th; 88 kegs; ask 88; order 888

18 Eight of the 88 cars score 8 or better on our Form 8 rating.

all figures learned

19 She did live at 818 Park, not 181 Park; or was it 181 Clark?

20 Put 1 with 8 to form 18; put 8 with 1 to form 81. Use 1881.

21 On May 1 at 8 a.m., 18 men and 18 women left Gate 8 for Rio.

SKILL BUILDING

14d Reinforcement
Key each line once; DS between groups. Repeat. Key with accuracy.

figures

22 Our 188 trucks moved 1881 tons on August 18 and December 18.

23 Send Mary 181 No. 188 panes for her home at 8118 Oak Street.

24 The 188 men in 8 boats left Docks 1 and 18 at 1 p.m., May 1.

25 pop was lap pass slaw wool solo swap Apollo wasp load plaque

26 Was Polly acquainted with the equipped jazz player in Texas?

27 The computer is a useful tool; it helps you to perform well.

14e Speed Builder
Key these lines in the game.

28 Did their form entitle them to the land?

29 Did the men in the field signal for us to go?

30 I may pay for the antique bowls when I go to town.

31 The auditor did the work right, so he risks no penalty.

32 The man by the big bush did signal us to turn down the lane.

| 1 | 2 | 3 | 4 | 5 | 6 | 7 | 8 | 9 | 10 | 11 | 12 |

53-d2

Letter

 BRADY

1. Make the following edits in the open document:
   - Revise the letter so that it will be formatted correctly as a modified block letter; indent paragraphs; remove extra space after paragraph in the inside address and closing lines.
   - Search for the name *Debauche*; each time it appears, replace it with *DeBauche*.
   - Use the Thesaurus to find a synonym for *statistics*. Replace *statistics* with the second synonym listed.
   - Make the following correction in the first sentence of paragraph 2:
     Brad Swinton, our new vice president of marketing, indicated. . .
   - Cut the following sentence from paragraph 2:
     I hope this will not be a problem for you.
   - Center the page vertically.
2. Check and close. (*53-d2*)

53-d3

Letter

1. Open *53-d2* and reformat it as a block style letter.
2. Check and close. (*53-d3*)

53-d4

Letter

1. Prepare another letter for Ms. DeBauche using the same address, salutation, and closing lines that were used in *53-d3*. Note that this letter does not contain an enclosure.
2. Key the letter below in block style format with open punctuation using *Word 2007* defaults.
3. Decrease the indent on the numbered items to position them at the left margin.
4. Search for *section*, and replace it each time it appears with *phase*.
5. Use the Thesaurus to find a synonym for *prolific*. Select the first option.
6. Center the page vertically.
7. Check and close. (*53-d4*)

October 11, 20--

Our team completed its preliminary review of your proposal today. Overall, we are very pleased with the approach you have taken.

Please plan to provide the following information at our meeting on October 18:

1. Please provide a more detailed pricing plan. We would like to have each section of the project priced separately specifying hourly rate and expenses rather than the one total sum quoted.

2. How many hours do you estimate will be necessary to complete each section of the project? When would your firm be able to begin the project?

We look forward to a very prolific meeting on October 18.

5 and 0

WARMUP 15a

Key each line twice.

For a series of capital letters, tap CAPS LOCK with the left little finger. Tap again to release.

alphabet	1	John Quigley packed the zinnias in twelve large, firm boxes.
1/8	2	Idle Motor 18 at 8 mph and Motor 81 at 8 mph; avoid Motor 1.
caps	3	Lily read BLITHE SPIRIT by Noel Coward. I read VANITY FAIR.
lock	4	Did they fix the problem of the torn panel and worn element?

| 1 | 2 | 3 | 4 | 5 | 6 | 7 | 8 | 9 | 10 | 11 | 12 |

15b

Technique Reinforcement
Reach up or down without moving your hands. Key each line once; repeat drill.

adjacent reaches

5 as oil red ask wet opt mop try tree open shred operas treaty

6 were pore dirt stew ruin faster onion alumni dreary mnemonic

7 The opened red hydrants were powerful, fast, and very dirty.

outside reaches

8 pop zap cap zag wasp equip lazy zippers queue opinion quartz

9 zest waste paper exist parquet azalea acquaint apollo apathy

10 The lazy wasp passed the potted azalea on the parquet floor.

NEW KEYS

15c 5 and 0

Key each line once.

5 Reach *up* with *left first* finger.

0 Reach *up* with *right fourth* finger.

5

11 5 5f f5 5 5; 5 fans; 5 feet; 5 figs; 5 fobs; 5 furs; 5 flaws

12 5 o'clock; 5 a.m.; 5 p.m.; is 55 or less; buy 55; 5 and 5 is

13 Call Line 555 if 5 fans or 5 bins arrive at Pier 5 by 5 p.m.

0

14 0 0; ;0 0 0; skip 0; plan 0; left 0; is below 0; I scored 0;

15 0 degrees; key 0 and 0; write 00 here; the total is 0 or 00;

16 She laughed at their 0 to 0 score; but ours was 0 to 0 also.

all figures learned

17 I keyed 550 pages for Invoice 05, or 50 more than we needed.

18 Pages 15 and 18 of the program listed 150, not 180, members.

19 On May 10, Rick drove 500 miles to New Mexico in car No. 08.

COMMUNICATION

53d
Composing and Editing

1. Compose a paragraph with at least two or three complete sentences to finish the three statements listed below.
2. Double-space the answers and indent each paragraph.
3. Print the paragraphs; use proofreaders' marks to edit the paragraphs carefully to improve your writing. Make the corrections.
4. Check and close. (*53d*)

TIP

Remember to proofread and preview each document as a SOP. You will not be reminded to do this.

1. **Currently, I live in** (name and describe the city, town, or area in which you live—indicate if it is a large city, small town, or rural area and provide other descriptive information about the locale).

2. **When friends from other locations come to visit me, the places I enjoy taking them are** (describe two or three places in your area that would be interesting to show to visitors).

3. **If I could pick one place in the United States to visit, it would be** (describe one place you would like to visit and explain why you would like to go there and what you would like to see and do while you are there).

APPLICATIONS

53-d1
Letter from Rough Draft

1. Use *Word 2003* style, Times New Roman font, and *Word 2003* default margins; key the letter below making all corrections noted.
2. Use the current date, block style, and open punctuation; add an enclosure notation and center the page.
3. Check and close. (*53-d1*)

Ms. Karen Bradley
228 High Ridge Road
Irmo, SC 29063-4187

Dear Ms. Bradley

Thank you for the opportunity to plan an exciting vacation for you and your family. We are certain that this trip will be one all of you will remember. The Greek Isles are a fun destination and you have selected outstanding pre- and post-cruise tours in Athens and Istanbul.

All of the travel arrangements have been confirmed, and a detailed itinerary and cruise brochure are enclosed. Please carefully review the itinerary to make certain that we have followed all of your instructions correctly. If any changes need to be made, please call us soon.

Your travel documents will be sent to you 2 weeks prior to departure. Please let us know if we can provide additional information for you.

Sincerely

Jane R. Todd
President

SKILL BUILDING

15d Textbook Keying
Key each line once; DS between 3-line groups.

improve figures

20 Read pages 5 and 8; duplicate page 18; omit pages 50 and 51.

21 We have Model 80 with 10 meters or Model 180 with 15 meters.

22 After May 18, French 050 meets in room 15 at 10 a.m. daily.

improve long reaches

23 Barb Abver saw a vibrant version of her brave venture on TV.

24 Call a woman or a man who will manage Minerva Manor in Nome.

25 We were quick to squirt a quantity of water at Quin and West.

15e Tab Review WP
1. Read the instructions to clear and set tabs.
2. Go to the Word Processor. Set a left tab at 4".
3. Practice the lines; tap TAB without watching your keyboard.

STANDARD PLAN | **for Setting and Clearing Tabs in the Word Processor**

Preset or default tabs are displayed on the Ruler. If necessary, display the Ruler in the Word Processor. (Choose the Show Ruler option on the Format menu.) Sometimes you will want to remove or clear existing tabs before setting new ones.

To clear and set tabs:

1. On the menu bar, click Format Tabs, and then Clear All Tabs.

2. To set tabs, select the type of tab you want to set (left, center, decimal, or right); enter the position and click Set.

Option: Click the tab button on the toolbar repeatedly to select the tab type. Then click the ruler where you want to set the tab.

Set tab 4"

	►Tab	Keyboarding
has become	►Tab	the primary
means of	►Tab	written communication
in business and	►Tab	in our personal lives.
Keyboarding is	►Tab	used by persons
in every profession	►Tab	and most job levels.

15f Timed Writing
Take a 2' writing on both paragraphs. End the lesson; go to the Word Processor to complete 15e.

all letters

	gwam	2'	3'
I thought about Harry and how he had worked for me for		6	4
10 years; how daily at 8 he parked his worn car in the lot;		12	8
then, he left at 5. Every day was almost identical for him.		18	12
In a quiet way, he did his job well, asking for little		23	15
attention. So I never recognized his thirst for travel. I		29	19
didn't expect to find all of those maps near his workplace.		35	23

Edit Letters

Key each line, striving for control. Repeat if desired.

alphabet 1 Jakob will save the money required for your next big cash prizes.
fig/sym 2 I saw Vera buy 13 7/8 yards of #240 cotton denim at $6.96 a yard.
3rd/4th 3 Zone 12 is impassable; quickly rope it off. Did you wax Zone 90?
easy 4 Did an auditor handle the formal audit of the firms for a profit?

| 1 | 2 | 3 | 4 | 5 | 6 | 7 | 8 | 9 | 10 | 11 | 12 | 13 |

SKILL BUILDING

53b Textbook Keying
1. Key the drill, concentrating on good keying techniques; tap ENTER twice after each 4-line group.
2. Repeat the drill if time permits.

1/2 fingers

5 Did bedlam erupt when they arrived after my speech ended quickly?
6 Joyce bought me a new bright red jacket for my birthday tomorrow.
7 Did Rebecca make the needlepoint cushion for the club room couch?
8 Much to the concern of our teacher, I did my homework on the bus.

3/4 fingers

9 Zam saw six small poodle puppies playing in the meadow last week.
10 Paxton saw a lazy lizard on the old wooden oar at Pawley's Plaza.
11 Zam Velasquez sells squid in six stores near the pool at the zoo.
12 Paul quizzed a shop owner about a patchwork quilt we saw in Waco.

all fingers

13 Jarvis Zackery played quarterback with six teams before retiring.
14 Jan Weitzel made grave errors, but he quickly fixed the problems.
15 Quinn Zack wrote just six poems and a short story before leaving.
16 Maxey Czajka will quit swimming because he performed very poorly.

53c Timed Writing
1. Key a 1' timed writing on each paragraph, working for speed.
2. Key a 3' timed writing, working for control.

all letters

	gwam	1'	3'

Have you ever thought about how you shake hands with — 11 | 4 | 51
people? One of the early impressions you make on other individuals — 24 | 8 | 56
is the way you greet them. Do you extend your hand immediately — 37 | 12 | 60
as a friendly gesture, or do you defer until the other person takes — 51 | 17 | 65
the initiative? — 54 | 18 | 66

When you prepare for an interview or an important meeting, — 12 | 22 | 70
it is very important for you to analyze the manner in which you — 25 | 26 | 74
shake hands. You can be sure that the individual in charge will — 37 | 30 | 78
examine the way in which you shake hands. Most people make a — 50 | 35 | 82
quick judgment about you that can be either positive or negative. — 63 | 39 | 87
To make that early impression a very favorable one, always use a — 76 | 43 | 91
firm, professional handshake that is neither limp nor bone crushing. — 90 | 48 | 95

1' | 1 | 2 | 3 | 4 | 5 | 6 | 7 | 8 | 9 | 10 | 11 | 12 | 13 |
3' | 1 | 2 | 3 | 4 |

LESSON 16

2 and 7

WARMUP 16a

Key each line twice.

alphabet 1 Perry might know I feel jinxed because I have missed a quiz.

figures 2 Channels 5 and 8, on from 10 to 11, said Luisa's IQ was 150.

caps lock 3 Ella Hill will see Chekhov's THE CHERRY ORCHARD on Czech TV.

easy 4 The big dog by the bush kept the ducks and hen in the field.

| 1 | 2 | 3 | 4 | 5 | 6 | 7 | 8 | 9 | 10 | 11 | 12 |

NEW KEYS

16b 2 and 7

Key each line once.

2 Reach *up* with *left third* finger.

7 Reach *up* with *right first* finger.

2

5 2 2s s2 2 2; has 2 sons; is 2 sizes; was 2 sites; has 2 skis

6 add 2 and 2; 2 sets of 2; catch 22; as 2 of the 22; 222 Main

7 Exactly at 2 on April 22, the 22nd Company left from Pier 2.

7

8 7 7j j7 7 7; 7 jets; 7 jeans; 7 jays; 7 jobs; 7 jars; 7 jaws

9 ask for 7; buy 7; 77 years; June 7; take any 7; deny 77 boys

10 From May 7 on, all 77 men will live at 777 East 77th Street.

all figures learned

11 I read 2 of the 72 books, Ellis read 7, and Han read all 72.

12 Tract 27 cites the date as 1850; Tract 170 says it was 1852.

13 You can take Flight 850 on January 12; I'll take Flight 705.

16c

Number Reinforcement
Key each line twice (slowly, then faster); DS between 2-line groups.

8/1 14 line 8; Book 1; No. 88; Seat 11; June 18; Cart 81; date 1881

2/7 15 take 2; July 7; buy 22; sell 77; mark 27; adds 72; Memo 2772

5/0 16 feed 5; bats 0; age 50; Ext. 55; File 50; 55 bags; band 5005

all 17 I work 18 visual signs with 20 turns of the 57 lenses to 70.

all 18 Did 17 boys fix the gears for 50 bicycles in 28 racks or 10?

APPLICATIONS

52-d1

Edit Document

 PUNCTUALITY

TIP

Use Show/Hide to facilitate editing.

WORKPLACE SUCCESS

1. Select the first paragraph below the title and apply Times New Roman, 12-point font; change line spacing to double (2.0); indent paragraphs.

2. Remove extra space after the paragraph. Then use the Format Painter to copy that format to the next two paragraphs.

3. Center the title and apply Arial, 14-point bold font.

4. In the third sentence of the first paragraph, *Punctuality-Not Performance-Determines Outcome!*, change the hyphens to em dashes; then apply italic format. Delete the quotation marks.

5. In the sentence that follows, replace the commas around *and by all accounts one who was unbeatable and assured to repeat the title* with em dashes.

6. Move paragraph 3 between paragraphs 1 and 2.

7. Find *weak* and replace it with *lame*.

8. Add the following below the last paragraph: **©2008 by Student's Name**. Right-align this information.

9. Select the last sentence of the document and change the text color to red.

10. Center the page vertically.

11. Use Full Screen Reading view to proofread the document.

12. Check and close. (*52-d1*)

WORKPLACE SUCCESS

Building Credibility

Very competent young people who have limited or no work experience often find it difficult to build credibility with managers and experienced employees. To bridge the credibility gap, they need to focus on four key factors:

1. **Expertise**—demonstrate in a confident manner the knowledge and skills they have acquired.

2. **Trust**—earn the respect and trust of managers and other employees by being honest and open. You must be believable. Use empathy and build rapport with colleagues.

3. **Consistency**—performing in a predictable, consistent manner gives managers and employees a feeling of comfort with the individual.

4. **Commitment**—managers and employees want to work with people who do what they say they will do and when they say they will do it. They trust people who understand the importance of punctuality and who will persevere until the job is done properly.

© PHOTODISC BLUE/GETTY IMAGES

16d Textbook Keying

Key each line once to review reaches; fingers curved and relaxed; wrists low. DS between groups.

3rd/4th
19 pop was lap pass slaw wool solo swap apollo wasp load plaque
20 Al's quote was, "I was dazzled by the jazz, pizza, and pool."

1st/2nd
21 bad fun nut kick dried night brick civic thick hutch believe
22 Kim may visit her friends in Germany if I give her a ticket.

3rd/1st
23 cry tube wine quit very curb exit crime ebony mention excite
24 To be invited, petition the six executive committee members.

16e Textbook Keying

Key each line once; DS between 3-line groups. Do not pause at the end of lines.

words: *think, say,* and *key* words

25 is do am lay cut pen dub may fob ale rap cot hay pay hem box
26 box wit man sir fish also hair giant rigor civic virus ivory
27 laugh sight flame audit formal social turkey bicycle problem

phrases: *think, say,* and *key* phrases

28 is it|is it|if it is|if it is|or by|or by|or me|or me|for us
29 and all|for pay|pay dues and|the pen|the pen box|the pen box
30 such forms|held both|work form|then wish|sign name|with them

easy sentences

31 The man is to do the work right; he then pays the neighbors.
32 Sign the forms to pay the eight men for the turkey and hams.
33 The antique ivory bicycle is a social problem for the chair.
    | 1 | 2 | 3 | 4 | 5 | 6 | 7 | 8 | 9 | 10 | 11 | 12 |

TECHNIQUE TIP

Think and key the words and phrases as units rather than letter by letter.

16f Timed Writing

Take a 2' timing on both paragraphs. Repeat the timing.

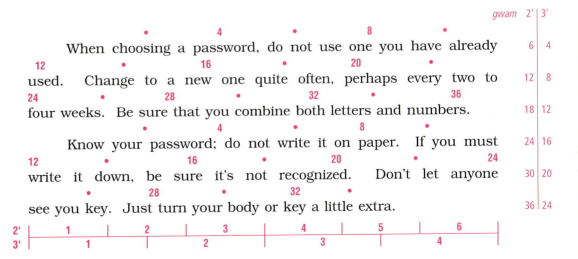

	gwam	2'	3'
When choosing a password, do not use one you have already		6	4
used. Change to a new one quite often, perhaps every two to		12	8
four weeks. Be sure that you combine both letters and numbers.		18	12
Know your password; do not write it on paper. If you must		24	16
write it down, be sure it's not recognized. Don't let anyone		30	20
see you key. Just turn your body or key a little extra.		36	24

2' | 1 | 2 | 3 | 4 | 5 | 6 |
3' | 1 | 2 | 3 | 4 |

THESAURUS

REVIEW/PROOFING/THESAURUS

Thesaurus

The Thesaurus is a tool that enables you to look up words and replace them with synonyms, antonyms, or related words. Many words have several different meanings. It is important to select the appropriate meaning before replacing a word.

To use the Thesaurus:

1. Position the insertion point in the word you wish to replace.

2. In the Proofing group on the Review tab, click Thesaurus to display the Research task pane.

3. If more than one meaning displays, select the appropriate meaning. Note that synonyms are listed first and then antonyms for each meaning.

4. Hold the mouse over the desired synonym or antonym, click the down arrow, and then click Insert.

TIP

An alternative way to use the Thesaurus is to position the insertion point in a word and right-click the mouse. Select Synonyms and then the desired word or Thesaurus to display the Research task pane.

DRILL 6   THESAURUS

1. Key the following words on separate lines:

   generous   data   smart   profit

2. Replace *generous* and *data* with synonyms.

3. Replace *smart* (meaning clever) with a synonym.

4. Key **smart** again (meaning elegant) on the next line and replace it with an antonym.

5. Replace *profit* with an antonym.

6. Check and close. (*52-drill6*)

COMMUNICATION ✳

52e
Applying Communication Knowledge

 TEAM WRITING

1. Print a copy of the open document and use proofreaders' marks to edit it. Note that this is a very rough draft that is packed with 25 errors.

2. Correct all keying, spelling, grammar, capitalization, number usage, and word usage errors.

3. At about 2", add the title: **STRATEGIES FOR TEAM WRITING**; center it, use Cambria 14-point font, and apply bold.

4. For side headings, use Cambria 12-point font and apply bold.

5. Change the bullets on the ten steps to numbering.

6. Key your name below the last line of the document; right-align it.

7. Insert the date and time below your name using the format of your choice.

8. Use Full Screen Reading view to proofread the document.

9. Check the document. (*52e*)

LESSON 17

4 and 9

WARMUP 17a

Key each line twice.

alphabet	1	Bob realized very quickly that jumping was excellent for us.
figures	2	Has each of the 18 clerks now corrected Item 501 on page 27?
shift keys	3	L. K. Coe, M.D., hopes Dr. Lopez can leave for Maine in May.
easy	4	The men paid their own firms for the eight big enamel signs.

NEW KEYS

17b 4 and 9

Key each line once.

4 Reach *up* with *left first* finger.

9 Reach *up* with *right third* finger.

4

5 4 4f f4 4 4 4; if 4 furs; off 4 floors; gaff 4 fish; 4 flags

6 44th floor; half of 44; 4 walked 44 flights; 4 girls; 4 boys

7 I order exactly 44 bagels, 4 cakes, and 4 pies before 4 a.m.

9

8 9 9l l9 9 9 9; fill 9 lugs; call 9 lads; Bill 9 lost; dial 9

9 also 9 oaks; roll 9 loaves; 9.9 degrees; sell 9 oaks; Hall 9

10 Just 9 couples, 9 men and 9 women, left at 9 on our Tour 99.

all figures learned

11 Memo 94 says 9 pads, 4 pens, and 4 ribbons were sent July 9.

12 Study Item 17 and Item 28 on page 40 and Item 59 on page 49.

13 Within 17 months he drove 85 miles, walked 29, and flew 490.

SKILL BUILDING

17c Textbook Keying

Key each line once.

14 My staff of 18 worked 11 hours a day from May 27 to June 12.

15 There were 5 items tested by Inspector 7 at 4 p.m. on May 8.

16 Please send her File 10 today at 8; her access number is 97.

17 Car 47 had its trial run. The qualifying speed was 198 mph.

18 The estimated score? 485. Actual? 190. Difference? 295.

CUSTOMIZE QUICK ACCESS TOOLBAR

In Lesson 27, you learned to use the Quick Access toolbar as a shortcut for saving documents and for the Undo and Redo commands. The Quick Access toolbar can be customized to add other functions that you use frequently.

To customize the Quick Access toolbar:

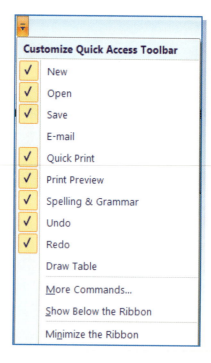

1. On the Quick Access toolbar, click the down arrow to display the Customize Quick Access Toolbar dialog box.

2. Click the desired command that you wish to add to the Quick Access toolbar. Note that the default commands Save, Undo, and Redo are already on the toolbar.

3. If you clicked New, Open, Quick Print, Print Preview, and Spelling and Grammar to add them to the toolbar, it would appear as shown below. Note you have to add one command at a time to the toolbar.

DRILL 5   CUSTOMIZE QUICK ACCESS TOOLBAR

1. Click the down arrow on the right side of the Quick Access toolbar.

2. Select New, Open, Quick Print, Print Preview, and Spelling & Grammar one at a time from the list of options available.

3. Check to see that the commands have been added to your Quick Access toolbar.

4. Open *52-drill2* using the Quick Access toolbar.

5. Key the paragraph shown below after the last paragraph in the document.

6. On the line below the last line on the document, key the drill name, *52-drill5*.

7. Use the Quick Access toolbar to check spelling and grammar, preview, and print the document.

8. Check and close. (*52-drill5*)

Follow-up activities vary depending on the type of presentation and the audience to whom the presentation is delivered. A presentation made within a company or to clients of a company is more likely to have follow-up activities other than questions and discussion than one made to an external audience. The follow-up activities required for an external audience such as members of a professional association are generally limited to questions and discussion.

17d

Technique Reinforcement
Key smoothly; tap the keys at a brisk, steady pace.

first finger

19 buy them gray vent guy brunt buy brunch much give huge vying

20 Hagen, after her July triumph at tennis, may try volleyball.

21 Verna urges us to buy yet another of her beautiful rag rugs.

second finger

22 keen idea; kick it back; ice breaker; decide the issue; cite

23 Did Dick ask Cecelia, his sister, if she decided to like me?

24 Suddenly, Micki's bike skidded on the Cedar Street ice rink.

third/fourth finger

25 low slow lax solo wax zip zap quips quiz zipper prior icicle

26 Paula has always allowed us to relax at La Paz and at Quito.

27 Please ask Zale to explain who explores most aquatic slopes.

17e Timed Writing

Take a 2' timing on both paragraphs. Repeat the timing.

all letters

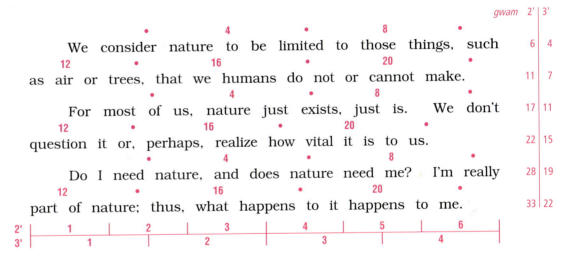

	gwam	2'	3'
We consider nature to be limited to those things, such		6	4
as air or trees, that we humans do not or cannot make.		11	7
For most of us, nature just exists, just is. We don't		17	11
question it or, perhaps, realize how vital it is to us.		22	15
Do I need nature, and does nature need me? I'm really		28	19
part of nature; thus, what happens to it happens to me.		33	22

17f Enrichment

TECHNIQUE TIP

Keep hands quiet and fingers well curved over the keys. Do not allow your fingers to bounce.

1. Click the Skill Building tab from the main menu and choose Technique Builder; select Drill 2.

2. Key Drill 2 from page 32. Key each line once striving for good accuracy.

3. The results will be listed on the Skill Building Report.

FIND AND REPLACE

HOME/EDITING/FIND AND REPLACE

① **Find**—locates text, formatting, footnotes, graphics, page breaks, and other items within a document. When text is located, it is highlighted.

② **Replace**—finds text, formatting, or other items within a document and replaces them with different text, formatting, or other items. Replaced text will have the same capitalization that the original text had.

To find text:

1. Click Find **①** and key the text you wish to locate in the Find what box **③**.
2. Click Find Next **④** to find the next occurrence of the text.

To replace text:

1. On the Home tab, click Replace **②** in the Editing group.
2. Key the text you wish to locate in the Find what box **③**.
3. Key the replacement text in the Replace with box **⑤**.
4. Click Find Next **④** to find the next occurrence of the text. Click Replace **⑥** to replace one occurrence or click Replace All **⑦** to replace all occurrences of the text.

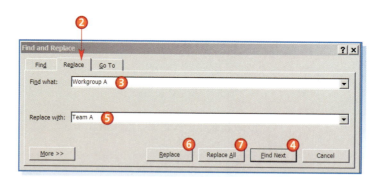

DRILL 4   **FIND AND REPLACE**   RESTRUCTURE

1. In the open document, find the word *restructuring* the first place it appears.
2. Find the second and third occurrences of *restructuring*.
3. Find *Workgroup A* and replace with *Team A*.

4. Note that the letter is formatted using the traditional *Word 2003* style, but the letter format is inconsistent. Edit the document so that the letter is formatted correctly as a block-style letter.
5. Check and close. (*52-drill4*)

LESSON 18

3 and 6

WARMUP 18a

Key each line twice.

alphabet	1 Jim Kable won a second prize for his very quixotic drawings.
figures	2 If 57 of the 105 boys go on July 29, 48 of them will remain.
easy	3 With the usual bid, I paid for a quantity of big world maps.

| 1 | 2 | 3 | 4 | 5 | 6 | 7 | 8 | 9 | 10 | 11 | 12 |

NEW KEYS

18b 3 and 6

Key each line once.

3 Reach *up* with *left second* finger.

6 Reach *up* with *right first* finger.

Note: Ergonomic keyboard users will use *left first* finger to key 6.

LEFT FINGERS   4 \ 3 \ 2 \ 1 \ 1 \ 2 \ 3 \ 4   RIGHT FINGERS

3

4 3 3d d3 3 3; had 3 days; did 3 dives; led 3 dogs; add 3 dips
5 we 3 ride 3 cars; take 33 dials; read 3 copies; save 33 days
6 On July 3, 33 lights lit 33 stands holding 33 prize winners.

6

7 6 6j 6j 6 6; 6 jays; 6 jams; 6 jigs; 6 jibs; 6 jots; 6 jokes
8 only 6 high; on 66 units; reach 66 numbers; 6 yams or 6 jams
9 On May 6, Car 66 delivered 66 tons of No. 6 shale to Pier 6.

all figures learned

10 At 6 p.m., Channel 3 reported the August 6 score was 6 to 3.
11 Jean, do Items 28 and 6; Mika, 59 and 10; Kyle, 3, 4, and 7.
12 Cars 56 and 34 used Aisle 9; Cars 2 and 87 can use Aisle 10.

SKILL BUILDING

18c
Keyboard Reinforcement
Key each line once; DS between 3-line groups.

TECHNIQUE TIP

Make the long reaches without returning to the home row between reaches.

long reaches

13 ce cede cedar wreck nu nu nut punt nuisance my my amy mystic
14 ny ny any many company mu mu mull lumber mulch br br furbish
15 The absence of receiving my umbrella disturbed the musician.

number review

16 set 0; push 4; Car 00; score 44; jot 04; age 40; Billet 4004
17 April 5; lock 5; set 66; fill 55; hit 65; pick 56; adds 5665
18 Her grades are 93, 87, and 100; his included 82, 96, and 54.

PASTE OPTIONS BUTTON

 The Paste Options button is a "smart tag" that appears when you paste an item from the Clipboard. It enables you to select the format you prefer to use.

To use the Paste option:

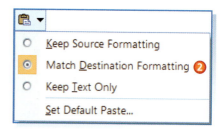

1. Point the mouse at the Paste Options button when it appears. Then select the down arrow ❶.

2. Select the desired option ❷. To format the text using the same format as the new document, click Match Destination Formatting. To format the text using the same format as the document from which the text was copied, click Keep Source Formatting.

DRILL 2   CLIPBOARD   EFFECTIVE PRES

1. In the open document, display formatting marks and the Clipboard.

2. Select the heading *Opening* and the paragraph that follows, and cut them.

3. Select the heading *Presentation Body* and the paragraph that follows, and cut them.

4. Select the heading *Closing* and the paragraph that follows, and cut them.

5. Place the insertion point on the line below the paragraph following the heading *Planning and Preparing Presentations*. Paste all items on the Clipboard at once.

6. Select the first sentence in the paragraph with the heading *Follow-up Activities* and cut it. Move the insertion point to the end of the paragraph.

7. On the Clipboard, click in the sentence you just cut and click the down arrow and select Paste. On the Paste Options button, choose Keep Source Formatting.

8. Add or delete extra spaces before or after sentences as necessary. Clear the Clipboard.

9. Preview and adjust line spacing if necessary.

10. Check and close. (*52-drill2*)

DRAG-AND-DROP EDITING

Another way to edit text is to use the mouse. With **drag and drop**, you can move or copy text using the mouse. To move copy, you must first select the text, then hold down the left mouse button, and drag the text to the desired location. The mouse pointer displays a rectangle indicating that copy is being moved. Release the mouse button to "drop" the text into the desired location.

Follow a similar procedure to copy (or duplicate) text. Hold down the left mouse button and the CTRL key, and drag the text to the desired location. A plus sign indicates the text is being copied.

DRILL 3   DRAG AND DROP   EFFECTIVE PRES

1. In the open document, use drag-and-drop editing to make the same changes you made in *52-drill2*.

2. Check and close. (*52-drill3*)

18d Textbook Keying

Key each line once; DS between 2-line groups; repeat.

word response: *think* and *key* words

19 he el id is go us it an me of he of to if ah or bye do so am

20 Did she enamel emblems on a big panel for the downtown sign?

stroke response: *think* and *key* each stroke

21 kin are hip read lymph was pop saw ink art oil gas up as mop

22 Barbara started the union wage earners tax in Texas in July.

combination response: vary speed but maintain rhythm

23 upon than eve lion when burley with they only them loin were

24 It was the opinion of my neighbor that we may work as usual.

18e Timed Writing

1. Key two 3' writings.
2. End the lesson but do not exit the software.

all letters

Goals: 1', 17–23 *gwam*
2', 15–21 *gwam*
3', 14–20 *gwam*

	gwam	2'	3'
I am something quite precious. Though millions of people		6	4
in other countries might not have me, you likely do. I have		12	8
a lot of power. For it is I who names a new president every		18	12
four years. It is I who decides if a tax shall be levied.		24	16
I even decide questions of war or peace. I was acquired at		30	20
a great cost; however, I am free to all citizens. And yet,		36	24
sadly, I am often ignored; or, still worse, I am just taken		42	28
for granted. I can be lost, and in certain circumstances I		48	32
can even be taken away. What, you may ask, am I? I am your		54	36
right to vote. Don't take me lightly.		58	39

COMMUNICATION ✳

18f Composition

1. Go to the Word Processor.

2. Introduce yourself to your instructor by composing two paragraphs, each containing about three sentences. Use proper grammatical structure. Do not worry about keying errors at this time.

3. Save the document as *xx-profile*. (Remember to replace *xx* with your initials.) It is not necessary to print the document. You will open and print it in a later lesson.

SPECIAL CHARACTERS

INSERT/SYMBOLS/SYMBOL

Special characters are inserted from the Symbols dialog box. Examples of special characters include:

Em dash —   En dash –   Copyright ©   Trademark ™

1. Repeat steps 1 and 2 for inserting symbols. (Click Symbol command and then More Symbols on Gallery to display the Symbols dialog box.)
2. Select the Special Characters tab **1**.
3. Select the special character desired **2**.
4. Click Insert **3** and then close.

DRILL 1   SYMBOLS AND SPECIAL CHARACTERS

1. Key the following lines as a numbered list; do not include the text in parentheses.
2. Insert the symbols and special characters shown.
3. Check and close. (*52-drill1*)

Special Characters

1. Parker House—Best Dining (em dash)
2. Pages 13–25 (en dash)
3. July 20 (nonbreaking space)
4. Brighten your day with a smile and ... (ellipsis)
5. Revise §2, ¶4. (Section 2, Paragraph 4)

Symbols

6. ☺ Have a nice day.
7. ⇨ Room 253
8. ✍ Sign here.
9. The size is 2 acres±.
10. The cost is 6€. (6 Euro)

OFFICE CLIPBOARD

HOME/CLIPBOARD/DIALOG BOX LAUNCHER

1 Clipboard   In Lesson 27, you worked with the commands from the Clipboard group. In this lesson, you will work with the Clipboard. Up to 24 segments of text or graphics that have been cut or copied can be stored on the Clipboard and then pasted individually or as a group into a document.

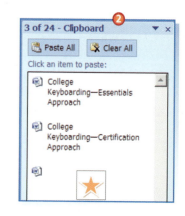

To use the Clipboard:

1. On the Home tab, click the Dialog Box Launcher **1** to display the Clipboard **2**. Each item that you cut or copy will display on the task pane.
2. To paste an item into a document **3**, click the item you want to paste and then click the down arrow and select Paste.

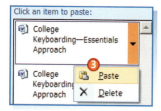

LESSON 19 — $ and - (hyphen), Number Expression

WARMUP 19a

Key each line twice.

alphabet 1	Why did the judge quiz poor Victor about his blank tax form?
figures 2	J. Boyd, Ph.D., changed Items 10, 57, 36, and 48 on page 92.
3rd row 3	To try the tea, we hope to tour the port prior to the party.
easy 4	Did he signal the authentic robot to do a turn to the right?

| 1 | 2 | 3 | 4 | 5 | 6 | 7 | 8 | 9 | 10 | 11 | 12 |

NEW KEYS

19b $ and -

Key each line once; DS between 2-line groups.

- = hyphen
-- = dash
Do not space before or after a hyphen or a dash.

$ Shift; then reach *up* with *left first* finger.

- (hyphen) Reach *up* with *right fourth* finger.

$

5 $ $f f$ $ $; if $4; half $4; off $4; of $4; $4 fur; $4 flats

6 for $8; cost $9; log $3; grab $10; give Rolf $2; give Viv $4

7 Since she paid $45 for the item priced at $54, she saved $9.

- (hyphen)

8 - -; ;- - - -; up-to-date; co-op; father-in-law; four-square

9 pop-up foul; big-time job; snap-on bit; one- or two-hour ski

10 You need 6 signatures--half of the members--on the petition.

all symbols learned

11 I paid $10 for the low-cost disk; high-priced ones cost $40.

12 Le-An spent $20 for travel, $95 for books, and $38 for food.

13 Mr. Loft-Smit sold his boat for $467; he bought it for $176.

SKILL BUILDING

19c

Keyboard Reinforcement
Key each line once; repeat the drill.

e/d 14	Edie discreetly decided to deduct expenses in making a deed.
w/e 15	Working women wear warm wool sweaters when weather dictates.
r/e 16	We heard very rude remarks regarding her recent termination.
s/d 17	This seal's sudden misdeeds destroyed several goods on land.
v/b 18	Beverley voted by giving a bold beverage to every brave boy.

52c Timed Writings

1. Key a 1' timed writing on each paragraph, working for speed.
2. Key a 3' timed writing, working for control.

all letters

A

Time is a perplexing commodity.   Frequently, we do not have | 12 | 4 | 45
adequate time to do the things required; yet we all have exactly the | 26 | 9 | 50
same amount of time.   The way we utilize time differs greatly. | 38 | 13 | 54

Seldom do we focus just on the quantity of time available because | 13 | 17 | 58
it is beyond our control.   Rather we tend to concentrate on the critical | 28 | 22 | 63
things that must be accomplished in the time that is available. | 40 | 26 | 67

Keep in mind that our efforts should be devoted primarily to | 12 | 30 | 71
enhancing the quality of the activities that occupy our time. Time, the | 27 | 35 | 76
most precious thing an individual spends, can never be regained once | 41 | 40 | 81
it has been lost. | 44 | 41 | 82

1' | 1 | 2 | 3 | 4 | 5 | 6 | 7 | 8 | 9 | 10 | 11 | 12 | 13 |
3' | | 1 | | 2 | | 3 | | 4 |

NEW FUNCTIONS

SYMBOLS AND SPECIAL CHARACTERS

INSERT/SYMBOLS/SYMBOL

52d

① Symbols and special characters that are not on your keyboard can be inserted using the Symbol command. Different types of symbols can be inserted depending on the font selected. Some of the symbols are scientific or mathematical and are generally located on the Symbols font. Other symbols are decorative and are generally located on the Wingdings fonts.

To insert symbols:

1. Position the insertion point where the symbol is to be inserted.

2. Click the Symbols command ① to display a gallery of symbols ②. If the symbol you want to insert is not shown on the Gallery, click More Symbols to display the Symbols dialog box.

3. Click on the Symbols tab to insert a symbol if it is not already selected ③.

4. Select a Symbol font for mathematical or scientific symbols or a Wingdings font ④ for decorative symbols.

5. Select the desired symbol ⑤; then click Insert ⑥ and close.

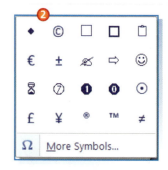

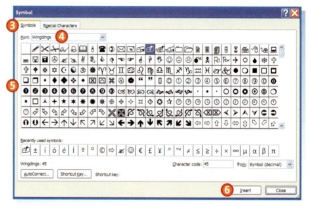

KEYBOARDING PRO DELUXE ▶ See References/Word commands/Lesson 52

19d Textbook Keying

Key each line once, working for fluid, consistent stroking. Repeat at a faster speed.

easy words

19 am it go bus dye jam irk six sod tic yam ugh spa vow aid dug
20 he or by air big elf dog end fit and lay sue toe wit own got
21 six foe pen firm also body auto form down city kept make fog

easy phrases

22 it is|if the|and also|to me|the end|to us|if it|it is|to the
23 if it is|to the end|do you wish|to go to|for the end|to make
24 lay down|he or she|make me|by air|end of|by me|kept it|of me

easy sentences

25 Did the chap work to mend the torn right half of the ensign?
26 Blame me for their penchant for the antique chair and panel.
27 She bid by proxy for eighty bushels of a corn and rye blend.

TECHNIQUE TIP

- Key the easy words as "words" rather than stroke by stroke.
- Key each phrase (marked by a vertical line) without pauses between words.

COMMUNICATION

19e Textbook Keying

1. Study the rules and examples at the right.
2. Key the sample sentences 28–33.
3. Change figures to words as needed in sentences 34–36.

NUMBER EXPRESSION: SPELL OUT NUMBERS

1. **First word in a sentence.** Key numbers ten and lower as words unless they are part of a series of related numbers, any of which are over ten.

    Three of the four members were present.

    She wrote 12 stories and 2 plays in five years.

2. The **smaller of two adjacent numbers** as words.

    SolVir shipped six 24-ton engines.

3. **Isolated fractions and approximate numbers.** Key as words **large round numbers that can be expressed as one or two words**. Hyphenate fractions expressed as words.

    She completed one-fourth of the experiments.

    Val sent out three hundred invitations.

4. **Preceding "o'clock."**

    John's due at four o'clock. Pick him up at 4:15 p.m.

28 **Six** or **seven** older players were cut from the **37**-member team.
29 I have **2** of **14** coins I need to start my set. Kristen has **9**.
30 Of **nine 24**-ton engines ordered, we shipped **six** last Tuesday.
31 Shelly has read just **one-half** of about **forty-five** documents.
32 The **six** boys sent well over **two hundred** printed invitations.
33 **One** or **two** of us will be on duty from **two** until **six** o'clock.
34 The meeting begins promptly at 9. We plan 4 sessions.
35 The 3-person crew cleaned 6 stands, 12 tables, and 13 desks.
36 The 3rd meeting is at 3 o'clock on Friday, February 2.

Editing Essentials

LEARNING OUTCOMES

- Build keying skill.
- Build editing skills.
- Edit letters.
- Edit memos and e-mail.
- Edit tables and reports.

LESSON 52 ▸ Editing Essentials

WARMUP 52a

Key each line, striving for control. Repeat if desired.

alphabet	1	Jim Daley gave us, in that box, a prize he won for his quick car.
figures	2	At 7 a.m., I open Rooms 18, 29, and 30; I lock Rooms 4, 5, and 6.
adjacent reaches	3	As Louis said, few questioned the points asserted by the porters.
easy	4	Did he vow to fight for the right to work as the Orlando auditor?

| 1 | 2 | 3 | 4 | 5 | 6 | 7 | 8 | 9 | 10 | 11 | 12 | 13 |

SKILL BUILDING

52b Textbook Keying
1. Key each line once, concentrating on good keying techniques; tap ENTER twice after each 3-line group.
2. Repeat the drill if time permits.

	5	James Carswell plans to visit Austin and New Orleans in December.
caps	6	Will Peter and Betsy go with Mark when he goes to Alaska in June?
	7	John Kenny wrote the book Innovation and Timing—Keys to Success.
	8	Jeanne arranges meeting room space in Massey Hall for committees.
double letters	9	Russell will attend to the bookkeeping issues tomorrow afternoon.
	10	Todd offered a free book with all assessment tools Lynette sells.
	11	Jane, a neighbor and a proficient auditor, may amend their audit.
balanced hand	12	Blanche and a neighbor may make an ornament for an antique chair.
	13	Claudia may visit the big island when they go to Orlando with us.

LESSON 20 # and /

and /

WARMUP 20a

Key each line twice (slowly, then faster).

alphabet	1 Freda Jencks will have money to buy six quite large topazes.
symbols	2 I bought 10 ribbons and 45 disks from Cable-Han Co. for $78.
home row	3 Dallas sold jade flasks; Sal has a glass flask full of salt.
easy	4 He may cycle down to the field by the giant oak and cut hay.

NEW KEYS

20b # and /

Key each line once.

= number sign, pounds
/ = diagonal, slash

Shift; then reach *up* with *left second* finger.

/ Reach *down* with *right fourth* finger.

#

5 # #e e# # # #; had #3 dial; did #3 drop; set #3 down; Bid #3

6 leave #82; sold #20; Lyric #16; bale #34; load #53; Optic #7

7 Notice #333 says to load Car #33 with 33# of #3 grade shale.

/

8 / /; ;/ / / /; 1/2; 1/3; Mr./Mrs.; 1/5/09; 22 11/12; and/or;

9 to/from; /s/ William Smit; 2/10, n/30; his/her towels; 6 1/2

10 The numerals 1 5/8, 3 1/4, and 60 7/9 are "mixed fractions."

all symbols learned

11 Invoice #737 cites 15 2/3# of rye was shipped C.O.D. 4/6/09.

12 B-O-A Company's Check #50/5 for $87 paid for 15# of #3 wire.

13 Our Co-op List #20 states $40 for 16 1/2 crates of tomatoes.

SKILL BUILDING

20c

Keyboard Reinforcement
Key each line once; work for fluency.

Option: In the Word Processor, key 30" writings on both lines of a pair. Work to avoid pauses.

gwam 30"

14 She did the key work at the height of the problem. 20

15 Form #726 is the title to the island; she owns it. 20

16 The rock is a form of fuel; he did enrich it with coal. 22

17 The corn-and-turkey dish is a blend of turkey and corn. 22

18 It is right to work to end the social problems of the world. 24

19 If I sign it on 3/19, the form can aid us to pay the 40 men. 24

DRILL 1

SUBJECT-VERB AGREEMENT

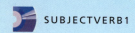

SUBJECTVERB1

1. Review the rules and examples on the previous page.
2. Follow the specific directions provided in the data file.
3. Preview, check, and print. (*subjectverb-drill1*)

DRILL 2

SUBJECT-VERB AGREEMENT

SUBJECTVERB2

1. Follow the specific directions provided in the data file.
2. Preview, check, and print. (*subjectverb-drill2*)

DRILL 3

SUBJECT/VERB AND CAPITALIZATION

1. Key the ten sentences at the right, choosing the correct verb and applying the correct capitalization.
2. Preview, check, and print. (*subjectverb-drill3*)

1. both of the curies (was/were) nobel prize winners.
2. each of the directors in the sales department (has/have) given us approval.
3. mr. and mrs. thomas funderburk, jr. (was/were) married on november 23, 1936.
4. my sister and her college roommates (plan/plans) to tour london and paris this summer.
5. our new information manager (suggest/suggests) the following salutation when using an attention line: ladies and gentlemen.
6. the body language expert (place/places) his hand on his cheek as he says, "touch your hand to your chin."
7. the japanese child (enjoy/enjoys) the american food her hosts (serve/serves) her.
8. all of the candidates (was/were) invited to the debate at boston college.
9. the final exam (cover/covers) chapters 1-5.
10. turn south onto interstate 20; then take exit 56 to bossier city.

DRILL 4

EDITING SKILLS

1. Key the paragraphs.
2. Correct all errors in grammar and capitalization.
3. Preview, check, and close. (*editing-drill4*)

This past week I visited the facilities of the magnolia conference center in isle of palms, south carolina, as you requested. bob bremmerton, group manager, was my host for the visit.

magnolia offers many advantages for our leadership training conference. The prices are reasonable; the facilities is excellent; the location is suitable. In addition to the beachfront location, tennis and golf packages are part of the group price.

COMMUNICATION

20d Textbook Keying: Number Usage Review

Key each line once. Decide whether the circled numbers should be keyed as figures or as words and make needed changes. Check your finished work with 19e, page 47.

20 Six or ⑦ older players were cut from the ㊲-member team.

21 I have ② of 14 coins I need to start my set. Kristen has ⑨.

22 Of ⑨ 24-ton engines ordered, we shipped ⑥ last Tuesday.

23 Shelly has read just ① half of about ㊺ documents.

24 The ⑥ boys sent well over ⑳⓪⓪ printed invitations.

25 ① or ② of us will be on duty from ② until ⑥ o'clock.

SKILL BUILDING

20e Timed Writing (WP)

1. Take a 3' writing on both paragraphs. If you finish the timing before time is up, repeat the timing.
2. End the lesson but do not exit the software.
3. Go to the Word Processor, and follow the directions at the right to build your speed on each paragraph by 4 words.

E
all letters

Goal: 16 *gwam*

			gwam
1/4'	1/2'	3/4'	1'
4	8	12	16
5	10	15	20
6	12	18	24
7	14	21	28
8	16	24	32
9	18	27	36
10	20	30	40

STANDARD PLAN | **for Guided Writing Procedures**

1. In the Word Processor, take a 1' writing on paragraph 1. Note your *gwam*.
2. Add four words to your 1' *gwam* to determine your goal rate.
3. Set the Timer for 1'. Set the Timer option to beep every 15".
4. From the table below, select from column 4 the speed nearest your goal rate. Note the ¼' point at the left of that speed. Place a light check mark within the paragraphs at the ¼' points.
5. Take two 1' guided writings on paragraphs 1 and 2. Do not save.
6. Turn the beeper off.

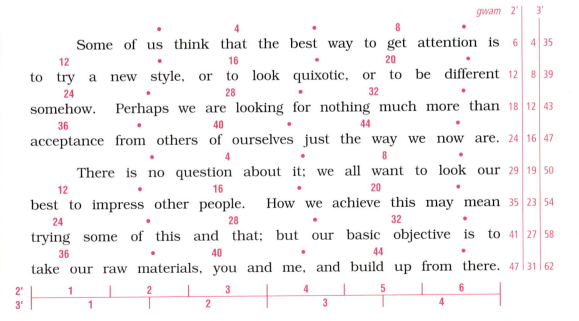

	gwam	2'	3'
Some of us think that the best way to get attention is		6	4 · 35
to try a new style, or to look quixotic, or to be different		12	8 · 39
somehow. Perhaps we are looking for nothing much more than		18	12 · 43
acceptance from others of ourselves just the way we now are.		24	16 · 47
There is no question about it; we all want to look our		29	19 · 50
best to impress other people. How we achieve this may mean		35	23 · 54
trying some of this and that; but our basic objective is to		41	27 · 58
take our raw materials, you and me, and build up from there.		47	31 · 62

2' | 1 | 2 | 3 | 4 | 5 | 6 |
3' | 1 | 2 | 3 | 4 |

Communication Skills

SUBJECT/VERB AGREEMENT

USE A SINGULAR VERB

1. With a **singular subject**. (The singular forms of *to be* include: am, is, was. Common errors with *to be* are: you was, we was, they was.)

> She monitors employee morale.
> You are a very energetic worker.
> A split keyboard is in great demand.

2. With most **indefinite pronouns**: *another, anybody, anything, everything, each, either, neither, one, everyone, anyone, nobody.*

> Each of the candidates has raised a considerable amount of money.
> Everyone is eager to read the author's newest novel.
> Neither of the boys is able to attend.

3. With singular subjects joined by *or/nor, either/or, neither/nor.*

> Neither your grammar nor punctuation is correct.
> Either Jody or Jan has your favorite CD.
> John or Connie has volunteered to chaperone the field trip.

4. With a **collective noun** (*family, choir, herd, faculty, jury, committee*) that acts as one unit.

> The jury has reached a decision.
> The council is in an emergency session.
> But:
> The faculty have their assignments. (Each has his/her own assignments.)

5. With words or phrases that express **periods of time**, **weights**, **measurements**, or **amounts of money**.

> Fifteen dollars is what he earned.
> Two-thirds of the money has been submitted to the treasurer.
> One hundred pounds is too much.

USE A PLURAL VERB

6. With a **plural subject**.

> The students sell computer supplies for their annual fundraiser.
> They are among the top-ranked teams in the nation.

7. With **compound (two or more) subjects** joined by *and*.

> Headaches and backaches are common worker complaints.
> Hard work and determination were two qualities listed by the references.

8. With *some, all, most, none, several, few, both, many,* and *any* when they refer to more than one of the items.

> All of my friends have seen the movie.
> Some of the teams have won two or more games.

% and !

WARMUP 21a

Key each line twice.

alphabet	1	Merry will have picked out a dozen quarts of jam for boxing.
fig/sym	2	Jane-Ann bought 16 7/8 yards of #240 cotton at $3.59 a yard.
1st row	3	Can't brave, zany Cave Club men/women next climb Mt. Zamban?
easy	4	Did she rush to cut six bushels of corn for the civic corps?

NEW KEYS

21b % and !

Key each line once.

% = **percent sign:** Use % with business forms or where space is restricted; otherwise, use the word "percent."

Space twice after the exclamation point!

% Shift; then reach *up* with *left first* finger.

SPACING TIP

- Do not space between a figure and the % or $ signs.
- Do not space before or after the dash.

%

5 % %f f% % %; off 5%; if 5%; of 5% fund; half 5%; taxes of 5%

6 7% rent; 3% tariff; 9% F.O.B.; 15% greater; 28% base; up 46%

7 Give discounts of 5% on rods, 50% on lures, and 75% on line.

!   reach *up* with the *left fourth* finger

8 ! !a a! ! ! !; Eureka! Ha! No! Pull 10! Extra! America!

9 Listen to the call! Now! Ready! Get set! Go! Good show!

10 I want it now, not next week! I am sure to lose 50% or $19.

all symbols

11 The ad offers a 10% discount, but this notice says 15% less!

12 He got the job! With Clark's Supermarket! Please call Mom!

13 Bill #92-44 arrived very late from Zyclone; it was paid 7/4.

21c

Keyboard Reinforcement
Key each line once; work for fluency.

all symbols

14 As of 6/28, Jeri owes $31 for dinner and $27 for cab fare.

15 Invoice #20--it was dated 3/4--billed $17 less 15% discount.

16 He deducted 2% instead of 6%, a clear saving of 6% vs. 7%.

combination response

17 Look at my dismal grade in English; but I guess I earned it.

18 Kris started to blend a cocoa beverage for a shaken cowhand.

19 Jan may make a big profit if she owns the title to the land.

51-d4

Table

1. Open *51-d1* and key the data in a new column B; adjust column widths.

    Publisher
    Bodwin
    American
    TWSS
    Bodwin
    TWSS
    American

2. Insert a new row above *Pommery Mountain* and add the following information.

    The Lion and the Mouse   American   2008   63,500.00   19.95

3. Continue to next document. (*51-d4*)

51-d5

Table with AutoFit and Remove Borders

1. Key the table. AutoFit the table to the contents. Key the source below the table.
2. Insert a column between columns A and B. Make the column 0.2" wide.
3. Remove all borders on the table. Center the table vertically and horizontally.
4. Check the test and close. (*51-d5*)

TIP

AutoFit resizes the column widths based on the size of the text in them.

STAGES OF LIFE SPAN DEVELOPMENT

Stage	Biological Development
Infancy and Toddlerhood: Birth to 2 years	Body doubles in height and quadruples in weight
Early Childhood: 2 to 6 years	Brain attains 90 percent of its adult weight by age 5
Middle Childhood: 7 to 9 years	Physical growth slows; slight height spurts occur
Late Childhood: 10 to 12 years	Boys lag behind girls in physical maturation
Early Adolescence: 13 to 15 years	Body continues to grow in height and weight
Late Adolescence: 16 to 19 years	Girls' motor performance peaks; boys' improve
Early Adulthood: 20 to 40 years	Physical functioning peaks at about age 30
Middle Adulthood: 40 to 65 years	Gradual changes in appearance
Late Adulthood: 65 years and over	Brain becomes smaller and functions slower

Source: www.learner.org

CHECKPOINT

Congratulations! You have successfully completed the lessons in Module 6. To check your understanding and for more practice, complete the objective assessment and performance assessment located on the textbook website at www.collegekeyboarding.com.

LESSON 22   (and) and Backspace Key

WARMUP 22a

Key each line twice.

alphabet	1 Avoid lazy punches; expert fighters jab with a quick motion.
fig/sym	2 Be-Low's Bill #483/7 was $96.90, not $102--they took 5% off.
caps lock	3 Report titles may be shown in ALL CAPS; as, BOLD WORD POWER.
easy	4 Do they blame me for their dismal social and civic problems?

| 1 | 2 | 3 | 4 | 5 | 6 | 7 | 8 | 9 | 10 | 11 | 12 |

NEW KEYS

22b

(and) (parentheses)

Key each line once.

(Shift; then reach *up* with the *right third* finger.

) Shift; then reach *up* with the *right fourth* finger.

( ) = parentheses
Parentheses indicate off-hand, aside, or explanatory messages.

5   ((l l((; (; Reach from l for the left parenthesis; as, ((.
6   )); ;))); Reach from ; for the right parenthesis; as,)).

( )

7   Learn to use parentheses (plural) or parenthesis (singular).
8   The red (No. 34) and blue (No. 78) cars both won here (Rio).
9   We (Galen and I) dined (bagels) in our penthouse (the dorm).

all symbols learned

10   The jacket was $35 (thirty-five dollars)--the tie was extra.
11   Starting 10/29, you can sell Model #49 at a discount of 25%.
12   My size 8 1/2 shoe--a blue pump--was soiled (but not badly).

22c Textbook Keying

Key each line once, keeping eyes on copy.

13   Jana has one hard-to-get copy of her hot-off-the-press book.
14   An invoice said that "We give discounts of 10%, 5%, and 3%."
15   The company paid bill 3/17 on 5/2/09 and bill 4/1 on 3/6/08.
16   The catalog lists as out of stock Items #230, #710, and #13.
17   Elyn had $8; Sean, $9; and Cal, $7. The cash total was $24.

51-d1
Table Formatted with Styles

1. Key the table; center column B; right-align column C; and set a decimal tab in column D. Center column heads. Italicize the book titles.
2. Format the table and apply Light Shading - Accent 2 table style.
3. Center the table vertically.
4. Continue to next document. (*51-d1*)

TIP

Remember to proofread and preview each document before you move to the next one.

LARSON LEARNING

Book Title	Publications	Sales	Unit Price
Adventures of Sally Boyer	2009	478,769.00	14.95
Tale of Five Cities	2008	91,278.00	32.50
New York, New York	2009	32,829.00	29.75
Horrell Hill Adventures	2008	39,412.00	29.50
Pommery Mountain	2009	194,511.00	33.75
Tom Creek's Adventures	2009	105,750.00	31.95

51-d2
Memo with Table

1. Key the memo; insert reference initials at the end of the memo.
2. Right-align column D and center columns B and C. Center column heads.
3. Adjust the spacing appropriately before and after the table.
4. Continue to next document. (*51-d2*)

TO: Brenda Cook | **FROM:** Marco Dominguez | **DATE:** June 19, 20-- | **SUBJECT:** Sales Report

A comparison of the sales figures for 2007 and 2008 is shown below. Figures look pretty good for all the regions except the Northern region. I am concerned about the decrease in sales for the Northern region; this has always been a high-growth area.

Region	2007 Sales	2008 Sales	% of Change
East	53,256	72,002	+18.55%
North	41,899	37,576	−4.07%
West	62,965	64,211	+2.88%
South	27,894	29,031	+3.55%

Please research the cause in the drop of sales for the Northern area. Let's get together next week and discuss how we can improve Northern sales for next year.

SKILL BUILDING

22d BACKSPACE Key

In the Word Processor, key the sentences using the BACKSPACE key to correct errors.

18 You should be interested in the special items on sale today.
19 If she is going with us, why don't we plan to leave now?
20 Do you desire to continue working on the memo in the future?
21 Did the firm or their neighbors own the autos with problems?
22 Juni, Vec, and Zeb had perfect grades on weekly query exams.
23 Jewel quickly explained to me the big fire hazards involved.

22e Timed Writing

1. Take a 3' timing on both paragraphs.
2. End the lesson; then go to the Word Processor and complete 22d and 22f.

E

all letters

	1'	3'
Most people will agree that we owe it to our children	10	4	28
to pass the planet on to them in better condition than we	22	7	32
found it. We must take extra steps just to make the quality	34	12	36
of living better.	38	13	37
If we do not change our ways quickly and stop damaging	11	16	41
our world, it will not be a good place to live. We can save	12	21	45
the ozone and wildlife and stop polluting the air and water.	35	25	49

1'	1	2	3	4	5	6	7	8	9	10	11	12
3'		1		2			3			4		

COMMUNICATION

22f Word Processor

1. Study the rules and examples at the right.
2. In the Word Processor, key the information below at the left margin. Tap ENTER as shown.

Your name ENTER
Current date ENTER
Number Expression ENTER

3. Key the sample sentences 24–28. Backspace to correct errors.
4. Save the file as *xx-22f*.

NUMBER EXPRESSION: EXPRESS AS FIGURES

1. **Money amounts** and **percentages, even when appoximate.** Spell out cents and percent except in statistical copy.

    The 16 percent discount saved me $145; Bill, 95 cents.

2. **Round numbers expressed in millions or higher with their word modifier.**

    Ms. Ti contributed $3 million.

3. **House numbers** (except house number One) and street names over ten. If a street name is a number, separate it from the house number with a dash.

    1510 Easy Street   One West Ninth Avenue   1592-11th Street

4. **Date following a month.** A date preceding the month is expressed in figures followed by "rd" or "th."

    June 9, 2009   March 3   4th of July

5. **Numbers used with nouns.**

    Volume 1   Chapter 6

24 Ask **Group 1** to read **Chapter 6** of **Book 11** (**Shelf 19, Room 5**).
25 All **six** of us live at **One Bay Road**, not at **126--56th Street**.
26 At **9 a.m.** the owners decided to close from **12 noon** to **1 p.m.**
27 Ms. Vik leaves **June 9**; she returns the **14th or 15th of July**.
28 The **16 percent** discount saves **$115**. A stamp costs **35 cents**.

LESSON 51 | Assessment

WARMUP 51a

Key each line, striving for control. Repeat if desired.

alphabet 1 Jacob Kazlowski and five experienced rugby players quit the team.

figures 2 E-mail account #82-4 is the account for telephone (714) 555-0108.

double letters 3 Anne will meet with the committee at noon to discuss a new issue.

easy 4 The men may pay my neighbor for the work he did in the cornfield.

| 1 | 2 | 3 | 4 | 5 | 6 | 7 | 8 | 9 | 10 | 11 | 12 | 13 |

SKILL BUILDING

51b Timed Writing
Take two 5' timed writings.

gwam 3' | 5'

	3'	5'

Whether any company can succeed depends on how well it fits — 4 | 2
into the economic system. Success rests on certain key factors that — 9 | 5
are put in line by a management team that has set goals for the — 13 | 8
company and has enough good judgment to recognize how best to — 17 | 10
reach these goals. Because of competition, only the best-organized — 21 | 13
companies get to the top. — 23 | 14

A commercial enterprise is formed for a specific purpose: that — 27 | 16
purpose is usually to equip others, or consumers, with whatever — 32 | 19
they cannot equip themselves. Unless there is only one provider, a — 36 | 22
consumer will search for a company that returns the most value in — 41 | 24
terms of price; and a relationship with such a company, once set — 45 | 27
up, can endure for many years. — 47 | 28

Thus our system assures that the businesses that manage to — 51 | 31
survive are those that have been able to combine successfully an — 55 | 33
excellent product with a low price and the best service—all in a place — 60 | 36
that is convenient for the buyers. With no intrusion from outside — 64 | 39
forces, the buyer and the seller benefit both themselves and each — 69 | 41
other. — 69 | 42

3' | 1 | 2 | 3 | 4 |
5' | 1 | 2 | 3 |

APPLICATIONS

51c
Assessment

 Continue

 Check

With *Keyboarding Pro DELUXE*: When you complete a document, proofread it, check the spelling, and preview for placement. When you are completely satisfied, click the Continue button to move to the next document. Click the Check button when you are ready to error-check the test. Review and/or print the document analysis results.

Without *Keyboarding Pro DELUXE*: Key the documents in sequence. When time has been called, proofread all documents again and identify errors.

LESSON 23

& and : (colon), Proofreaders' Marks

WARMUP 23a

Key each line twice.

alphabet 1 Roxy waved as she did quick flying jumps on the trapeze bar.

symbols 2 Ryan's--with an A-1 rating--sold Item #146 (for $10) on 2/7.

space bar 3 Mr. Fyn may go to Cape Cod on the bus, or he may go by auto.

easy 4 Susie is busy; may she halt the social work for the auditor?

| 1 | 2 | 3 | 4 | 5 | 6 | 7 | 8 | 9 | 10 | 11 | 12 |

NEW KEYS

23b & and : (colon)
Key each line once.

& = ampersand: The ampersand is used only as part of company names.

Colon: Space twice after a colon except when used within a number for time.

& Shift; then reach *up* with *right first* finger.

: (colon) Left shift; then tap key with *right fourth* finger.

& (ampersand)

5 & &j j& & & &; J & J; Haraj & Jay; Moroj & Jax; Torj & Jones

6 Nehru & Unger; Mumm & Just; Mann & Hart; Arch & Jones; M & J

7 Rhye & Knox represent us; Steb & Doy, Firm A; R & J, Firm B.

: (colon)

8 : :; ;: : : :; as: for example: notice: To: From: Date:

9 in stock: 8:30; 7:45; Age: Experience: Read: Send: See:

10 Space twice after a colon, thus: To: No.: Time: Carload:

all symbols learned

11 Consider these companies: J & R, Brand & Kay, Uper & Davis.

12 Memo #88-89 reads as follows: "Deduct 15% of $300, or $45."

13 Bill 32(5)--it got here quite late--from M & N was paid 7/3.

23c
Keyboard Reinforcement
Key each line twice; work for fluency.

double letters

14 Di Bennett was puzzled by drivers exceeding the speed limit.

15 Bill needs the office address; he will cut the grass at ten.

16 Todd saw the green car veer off the street near a tall tree.

figures and symbols

17 Invoice #84 for $672.91, plus $4.38 tax, was due on 5/19/08.

18 Do read Section 4, pages 60-74 and Section 9, pages 198-225.

19 Enter the following: (a) name, (b) address, and (c) tax ID.

The items you requested on Purchase Order 5122 are in stock and will be shipped from our warehouse today. The shipment will be transported via Romulus Delivery System and is expected to arrive at your location in five days.

Item Number	Description	Unit Price
329-8741	Lordusky locking cabinet	265.00
336-1285	Anchorage heavy duty locking cabinet	465.00
387-6509	Lordusky locking cabinet (unassembled)	195.00

xx

50-d3

Block Letter with Table

1. Key the block letter below with open punctuation. Supply necessary letter parts.
2. Center the data in column A; set a decimal tab in column D.
3. From the Design tab, apply the table style Light Grid - Accent 2.
4. Adjust column width and center table horizontally on the page. (**Note:** Before you key the second paragraph, select the paragraph marker below the table and add extra space above it.)
5. Click the ¶ following the table. In the Paragraph group on the Home tab, click the Line Spacing drop-list arrow. Choose *Add Space Before Paragraph*, and then key the last paragraph. The letter is from **Veejah Patel, Collections Manager**.
6. Center letter vertically on the page.
7. Check and close. (*50-d3*)

Ms. Beatrice Snow | Collections Manager | Precision Office Products | 2679 Orchard Lake Road | Farmington Hills, MI 48297-5534

Thank you for allowing International Financial Systems to assist you in managing your delinquent accounts. We provide you with the fastest interface to International Systems Collection Services. The activity report for last month is shown below.

Client Number	Last Name	First Name	Current Balance
1487	Rodriguez	Delia	1,576.00
1679	Kim	Lisa	954.35
1822	Batavia	Kirsten	1,034.21
1905	Vokavich	Kramer	832.09

Please verify the accuracy of the names transmitted by your billing office. If you find any transmission errors, please contact Joseph Kerning at 888-555-0134 immediately.

SKILL BUILDING

23d **Textbook Keying**
Key each line once; work for fluency.

20 *Jane may work with an auditing firm if she is paid to do so.*
21 *Pam and eight girls may go to the lake to work with the dog.*
22 *Clancy and Claudia did all the work to fix the sign problem.*
23 *Did Lea visit the Orlando land of enchantment or a neighbor?*
24 *Ana and Blanche made a map for a neighbor to go to the city.*
25 *Sidney may go to the lake to fish with worms from the docks.*
26 *Did the firm or the neighbors own the auto with the problem?*

| 1 | 2 | 3 | 4 | 5 | 6 | 7 | 8 | 9 | 10 | 11 | 12 |

23e **Timed Writing**
Take a 3' timing on both paragraphs. Repeat.

all letters

Is how you judge my work important? It is, of course; **11 | 4 | 26**
I hope you recognize some basic merit in it. We all expect **23 | 8 | 30**
to get credit for good work that we conclude. **32 | 11 | 33**

I want approval for stands I take, things I write, and **11 | 14 | 36**
work I complete. My efforts, by my work, show a picture of **23 | 18 | 41**
me; thus, through my work, I am my own unique creation. **34 | 22 | 44**

gwam 1' | 3'

| 1' | 1 | 2 | 3 | 4 | 5 | 6 | 7 | 8 | 9 | 10 | 11 | 12 |
| 3' | | 1 | | 2 | | 3 | | 4 | |

COMMUNICATION

23f **Edit Text** (WP)
1. Read the information about proofreaders' marks.
2. In the Word Processor, key your name, class, and **23f** at the left margin. Then key lines 27–32, making the revisions as you key. Use the BACKSPACE key to correct errors.
3. Save as *xx-23f* and print.

Proofreaders' marks are used to identify mistakes in typed or printed text. Learn to apply these commonly used standard proofreaders' marks.

Symbol	Meaning	Symbol	Meaning
——	Italic	◯ sp	Spell out
～～	Bold	¶	Paragraph
Cap or ≡	Capitalize	#	Add horizontal space
∧	Insert	/ or lc	Lowercase
⟋	Delete	◡	Close up space
⊏	Move to left	～	Transpose
⊐	Move to right	stet	Leave as originally written

27 We miss 50% in life's rewards by refusing to new try things.

28 do it now--today--then tomorrow's load will be 100%% lighter.

29 Satisfying work- whether it pays $40 or $400- is the pay off.

30 Avoid mistakes: confusing a #3 has cost thousands.

31 Pleased most with a first-rate job is the person who did it.

32 My wife and/or me mother will except the certifi cate for me.

NOTEBOOK SECURITY GUIDELINES

Choose an easy-to-use security system.	Select a security system that is easy to use. If the security system is difficult to use and requires complicated steps, users will either not use it or look for ways to defeat it.
Assign someone to be in charge of notebook security.	One or more persons in the company should be responsible for monitoring the hardware and software on notebook computers. This person needs to be in charge of disseminating security rules and making sure that the rules are followed.
Apply several levels of security.	Different levels of security should be applied to different levels of employees. A CEO or an engineer working in the company's R & D department may be working with data that will require a higher level of security than someone in the art department. Don't bog down the artist with the high level of security needed for the CEO.
Most laptop/notebook thefts are opportunistic.	Train users to be alert and to keep an eye on their computers at all times. Remind them to use extra caution when passing through airports and staying in hotels.
Hold users responsible for their computers.	Encourage users to take precautions, and punish those who are careless by taking away laptop privileges.

50-d2

Memo with Table

1. Key the memo on the next page to Roberto Perez from Marcia Lewis. The subject is Purchase Order 5122. Insert the current date.

2. Center the data in columns A and C. Adjust column width so that the text fits on one line. Apply the Colorful List - Accent 1 table style.

3. Click the ¶ following the table. In the Paragraph group on the Home tab, click the Line Spacing drop-list arrow. Choose Add Space Before Paragraph, and then key your reference initials.

4. Check and close. (*50-d2*)

LESSON 24

Other Symbols

WARMUP 24a

Key each line twice.

alphabet 1 Pfc. Jim Kings covered each of the lazy boxers with a quilt.

figures 2 Do problems 6 to 29 on page 175 before class at 8:30, May 4.

" 3 They read the poems "September Rain" and "The Lower Branch."

easy 4 When did the busy girls fix the tight cowl of the ruby gown?

| 1 | 2 | 3 | 4 | 5 | 6 | 7 | 8 | 9 | 10 | 11 | 12 |

NEW KEYS

24b Textbook Keying

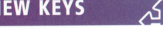

Key each pair of lines once;
DS between 2-line groups.

Become familiar with these symbols:

@   at
<   less than
>   greater than
*   asterisk
+   plus sign (use a hyphen for minus and x for "times")
=   equals
[ ] left and right bracket

@   shift; reach *up* with *left third* finger to @

5 @ @s s@ @ @; 24 @ .15; 22 @ .35; sold 2 @ .87; were 12 @ .95

6 You may contact Luke @: LJP@rx.com or fax @ (602) 555-0101.

<   shift; reach *down* with *right second* finger to <
>   shift; reach *down* with *right third* finger to >

7 Can you prove "a > b"?   If 28 > 5, then 5a < x.   Is a < > b?

8 E-mail Al ajj@crewl.com and Matt mrw10@scxs.com by 9:30 p.m.

*   shift; reach *up* with *right second* finger to *

9 * *k k8* * *; aurelis*; May 7*; both sides*; 250 km.**; aka*

10 Note each *; one * refers to page 29; ** refers to page 307.

+   shift; reach *up* with *right fourth* finger to +

11 + ;+ +; + + +; 2 + 2; A+ or B+; 70+ F. degrees; +xy over +y;

12 The question was 8 + 7 + 51; it should have been 8 + 7 + 15.

=   reach *up* with *right fourth* finger to =

13 = =; = = =; = 4; If 14x = 28, x = 2; if 8x = 16, then x = 2.

14 Change this solution (where it says "= by") to = bx or = BX.

[ ] reach *up* with *right fourth* finger to [and]

15 Mr. Wing was named.   [That's John J. Wing, ex-senator.   Ed.]

16 We [Joseph and I] will be in Suite #349; call us @ 555-0102.

WARMUP 50a

Key each line, striving for control. Repeat if desired.

alphabet   1   Jerrillyn quickly moved the six dozen big pink and white flowers.

double letters   2   Add cherries and green and yellow peppers to May's shopping cart.

1st/2nd fingers   3   The task was too big for us to finish in one day; we need a week.

balanced hand   4   I am busy, but I can make the formal amendment to the title form.

50b

Application Review

Word's default Normal style inserts a 10 point space after a paragraph and uses 1.15 line spacing. However, *Word* defaults to single spacing in a table and no spacing after a paragraph. Therefore, when a table is keyed within a document, extra spacing needs to be inserted below the table to match the spacing above the table. The extra space can easily be inserted by first clicking on the paragraph marker (¶) below the table, clicking the Line Spacing drop-list arrow, and choosing Add Space Before Paragraph.

The items you requested on Purchase Order 5122 are in stock and will be shipped from our warehouse today.

Item Number	Description	Unit Price
329-8741	Lordusky lock	265.00
336-1285	Anchorage	465.00
387-6509	Locking cab	195.00

¶

Please call us if we can assist you any further.

xx   **Select this ¶ and choose Add Space Before Paragraph**

APPLICATIONS

50-d1

Table Without Borders

The Table feature can be used to create an attractive report. The row and column structure allows you to organize and present text in an attractive format that is easy to read. After the table is keyed, the borders are removed so that it will resemble a report.

1. Key the main heading on the next page and format it appropriately. Position the head at approximately 2".

2. Insert a three-column, five-row table.

3. Click the cursor in column B. Click the cursor in the Table Column Width box. Key **.2** in the Width box. This narrow column is used to separate the text in columns A and C.

4. Click the cursor in column A. Key **2.05** in the Width box. Make the width of column C **3.8**.

5. Key the text in columns A and C. Do not key in column B.

6. Bold the text in column A.

7. Insert a blank row below each row except the last.

8. Remove the table borders by selecting the entire table; then click the Table Design tab. Click the Borders drop-list arrow and select No Border.

9. Check and close. (*50-d1*)

24c Rhythm Builder
Key each line once.

double letters
17 feel pass mill good miss seem moons cliffs pools green spell
18 Assets are being offered in a stuffy room to two associates.

balanced hand
19 is if of to it go do to is do so if to to the it sign vie to
20 Pamela Fox may wish to go to town with Blanche if she works.

one hand
21 date face ere bat lip sew lion rear brag fact join eggs ever
22 get fewer on; after we look; as we agree; add debt; act fast

combination
23 was for|in the case of|they were|to down|mend it|but pony is
24 They were to be down in the fastest sleigh if you are right.

| 1 | 2 | 3 | 4 | 5 | 6 | 7 | 8 | 9 | 10 | 11 | 12 |

24d Edited Copy
1. In the Word Processor, key your name, class, and date at the left margin, each on a separate line.
2. Key each line, making the corrections marked with proofreaders' marks.
3. Correct errors using the BACKSPACE key.
4. Save as *xx-24d*.

25 Ask Group 1 to read Chater 6 of Book 11 (Shelf 19,Room 5).

26 All 6 of us live at One Bay road, not at 126 -56th Street.

27 AT 9 a.m. the owners decided to close form 12 noon to 1 p.m.

28 Ms. Vik leaves June 9; she returns the 14 or 15 of July.

29 The 16 per cent discount saves 115. A stamp costs 35 cents.

30 Elin gave $300,000,000; our gift was only 75 cents.

24e Timed Writing
Take a 3' timing on both paragraphs. Repeat.

gwam 1' | 3'

Why don't we like change very much? Do you think that just maybe we want to be lazy; to dodge new things; and, as much as possible, not to make hard decisions?

We know change can and does extend new areas for us to enjoy, areas we might never have known existed; and to stay away from all change could curtail our quality of life.

	1'	3'
	11	4	26
	23	8	30
	32	11	33
	11	14	36
	24	18	40
	34	22	44

| 1' | 1 | 2 | 3 | 4 | 5 | 6 | 7 | 8 | 9 | 10 | 11 | 12 |
| 3' | | 1 | | 2 | | 3 | | 4 | |

24f Composition
1. In the Word Processor, open the file *xx-profile* that you created in Lesson 18.
2. Position the insertion point at the end of the last paragraph. Tap ENTER twice.
3. Key an additional paragraph that begins with the following sentence:
   Thank you for allowing me to introduce myself.
4. Finish the paragraph by adding two or more sentences that describe your progress and satisfaction with keyboarding.
5. Correct any mistakes you have made. Click Save to resave the document. Print.
6. Mark any mistakes you missed with proofreaders' marks. Revise the document, save, and reprint. Submit to your instructor.

49-d4

Table with Indented Lines and Decimal Tab

1. Key the table below. Adjust column width attractively so that each entry fits on one line. Column A: Set a left tab at .25" for the indented lines; press CTRL + TAB to indent lines.

2. Use a decimal tab to right-align numbers; set the tab so that the column appears centered below the column head.

3. Apply Black, Text 1 shading to row 1. Apply White, Background 2, Darker 10% shading to rows 2 and 5.

4. Center the table vertically on the page. Check and close. (*49-d4*)

EFFECTS OF CRONIX ON PATIENTS

Body Systems	Cronix + Aspirin	Placebo + Aspirin
Central nervous system		
Headache	867	402
Dizziness	1,084	839
Gastrointestinal system disorders		
Abdominal pain	317	130
Dyspepsia	62	1,017
Diarrhea	64	9

49-d5

Internet Activity

1. Go to http://www.50states.com/flower. Look up the official state flower for Michigan, Mississippi, and South Carolina. Write the state flowers on a sheet of paper.

2. Go to http://www.50states.com/bird and write down the official state bird for the same states listed in step 1.

3. Open *46-d4*. Insert the three states with their official bird and flower in the table. Insert the rows so that the states will be in correct alphabetical order.

4. Change the row height of the entire table to .3. Center the text vertically in the cells.

5. Adjust column width and center table horizontally. Change the main heading to 14 point and the secondary heading to 12 point.

6. Check and close. (*49-d5*)

Assessment

WARMUP 25a

Key each line twice.

alphabet	1	My wife helped fix a frozen lock on Jacque's vegetable bins.
figures	2	Sherm moved from 823 West 150th Street to 9472--67th Street.
double letters	3	Will Scotty attempt to sell his accounting books to Elliott?
easy	4	It is a shame he used the endowment for a visit to the city.

| 1 | 2 | 3 | 4 | 5 | 6 | 7 | 8 | 9 | 10 | 11 | 12 |

25b Reach Review
Key each line once; repeat.

TECHNIQUE TIP

Keep arms and hands quiet as you practice the long reaches.

n/y	5	deny many canny tiny nymph puny any puny zany penny pony yen
	6	Jenny Nyles saw many, many tiny nymphs flying near her pony.
b/r	7	bran barb brim curb brat garb bray verb brag garb bribe herb
	8	Barb Barber can bring a bit of bran and herbs for her bread.
c/e	9	cede neck nice deck dice heck rice peck vice erect mice echo
	10	Can Cecil erect a decent cedar deck? He erects nice condos.
n/u	11	nun gnu bun nut pun numb sun nude tuna nub fun null unit gun
	12	Eunice had enough ground nuts at lunch; Uncle Launce is fun.

25c Timed Writing
Key two 3' writings. Strive for accuracy.

all letters

Goal: 3', 19–27 gwam

	gwam	3'
The term careers can mean many different things to	3	51
different people. As you know, a career is much more than a	8	55
job. It is the kind of work that a person has through life.	12	59
It includes the jobs a person has over time. It also involves	16	63
how the work life affects the other parts of our life. There	20	67
are as many types of careers as there are people.	23	71
Almost all people have a career of some kind. A career	27	74
can help us to reach unique goals, such as to make a living	31	79
or to help others. The kind of career you have will affect	35	83
your life in many ways. For example, it can determine where	39	87
you live, the money you make, and how you feel about yourself.	44	91
A good choice can thus help you realize the life you want.	47	95

| 3' | 1 | 2 | 3 | 4 |

49-d1 and 49-d2

Table with Merge Row, Table Style, and Changing Row Height

TIP

To key the bullets with extra space, key the text and tap ENTER between each line. Then select the text, click the Bullets button, and click the Decrease Indent button.

1. Create a three-column, eight-row table using the data below.
2. Merge the cells in row 1. Center the main heading, tap ENTER, and key the first paragraph in row 1 (left aligned). Leave row 2 blank.
3. Key the column heads in row 3 and change the row height to .3".
4. Key **Obtain Driving Directions** in row 4. Leave rows 5 and 7 blank.
5. Key the remainder of the table. Center the table vertically and horizontally. Check and close. (*49-d1*)
6. Open *49-d1*; bold the column headings; center them horizontally and vertically. Change the main heading to 14 point.
7. Apply Light Shading - Accent 4 style to the table.
8. Check and close. (*49-d2*)

49-d3

Remove Table Borders

1. Open *49-d1*.
2. Select the entire table. Remove the outer borders of the table.
3. Check and close. (*49-d3*)

MOBILE PHONE: JACK OF ALL TRADES		
Cell phones have the capability of doing more than just calling people. New technology is now producing faster chips, bigger and brighter screens, and Internet data capability. The gadget that you carry with you can do so much more than just make phone calls.		
Additional Services	Description of Service	Service Provider
Obtain Driving Directions	GPS system for the car can be very expensive. Several services have added Wi-Fi "hotspot" finders to their mobile mapping service so that you can get driving directions on your cell phone for just a couple of extra dollars per month.	• StreetFinder just launched its mobile version called Street Finder Navigator. • Telecomm • Phone Nav
Get Extra Money	You can now turn your cell phone into a digital wallet. Some banking systems allow you to use your cell phone to transfer money from your bank account to a credit or debit card.	• International Express • AmeriCard
Access Computer Files	If you left a file on a home or work computer, you can remotely access that computer and fetch the file. Software is now being developed that will also allow you to access computers that are not turned on.	• Computer Transcender • Hitch Hiker Express

25d Textbook Keying
Key each line once; DS between groups.

Key with precision and without hesitation.

13 is if he do rub ant go and am pan do rut us aid ox ape by is
14 it is|an end|it may|to pay|and so|aid us|he got|or own|to go
15 Did the girl make the ornament with fur, duck down, or hair?
16 us owl rug box bob to man so bit or big pen of jay me age it
17 it|it is|time to go|show them how|plan to go|one of the aims
18 It is a shame they use the autobus for a visit to the field.
| 1 | 2 | 3 | 4 | 5 | 6 | 7 | 8 | 9 | 10 | 11 | 12 |

25e Figure Check
In the Word Processor, key two 3' writings at a controlled rate. Save the timings as *xx-25e-t1* and *xx-25e-t2*

E

all letters/figures

Goal: 3' 16–14 *gwam*.

gwam 3'

Do I read the stock market pages in the news? Yes; and — 4 | 35
at about 9 or 10 a.m. each morning, I know lots of excited — 8 | 39
people are quick to join me. In fact, many of us zip right — 12 | 43
to the 3rd or 4th part of the paper to see if the prices of — 16 | 47
our stocks have gone up or down. Now, those of us who are — 19 | 51
"speculators" like to "buy at 52 and sell at 60"; while the — 23 | 55
"investors" among us are more interested in a dividend we — 27 | 59
may get, say 7 or 8 percent, than in the price of a stock. — 31 | 62

3' | 1 | 2 | 3 | 4 |

COMMUNICATION

25f Edited Copy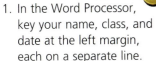
1. In the Word Processor, key your name, class, and date at the left margin, each on a separate line.
2. Key the paragraphs and make the corrections marked with proofreaders' marks. Use the BACKSPACE key to correct errors.
3. Check all number expressions and correct any mistakes.
4. Save as *xx-25f*.

Last week the healthy heart foundation relased the findings of a study that showed exercise diet and if individuals don't smoke are the major controllable factors that led to a healthy heart. Factors such as heredity can not be controlled. The study included 25 to 65 year old males as well as females. The study also showed that just taking a walk benefits our health. Those who walked an average of 2 to 3 hours a week were more then 30 percent less likely to have problems than those who did no exercise.

DECIMAL TABS

Decimal tabs can be used to align numbers containing decimals in a column as shown in column A in the table below. They can also be used to right-align numbers in a column. You have been using the Align Right button to right-align the numbers in the column. Column B below shows an example of this. Column C shows the numbers right-aligned using a decimal tab. Setting a decimal tab allows you to keep the numbers right aligned and make the numbers appear centered in the column.

If the tab for the column needs to be moved, you must first select all the numbers in the column before moving the tab. Otherwise the change will only take place in the cell the insertion point is in.

Numbers with Decimals	Use Align-Right Feature	Use Decimal Tab
2.1	56	56
10.75	100	100
325.333	2,050	2,050

To set a decimal tab in a column:

1. Click the Tab Alignment button at the left edge of the Ruler until the decimal tab ❶ displays.

2. Select the column or the cells in the column where the decimal tab will be used.

3. Click the Horizontal Ruler where you want to set the tab.

4. Tap TAB to move to the decimal tab; then key the number. If you need to move the decimal tab, first select the column before moving the tab marker on the Ruler.

DRILL 4　　SET DECIMAL TABS

1. Key **ALIGN NUMBERS USING A DECIMAL TAB** as the main heading in uppercase, bold, 14 point.

2. Create the table shown above (*Numbers with Decimals*, etc.)

3. Select cells A2–A4 and set a decimal tab at 1" on the Horizontal Ruler.

4. Select cells B2–B4 and click the Align Text Right button or press CTRL + R.

5. Select cells C2–C4 and set a decimal tab at 5". The numbers automatically align-right with the decimal tab. Tap TAB before keying each number.

6. Select cells C2–C4; move the decimal tab on the Ruler to 5.5".

7. Center the table vertically on the page.

8. Check and close. (*49-drill4*)

2 Skill Builder

Skill Building   Technique Builder

Select the Skill Building tab from the Main menu and then Technique Builder. Select the drill and follow the directions in the book.

DRILL 8

OPPOSITE HAND REACHES
Key each line once and DS between groups of lines. Key at a controlled rate; concentrate on the reaches.

i/e

1 ik is fit it sit laid site like insist still wise coil light
2 ed he ear the fed egg led elf lake jade heat feet hear where
3 lie kite item five aide either quite linear imagine brighter
4 Imagine the aide eating the pears before the grieving tiger.

w/o

5 ws we way was few went wit law with weed were week gnaw when
6 ol on go hot old lot joy odd comb open tool upon money union
7 bow owl word wood worm worse tower brown toward wrote weapon
8 The workers lowered the brown swords toward the wood weapon.

DRILL 9

PROOFREADERS' MARKS
Key each line once and DS after each sentence. Correct the sentence as edited, making all hand-written corrections. Do not key the numbers.

≡ Capitalize
／ Change letter
⊂ Close up space
ᐟ Delete
∧ Insert
ℓ𝑐 Lowercase
Space
∩ Transpose

1. When a writer create the preliminary version of a document, they are concentrating on conveying the intended ideas.
2. This ver sion of a preliminary document is called a rough.
3. After the draft is created, the Writer edits refines the copy.
4. Sometimes proofreader's marks are used to edit the draft.
5. The changes will them be make to the original. editing
6. After the changes have been made, then the Writer reads the copy.
7. Edit ing and proofreading requires alot of time and effort.
8. An attitude of excellance is required to produce error free message.

DRILL 10

PROOFREADING
Compare your sentences in Drill 9 with Drill 10. How did you do? Now key the paragraph for fluency. Concentrate on keying as accurately as possible.

When a writer creates the preliminary version of a document, he or she is concentrating on conveying ideas. This preliminary version is called a rough draft. After the draft is created, the writer edits or refines the copy. Proofreaders' marks are used to edit the rough draft. The editing changes will be made to the original. Then the writer reads the copy again. Editing requires a lot of time and effort. An attitude of excellence is required to produce an error-free message.

REMOVE TABLE BORDERS

 The Table feature allows text and data to be easily aligned in columns and rows. There may be times when you need to use the Table feature, but may not want the "boxed in" look that tables create. You can remove some or all of the borders to give a table a more "open" look.

To remove table borders:

TABLE TOOLS/DESIGN/TABLE STYLES/NO BORDER

1. Click the table move handle to select the entire table.
2. Click the Borders drop list arrow in the Table Tools Design tab.
3. Click No Border to remove the table gridlines.

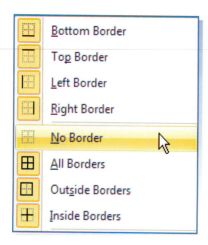

DRILL 3 **REMOVE TABLE BORDERS** ESTIMATES

1. In the header, replace the word *Estimates* with your name.
2. Replace the words *Prerecorded Document* with **49-drill3a**.
3. Under Header & Footer Tools, on the Design tab, in the Close group, click Close Header & Footer.
4. Click the Table Move handle to select the entire table.
5. Remove all borders in the table. Center the table vertically on the page and print. (*49-drill3a*)
6. Change the drill number in the header to *49-drill3b*. Click the Table Move handle to select the entire table. From the Borders drop-list menu, choose Inside Borders.
7. Check and close. (*49-drill3b*)

ASSESS SKILL GROWTH:

1. Select the Timed Writing tab from the Main menu.

Timed Writings

2. Select the writing number such as Writing 8.
3. Select 3' as the length of the writing.
4. Repeat the timing if desired.

WORD PROCESSOR OPTION:

1. Key 1' writings on each paragraph of a timing. Note that paragraphs within a timing increase by two words.
   Goal: to complete each paragraph.
2. Key a 3' timing on the entire writing.

E

all letters

Writing 8

	1'	3'
Any of us whose target is to achieve success in our professional	13	4
lives will understand that we must learn how to work in harmony	26	8
with others whose paths may cross ours daily.	35	12
We will, unquestionably, work for, with, and beside people, just	13	16
as they will work for, with, and beside us. We will judge them,	26	20
as most certainly they are going to be judging us.	38	24
A lot of people realize the need for solid working relations and	13	28
have a rule that treats others as they, themselves, expect to be	26	33
treated. This seems to be a sound, practical idea for them.	40	37

Writing 9

	1'	3'
I spoke with one company visitor recently; and she was very much	13	4
impressed, she said, with the large amount of work she had noted	26	9
being finished by one of our front office workers.	36	12
I told her how we had just last week recognized this very person	13	16
for what he had done, for output, naturally, but also because of	26	21
its excellence. We know this person has that "magic touch."	38	25
This "magic touch" is the ability to do a fair amount of work in	13	29
a fair amount of time. It involves a desire to become ever more	26	34
efficient without losing quality--the "touch" all workers should	39	38
have.	40	38

Writing 10

	1'	3'
Isn't it great just to untangle and relax after you have keyed a	13	4
completed document? Complete, or just done? No document is	25	8
quite complete until it has left you and passed to the next step.	38	13
There are desirable things that must happen to a document before	13	17
you surrender it. It must be read carefully, first of all, for	26	22
meaning to find words that look right but aren't. Read word for	39	26
word.	40	26
Check all figures and exact data, like a date or time, with your	13	31
principal copy. Make sure format details are right. Only then,	26	35
print or remove the work and scrutinize to see how it might look	39	39
to a recipient.	42	40

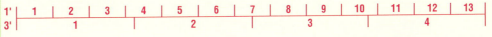

1' | 1 | 2 | 3 | 4 | 5 | 6 | 7 | 8 | 9 | 10 | 11 | 12 | 13 |

3' | 1 | 2 | 3 | 4 |

CHANGE ROW HEIGHT AND CENTER TEXT VERTICALLY IN CELL

The height of a row can be increased to draw more attention to a specific row. In Lesson 48, you learned to merge cells in the first row and place the main heading in the row. Greater emphasis can be placed on that row by increasing the row height. You can also increase the row height for an entire table. This will make the table more attractive and easier to read.

The default settings align text at the top of the cell. After increasing row height, you will want to center the text vertically in the cells to enhance the appearance of your table.

To change row height and center text vertically in cell:
TABLE TOOLS/LAYOUT/CELL SIZE/TABLE ROW HEIGHT

1. Click the insertion point in the cell in which the height will be altered.
2. Under Table Tools, click the Layout tab.
3. Increase or decrease the cell height by clicking the spin arrows in the Table Row Height box ❶.
4. Click the appropriate Center alignment button in the Alignment group ❷ to center the text vertically in the cell or row.

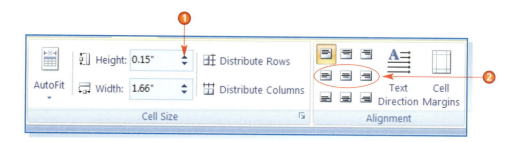

Note: You can also increase row height by dragging the top or bottom border of the row away from the text.

 **KEYBOARDING PRO DELUXE** ▶ See References/Word commands/Lesson 49

| DRILL 2 | CHANGE ROW HEIGHT | ESTIMATES |

1. Double-click the word *Estimates* in the page header. Replace *Estimates* with your name.
2. Replace the words *Prerecorded Document* with **49-drill2**.
3. Under Header & Footer Tools, on the Design tab, in the Close group, click Close Header & Footer.
4. Insert a row above row 1. Merge the cells in the new row 1.

5. Cut the main heading and paste it in the new row 1. Apply Heading 1 style; change spacing before and after paragraph to 0.
6. Change the height of row 1 to .4".
7. Click the Align Center button to center the text vertically in the row. Center the table vertically on the page.
8. Check and close. (*49-drill2*)

Writing 11

Anyone who expects some day to find an excellent job should   4 | 34
begin now to learn the value of accuracy. To be worth anything,   8 | 38
completed work must be correct, without question. Naturally, we   13 | 43
realize that the human aspect of the work equation always raises   17 | 47
the prospect of errors; but we should understand that those same   20 | 51
errors can be found and fixed. Every completed job should carry   26 | 56
at least one stamp; the stamp of pride in work that is exemplary.   30 | 60

Writing 12

No question about it: Many personal problems we face today   4 | 34
arise from the fact that we earthlings have never been very wise   8 | 38
consumers. We haven't consumed our natural resources well; as a   13 | 43
result, we have jeopardized much of our environment. We excused   17 | 47
our behavior because we thought that our stock of most resources   20 | 51
had no limit. So, finally, we are beginning to realize just how   26 | 56
indiscreet we were; and we are taking steps to rebuild our world.   30 | 60

Writing 13

When I see people in top jobs, I know I'm seeing people who   4 | 34
sell. I'm not just referring to employees who labor in a retail   8 | 38
outlet; I mean those people who put extra effort into convincing   13 | 43
others to recognize their best qualities. They, themselves, are   17 | 47
the commodity they sell; and their optimum tools are appearance,   20 | 51
language, and personality. They look great, they talk and write   26 | 56
well; and, with candid self-confidence, they meet you eye to eye.   30 | 60

3' | 1 | 2 | 3 | 4 |

LESSON 49 — Format Tables

WARMUP 49a

Key each line, striving for control. Repeat if desired.

1/2 fingers	1	The five men and women in the jury box quickly spotted Al dozing.
one hand	2	Jimmy saw him carve a great pumpkin; John deserved better awards.
figures	3	Models 150, 279, 384, and 601 were assembled in plant number 851.
balanced hand	4	The problem is Papa paid the neighbor for the gyro and the mango.

NEW FUNCTIONS

49b

SHADING

The Shading tool can be used to add color or degrees of gray shading to portions of your table. The shading tool can be found in the Paragraph group of the Home tab as well as in the Table Styles group on the Design tab under Table Tools.

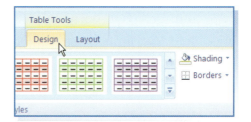

To apply shading to cell(s):

TABLE TOOLS/DESIGN/TABLE STYLES/SHADING

1. Select the cell or cells to be shaded.
2. Under Table Tools, on the Design tab, click the Shading drop-list arrow. You can also access the Shading drop-list arrow from the Paragraph group in the Home tab. The Theme Colors pallet displays.
3. Move the mouse pointer over the colors to see the name of each.
4. Click the color desired.

DRILL 1   SHADING

 ESTIMATES

1. In the open document, double-click the word *Estimates* in the page header. Replace *Estimates* with your name.
2. Replace the words *Prerecorded Document* with **49-drill1**.
3. Under Header & Footer Tools, on the Design tab, in the Close group, click Close Header & Footer.
4. Format the table and center it vertically on the page. Apply White, Background 1, Darker 25% to row 1.
5. Check and close. (*49-drill1*)

Writing 14

What do you expect when you travel to a foreign country? Quite a few people realize that one of the real joys of traveling is to get a brief glimpse of how others think, work, and live.

The best way to enjoy a different culture is to learn as much about it as you can before you leave home. Then you can concentrate on being a good guest rather than trying to find local people who can meet your needs.

Writing 15

What do you enjoy doing in your free time? Health experts tell us that far too many people choose to be lazy rather than to be active. The result of that decision shows up in our weight.

Working to control what we weigh is not easy, and seldom can it be done quickly. However, it is quite important if our weight exceeds what it should be. Part of the problem results from the amount and type of food we eat.

If we want to look fit, we should include exercise as a substantial part of our weight loss plan. Walking at least thirty minutes each day at a very fast rate can make a big difference both in our appearance and in the way we feel.

Writing 16

Doing what we like to do is quite important; however, liking what we have to do is equally important. As you ponder both of these concepts, you may feel that they are the same, but they are not the same.

If we could do only those things that we prefer to do, the chances are that we would do them exceptionally well. Generally, we will take more pride in doing those things we like doing, and we will not quit until we get them done right.

We realize, though, that we cannot restrict the things that we must do just to those that we want to do. Therefore, we need to build an interest in and an appreciation of all the tasks that we must do in our positions.

| 1' | 1 | 2 | 3 | 4 | 5 | 6 | 7 | 8 | 9 | 10 | 11 | 12 |
| 3' | | 1 | | 2 | | | 3 | | | 4 | | |

1. Create a six-column, ten-row table. Merge the cells in rows 1 and 2 as needed.
2. Key the main heading in 14-point font, bold, uppercase.
3. Center the table vertically. Check and close. (*48-d4*)

CANADA GEOGRAPHICAL INFORMATION					
Key Islands		Key Mountains		Key Lakes	
Island	**Sq. Miles**	**Mountain**	**Height**	**Lake**	**Sq. Miles**
Baffin	195,928	Logan	19,524	Superior	31,700
Victoria	83,897	St. Elias	18,008	Huron	23,000
Ellesmere	75,767	Lucania	17,147	Great Bear	12,095
Newfoundland	42,031	Fairweather	15,300	Great Slave	11,030
Banks	27,038	Waddington	13,104	Erie	9,910
Devon	21,331	Robson	12,972	Winnipeg	9,416
Melville	16,274	Columbia	12,294	Ontario	7,540

WORKPLACE SUCCESS

Staying Fit on the Job

© IMAGE100/JUPITERIMAGES

People often say that they do not exercise because they are stuck at the office most of the day and do not have time. Daily exercise is important; even a little exercise is better than no exercise at all. Exercise and movement is not only good for the heart, but also good for your bones and joints.

Here are some suggestions on how you can incorporate exercise into your workday:

- Park farther away—whether you take the bus, train, or car for your morning commute—than you need to. Steps add up and pounds go down.

- Use the stairs instead of the elevator. If the stairs are too much for you, then try a combination of stairs and elevator.

- Get up and walk to deliver a message or document rather than make a phone call or send an e-mail down the hall.

- Take a break each hour to stand, stretch, and walk around.

Writing 17

Many people like to say just how lucky a person is when   11 | 4 | 29
he or she succeeds in doing something well. Does luck play a   24 | 8 | 33
large role in success? In some cases, it might have a small   36 | 12 | 37
effect.   37 | 13 | 38

Being in the right place at the right time may help, but   11 | 16 | 41
hard work may help far more than luck. Those who just wait for   24 | 20 | 46
luck should not expect quick results and should realize luck   36 | 24 | 50
may never come.   39 | 26 | 51

1' | 1 | 2 | 3 | 4 | 5 | 6 | 7 | 8 | 9 | 10 | 11 | 12 |
3' | 1 | 2 | 3 | 4 |

Writing 18

New golfers must learn to zero in on just a few social   11 | 4 | 39
rules. Do not talk, stand close, or move around when another   23 | 8 | 44
person is hitting. Be ready to play when it is your turn.   35 | 12 | 47

Take practice swings in an area away from other people.   11 | 15 | 51
Let the group behind you play through if your group is slow.   24 | 20 | 55
Do not rest on your club on the green when waiting your turn.   36 | 23 | 59

Set your other clubs down off the green. Leave the green   12 | 27 | 63
quickly when done; update your card on the next tee. Be sure   24 | 31 | 67
to leave the course in good condition. Always have a good time.   37 | 36 | 72

1' | 1 | 2 | 3 | 4 | 5 | 6 | 7 | 8 | 9 | 10 | 11 | 12 |
3' | 1 | 2 | 3 | 4 |

Writing 19

Do you know how to use time wisely? If you do, then its   11 | 4 | 51
proper use can help you organize and run a business better.   24 | 8 | 55
If you find that your daily problems tend to keep you from   35 | 12 | 59
planning properly, then perhaps you are not using time well.   48 | 16 | 63
You may find that you spend too much time on tasks that are   60 | 20 | 67
not important. Plan your work to save valuable time.   70 | 24 | 70

A firm that does not plan is liable to run into trouble.   12 | 27 | 74
A small firm may have trouble planning. It is important   23 | 31 | 78
to know just where the firm is headed. A firm may have a   35 | 35 | 82
fear of learning things it would rather not know. To say   46 | 39 | 86
that planning is easy would be absurd. It requires lots of   58 | 43 | 90
thinking and planning to meet the expected needs of the firm.   70 | 47 | 94

1' | 1 | 2 | 3 | 4 | 5 | 6 | 7 | 8 | 9 | 10 | 11 | 12 |
3' | 1 | 2 | 3 | 4 |

48-d1

Create Table

1. Key the table below; right-align column C. Center vertically on the page.
2. Check and close. (*48-d1*)

SAFETY AWARDS

Award Winners	Department	Amount
Lorianna Mendez	Accounting	2,000
William Mohammed	Marketing	800
Cynthia Khek	Engineering	1,500
Charles Pham	Purchasing	1,000

48-d2

Insert Column

1. Open *48-d1* if it is not already displayed on the screen.
2. Click the insertion point in cell B1 and insert a column to the right.
3. Insert the following text left-aligned in the column and print.

   Division
   Commercial
   Space Shuttle
   Military
   Commercial

4. Check and close. (*48-d2a*)
5. Open *48-d2a* and insert a blank row above row 1. Merge the cells in the new row 1.
6. Cut the title *SAFETY AWARDS* and paste it in row 1. Keep the font size 14 point.
7. Check and close. (*48-d2b*)

48-d3

Insert Row

1. Open *48-d2b*, insert a row after Lorianna Mendez, and add the following information:
   Robert Ruiz, Research, Military, 2,250
2. Insert a row at the end of the table; add the following information:
   Franklin Cousins, Security, Space Shuttle, 500
3. Delete the row for William Mohammed. Check and close. (*48-d3*)

Writing 20

	3'	5'

If asked, most people will agree that some people have far more creative skills than others, and they will also say that these skills are in great demand by most organizations. A follow-up question is in order. Are you born with creative skills or can you develop them? No easy answer to that question exists, but it is worth spending a bit of time pondering.

	3'	5'
(line 1)	4	2 21
(line 2)	8	5 34
(line 3)	12	7 37
(line 4)	17	10 39
(line 5)	21	13 42
(line 6)	24	15 44

If creative skills can be developed, then the next issue is how can you develop these skills. One way is to approach each task with a determination to solve the problem and a refusal to accept failure. If the normal way of doing a job does not work, just keep trying things never tried before until you reach a good solution. This is called thinking outside the box.

	3'	5'
	28	17 46
	32	19 49
	37	22 51
	41	25 54
	45	27 56
	49	29 58

3' | 1 | 2 | 3 | 4 |
5' | 1 | 2 | 3 |

Writing 21

	1'	3'

Figures are not as easy to key as many of the words we use. Balanced-hand figures such as 16, 27, 38, 49, and 50, although fairly easy, are slower to key because each one requires longer reaches and uses more time per stroke.

	1'	3'
	12	4 36
	25	8 40
	37	12 44
	45	16 46

Figures such as 12, 45, 67, and 90 are even more difficult because they are next to one another and each uses just a single hand to key. Because of their size, bigger numbers such as 178, 349, and 1,220 create extra speed losses.

	1'	3'
	12	20 50
	25	25 54
	39	29 59
	45	32 61

1' | 1 | 2 | 3 | 4 | 5 | 6 | 7 | 8 | 9 | 10 | 11 | 12 | 13 |
3' | 1 | 2 | 3 | 4 |

Writing 22

SKILL TRANSFER
1. Set the timer for 2'. Take a 2' writing on paragraph 1.
2. Set the timer for 2'. Take a 2' writing on paragraph 2.
3. Take 2 or more 2' writings on the slower paragraph.

	1'	2'

Few people attain financial success without some kind of planning. People who realize the value of prudent spending and saving are those who set up a budget. A budget helps individuals determine just how much they can spend and how much they can save so that they will not squander their money recklessly.

	1'	2'
	11	6
	24	12
	36	18
	49	24
	61	31

Keeping records is a *vital* ~~crucial~~ part of *a* budget. *A detailed* ~~Complete~~ records *of all* income and expenses over a period of *several* ~~a number of~~ months *will* ~~can~~ help *to* determine what bills, *like utilities* ~~as water~~ or rent, are *fixed* ~~static~~ and which are flexible. To get the most out of your income, *focus* ~~pay~~ attention *on* ~~to~~ the items that you can *be changed* ~~modify~~.

	1'	2'
	12	6
	24	12
	37	18
	49	25
	61	30

1' | 1 | 2 | 3 | 4 | 5 | 6 | 7 | 8 | 9 | 10 | 11 | 12 |
2' | 1 | 2 | 3 | 4 | 5 | 6 |

MERGE AND SPLIT CELLS

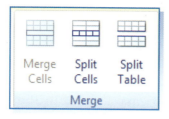

Merging is the process of combining two or more table cells located in the same row or column into a single cell. Cells can be joined horizontally or vertically. For example, you can merge several cells horizontally to create a table heading that spans several columns. A cell or several selected cells can be divided into multiple cells and columns by using the Split Cells feature.

To merge cells:

TABLE TOOLS/LAYOUT/MERGE/MERGE CELLS

1. Select the cells that are to be merged.

2. Under Table Tools, click the Layout tab. Then click Merge Cells in the Merge group.

To split cells:

TABLE TOOLS/LAYOUT/MERGE/SPLIT CELLS

1. Click in the cell that is to be divided into multiple cells. If multiple cells are to be split, select the cells.

2. Under Table Tools, click the Layout tab. Then click Split Cells in the Merge group.

3. Enter the number of columns or rows that the selected cells are to be split into.

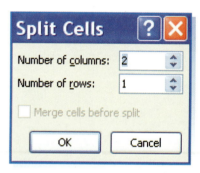

DRILL 2 **INSERT COLUMNS AND ROWS**

1. Create a two-column, five-row table.

2. Merge the cells in row 1. Key the main heading shown on the next page in 14-point font, uppercase; center and bold it.

3. Center **Course Name** in cell B1. Center **Enrollment Figures** in cell B2. Bold row 2.

4. Select cells B3–B5; split these cells into two columns and three rows.

5. Center and bold **Undergraduates** in cell B3. Center and bold **Graduates** in cell B4.

6. Select cells A2 and A3; merge the cells. In the Alignment group, click the Align Center button to center *Course Name*.

7. Key the table. Adjust column width.

8. Center the table vertically and horizontally on the page.

9. Check and close. (*48-drill2*)

FINAL SEAT COUNT		
Course Name	Enrollment Figures	
	Undergraduates	Graduates
English Reading and Composition	12,875	97
Medical Microbiology	782	1,052

1

Internet Activities

Activity 1
Open Internet Explorer

KNOW YOUR BROWSER

The Internet is a global collection of computers linked together to share information. The World Wide Web is a part of the Internet that consists of website located on different computers around the world. A Web browser, such as Internet Explorer, is a program that allows you to "browse the Web." The browser enables you to find, load, view, and print Web pages.

TO LAUNCH INTERNET EXPLORER:

1. Click the Start button on the taskbar to display the Start menu.
2. Point to All Programs, and then click Internet Explorer in the submenu.
3. The Internet Explorer menu bar displays.
   a. The Standard Buttons toolbar contains buttons for frequently used commands. If the toolbar is not visible on your screen, click View, Toolbars, Standard Buttons.
   b. The Address Bar displays the address of the current page. If the Address Bar is not visible on your screen, click View, Toolbars, Address Bar.

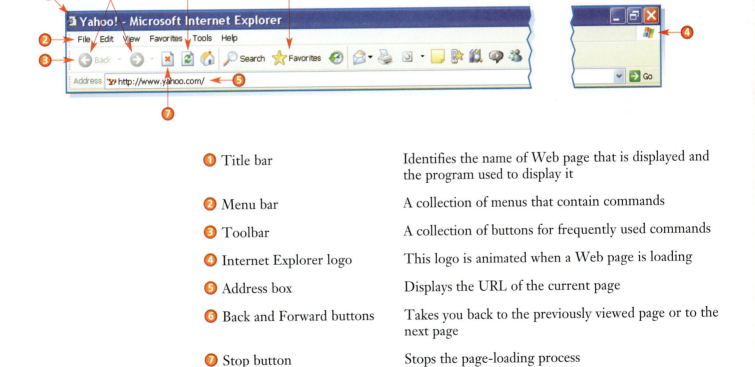

❶ Title bar	Identifies the name of Web page that is displayed and the program used to display it
❷ Menu bar	A collection of menus that contain commands
❸ Toolbar	A collection of buttons for frequently used commands
❹ Internet Explorer logo	This logo is animated when a Web page is loading
❺ Address box	Displays the URL of the current page
❻ Back and Forward buttons	Takes you back to the previously viewed page or to the next page
❼ Stop button	Stops the page-loading process
❽ Refresh button	Reloads the current page
❾ Favorites button	Contains a list of bookmarked pages

INSERT AND DELETE COLUMNS AND ROWS

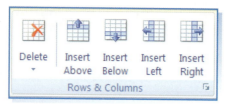

Columns can be added to the left or right of existing columns. Rows can be added above or below existing rows. A row can also be added at the end of the table by clicking the insertion point in the last cell and tapping TAB.

To insert rows or columns in a table:
TABLE TOOLS/LAYOUT/ROWS & COLUMNS

1. Click the insertion point where the new row or column is to be inserted. If several rows or columns are to be inserted, select the number you want to insert.
2. Under Table Tools, click the Layout tab.
3. From the Rows & Columns group, click Insert Above, Insert Below, Insert Left, or Insert Right as appropriate.

To delete rows or columns in a table:
TABLE TOOLS/LAYOUT/ROWS & COLUMNS

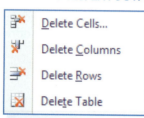

1. Click the insertion point in the row or column to be deleted. If more than one row or column is to be deleted, select them first.
2. In the Rows & Columns group, click the Delete button. Select the appropriate item to be deleted in the drop down menu that displays.

KEYBOARDING PRO DELUXE See References/Word commands/Lesson 48

DRILL 1   INSERT COLUMNS AND ROWS   ESTIMATES

1. In the open document, insert the following rows so that the items are in correct alphabetical order. The total should be the last row in bold.

Appliances (allowance)	12,000	12,000
Sinks and fixtures	3,500	3,225
Total	$59,575	$65,650

2. Center the table vertically on the page. Preview and check the document. (48-drill1a)

3. Delete the "Sinks and fixtures" row. Recalculate the total in columns B and C.

4. Insert a column between columns B and C. Key the data below in the new column.

Designs by Pat
$12,000
22,100
7,950
1,600
$43,650

5. Check and close. (48-drill1b)

DRILL 1

LAUNCH INTERNET EXPLORER

1. Launch Internet Explorer.
2. Locate the address box at the top of the screen. The address that currently displays in the box is your current home page; that is the page your browser goes to when you first open it.
3. Click your mouse in the address box to highlight the address. With the address highlighted, key the following address http://www.whitehouse.gov.
4. Tap ENTER. Notice the movement of the logo as the site is being located. If it takes a long time for the pages to load, you can click the Stop button to cancel the loading.

WEB ADDRESS

Each Web page has a unique address, which is commonly called the URL or Uniform Resource Locator. The URL is composed of one or more domains separated by periods. In the address, http://www.whitehouse.gov, the protocol is *http://*; the location of the website is *www.* (World Wide Web); the name of the website is *Whitehouse*; and the domain is *.gov* (U.S. government). Other domains include educational institution (.edu), commercial organizations (.com), military sites (.mil), and other organizations (.org).

DRILL 2

VISIT WEBSITES
1. Go to each of these websites.
2. Write the name of the Web page as it appears in the title bar.

1. http://www.house.gov _____
2. http://www.fbla.org _____
3. http://www.army.mil _____
4. http://www.news.com _____

DRILL 3

USE TOOLBAR BUTTONS

1. Open the following websites:

   http://www.cnn.com

   http://senate.gov

   http://nike.com

2. Click the Back button twice. The _____ website displays.
3. Click the Forward button once. The _____ website displays.
4. Print the active Web page.

LESSON 48 Change Table Structure

WARMUP 48a

Key each line, striving for control. Repeat if desired.

alphabet	1	Jacqueline quickly moved up front and seized the big pile of wax.
1st/2nd fingers	2	I went to the baseball game to see Ginger hit the first home run.
3rd row	3	I should go to the store with Paul to get eggs for the apple pie.
balanced hand	4	Did the neighbor and his visitor roam down to the town for clams?

SKILL BUILDING

48b Textbook Keying
1. Key the drill, concentrating on good keying techniques.
2. Repeat the drill if time permits.

direct reaches	5	June and my brother, Bradly, received advice from junior umpires.
	6	My bright brother received minimum reward for serving many years.
adjacent reaches	7	Clio and Trey were sad that very few voters were there last week.
	8	Western attire was very popular at the massive auction last week.
double letters	9	Tommie Bennett will go to a meeting in Dallas tomorrow afternoon.
	10	Lee will meet Joanne at the swimming pool after accounting class.

NEW FUNCTIONS

48c

CHANGE TABLE STRUCTURE

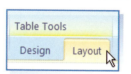

Word makes it easy to alter the structure of an existing table. Columns, rows, and cells can easily be inserted or deleted in a table. Cells can be joined or merged horizontally or vertically to make the table more attractive and easier to read.

Changes to a table structure are made in the Layout ribbon under Table Tools.

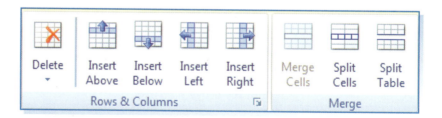

BOOKMARK A FAVORITE WEBSITE

Web pages that you display often can be added to a Favorites list. This will allow you to open the Favorites list and click the link to display the page you want; it saves you from having to key the Web address each time.

TO ADD WEB PAGE TO THE FAVORITES LIST:

1. Display the Web page on the screen.
2. Click Favorites on the Internet Explorer menu bar.
3. Select Add to Favorites from the drop-down menu. The Add Favorite dialog box displays.
4. The name of the Web page displays in the Name box. Click OK.

TO OPEN ONE OF YOUR FAVORITE PAGES:

1. Launch Internet Explorer.
2. Click the Favorites menu (or click the Favorites button to display the Favorites menu).
3. Select the page you want to open. As your list of favorite pages grows longer, you can organize it by moving pages into subfolders.

DRILL 4

VISIT WEBSITES

1. Open these websites and add them to your Favorites list.
   a. http://www.weather.com
   b. http://www.cnn.com
2. Use the Favorites list to go to the following websites to find answers to the questions below:
   a. The Weather Channel—What is today's temperature in your city? _____
   b. CNN—What is today's top news story? _____

Activity 2
Set Up E-mail Addresses

ELECTRONIC MAIL

Electronic mail or **e-mail** refers to electronic messages sent by one computer user to another. To be able to send or receive e-mail, you must have an e-mail address, an e-mail program, and access to the Internet or an intranet (in-house network).

Many search engines such as Yahoo, Google, Excite, Lycos, and others provide free e-mail via their websites. These e-mail programs allow users to set up an e-mail address and then send and retrieve e-mail messages. To set up an account and obtain an e-mail address, the user must (1) consent to the terms to the agreement, (2) complete an online registration form, and (3) compose an e-mail name and password.

DRILL 1

SET UP E-MAIL

1. Click the Search button on the browser's toolbar.
2. Click a search engine that offers free e-mail.
3. Follow the directions to set up an e-mail account.

General Guidelines	Example
Use words for numbers that precede o'clock.	Mail pickup is at 11 and 2 o'clock. I need to be home by 6 o'clock.
Use figures for times with a.m. or p.m. and days when they follow the month.	The store closes at nine p.m. Tarian was born on February 23, 2007. Classes begin on August 23, 2008.
Use ordinals for the day when it precedes the month.	The next Board of Directors meeting will be held on the tenth of August. Taxes are due on the fifteenth of April.

47-d3

Text Table

1. Create a two-column, ten-row table. Key the table using wordwrap.
2. Drag the left border of the table to make column A narrower.
3. Apply the Colorful List - Accent 5 style. Center the table horizontally.
4. Bold column heads and change the main heading to 14-point font.
5. Center the table on the page.
6. Check and close. (*47-d3*)

MACKINNON'S CLASSES OF EXPERT SYSTEMS

Class	Area of Classification
Configuration	Assemble proper components of a modern expert computer system in the proper way.
Diagnosis	Expert system infers underlying problems based on observed evidence.
Instruction	Intelligent teaching so that an inquirer can ask *why*, *how*, and *what if* questions just as if a human were teaching.
Interpretation	Expert system explains observed data.
Monitoring	Ability to compare observed data to expected data to judge performance.
Planning	Devise actions to produce a desired outcome.
Prognosis	Ability to predict the outcome of any given situation.
Remedy	Prescribe treatment for a given problem.
Control	Regulate a process. May require interpretation, diagnosis, monitoring, planning, prognosis, and remedies.

Send E-mail Message

To send an e-mail message, you must have the address of the computer user you want to write. Business cards, letterheads, directories, etc., now include e-mail addresses. Often a telephone call is helpful in obtaining e-mail addresses. An e-mail address includes the user's login name followed by @ and the domain (sthomas@yahoo.com).

Creating an e-mail message is quite similar to preparing a memo. The e-mail header includes TO, FROM, and SUBJECT. Key the e-mail address of the recipient on the TO line, and compose a subject line that concisely describes the theme of your message. Your e-mail address will automatically display on the FROM line.

DRILL 2

1. Open the search engine used to set up your e-mail account. Click E-mail or Mail. (Terms will vary.)

2. Key your e-mail name and password when prompted.

E-mail Message 1

3. Key the e-mail address of your instructor or another student. Compose a brief message describing the weather in your city (from Activity 1, Drill 4). Include a descriptive subject line. Send the message.

E-mail Message 2

4. Key your e-mail address. The subject is **Journal Entry for March 29, 20--**. Compose a message to show your reflections on how keyboarding is useful to you. Share your progress in the course and your plan for improving this week. Send the message.

Respond to Messages

Replying to e-mail messages

Reading one's e-mail messages and responding promptly are important rules of netiquette (etiquette for the Internet). However, avoid responding too quickly to sensitive situations.

Forwarding e-mail messages

Received e-mail messages are often shared or forwarded to other e-mail users. Be sure to seek permission from the sender of the message before forwarding it to others.

DRILL 3

1. Open your e-mail account if it is not open.

2. Read your e-mail messages and respond immediately and appropriately to any e-mail messages received from your instructor or fellow students. Click Reply to answer the message.

3. Forward the e-mail message titled *Journal Entry for March 29, 20--* to your instructor.

4. Delete all read messages.

Attach a Document to an E-mail Message

Electronic files can be attached to an e-mail message and sent to another computer electronically. Recipients of attached documents can transfer these documents to their computers and then open them for use.

DRILL 4

1. Open your e-mail account if it is not open.

2. Create an e-mail message to your instructor that states your homework is attached. The subject line should include the specific homework assignment (**xx-profile**, for example).

3. Attach the file by clicking Attach (or the appropriate button; email programs may vary). Use the browser to locate the homework assignment.

4. Send the e-mail message with the attached file.

TABLE FORMAT GUIDES

1. Position the table (or main heading) at about 2", or center the table vertically on the page.

2. Headings: Main heading: center, bold, uppercase, 14-point font; and then tap ENTER. Secondary heading: center, bold, 12-point font; capitalize each word. Center and bold all column headings. If styles are applied to main and secondary headings, adjust spacing as needed.

3. Adjust column width attractively, and center the table horizontally.

4. Align text within the cells at the left. Align numbers at the right. Align decimal number of varying lengths at the decimal point.

5. When a table is within a document, the same amount of blank space should display before and after the table as between paragraphs.

APPLICATIONS

47-d1
Create Table and Apply Style

1. Key the table below. Format the main heading appropriately. Adjust column width and center column heads.

2. Right-align column C. Apply Medium Grid 1 - Accent 6 table style.

3. Center the table vertically and horizontally on the page.

4. Check and close. (*47-d1*)

MAJOR METROPOLITAN AREAS OF CANADA

City	Province	Population
Toronto	Ontario	5,427,250
Montreal	Quebec	3,921,375
Vancouver	British Columbia	2,285,750
Ottawa	Ontario	1,893,987
Winnipeg	Manitoba	685,957
Quebec	Quebec	1,097,982
Hamilton	Ontario	757,250

47-d2
Applying Communication Knowledge

1. Key **NUMBER EXPRESSION** as the main heading. Key **Times and Dates** as the secondary heading. Format the headings appropriately.

2. Key the table on the next page. Do not adjust column width.

3. Column A contains guidelines for using figures and words when keying dates and times. Key the examples in column B to comply with the guidelines.

4. Apply Medium Shading 1 - Accent 2 table style. The table style will bold the text in column A.

5. Apply italics to column B. Bold column heads. Center the table on the page horizontally and vertically.

6. Check and close. (*47-d2*)

Level 2

FORMATTING ESSENTIALS

LEARNING OUTCOMES

Keyboarding
- To key fluently using good keying techniques.
- To key about 40 words per minute with good accuracy.

Document Design Skills
- To format memos, e-mails, letters, reports, and tables appropriately.
- To apply basic design skills to newsletters and announcements.
- To enhance documents with basic graphics.

Word Processing Skills
- To learn the essential word processing commands.
- To create, edit, and format documents effectively.

Communication Skills
- To review and improve basic communication skills.
- To compose e-mails, memos, and other documents.
- To proofread effectively, apply proofreaders' marks, and revise text.

1. Open *46-drill2*.
2. Display the widths of the columns by pointing to the ruler, holding down the ALT key, and clicking the left mouse button.

3. Use the mouse to adjust column width. Leave approximately 0.5" to .75" between the longest line and the border in each column.
4. Center the table horizontally on the page. Check and close. (*47-drill1*)

NEW FUNCTIONS

47e

TABLE STYLES

Microsoft Word has preformatted table styles that you can use to make your tables more attractive. The styles contain a combination of font attributes, color, shading, and borders to enhance the appearance of the table.

Under Table Tools, click the Design tab to access the Table Styles group ❶. As you move the mouse over each style, you will also see your table formatted in that style. A tab also displays with the name of the style. Additional styles display when you click the More button ❷.

To apply Table Styles:

TABLE TOOLS/DESIGN/TABLE STYLES

1. Display the table on the screen. Click the insertion point in the body of the table to display the Table Tools tabs.
2. Click the Design tab to display the Table Styles group.
3. Move the mouse over each table style until you find the desired style. View more styles by clicking the More arrow; then use the scroll bar to view the available styles.
4. Click the style to apply it to the table.
5. Click the Layout tab. From the Table group, select Properties and recenter the table on the page.

1. Open *47-drill1*. Click in the table.
2. Click the Design tab. Apply the Colorful List – Accent 1 style to the table.

3. Click the Layout tab; then select Properties. Recenter the table horizontally on the page.
4. Check and close. (*47-drill2*)

The Transition—*Word 2003* to *Word 2007*

The transition from *Word 2003* to *Word 2007* will be significantly different for students, instructors, and for industry than the transition from previous versions of *Word* to new versions. Three factors account for the differences:

1. The user interface that replaces toolbars and menus with a ribbon is totally new.
2. The new XML default file format (.docx) is not backward compatible with previous versions of *Word*.
3. The formatting defaults have changed significantly from *Word 2003*.

USER INTERFACE

The Ribbon consists of three basic components:

1. Tabs are listed across the top of the Ribbon (Home, Insert, Page Layout, etc.). Each tab displays a different ribbon.
2. Groups are listed at the bottom of the Ribbon (Clipboard, Font, Paragraph, etc.) and contain a variety of related commands. The groups are different on each ribbon that is displayed by a tab.
3. Commands are the related functions that are located in each group.

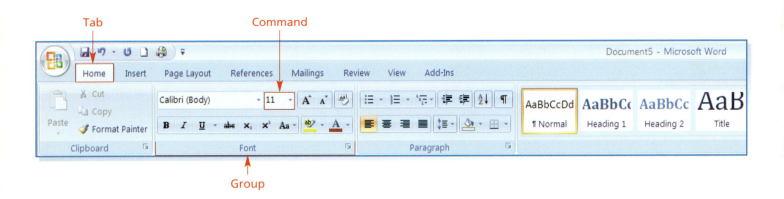

The new user interface is easier to learn. The system is intuitive, and the use of groups facilitates the learning of related commands.

DEFAULT FILE FORMAT

The default file format presents a major challenge to industry during the transition period, but it is transparent to the user and is very simple to learn. The challenge to industry is that documents stored in previous formats will have to be converted to the new XML format. It also presents a problem when one organization sends a *Word 2007* document to an organization that is using a previous version of *Word*. Unless the document is stored in a 1997–2003 compatible format, the recipient will not be able to open the *Word 2007* document. Documents stored in a compatible format cannot be edited or use new features of *Word 2007* such as Smart Art. Since you are not likely to be sending documents from the classroom to other organizations, the default file format is not an issue.

ADJUST COLUMN WIDTH

Tables extend from margin to margin when they are created, regardless of the width of the data in the columns. Some tables, however, would be more attractive and easier to read if the columns were narrower. Column widths can be changed manually using the mouse or automatically using AutoFit. Using the mouse enables you to adjust the widths as you like. Once you change the width of a table, you will need to center it horizontally.

Column width ──────────────────→

Column marker ──────────

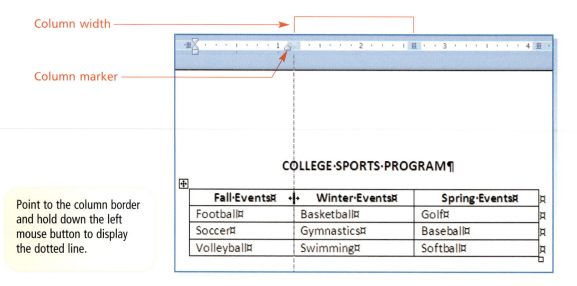

Point to the column border and hold down the left mouse button to display the dotted line.

To adjust column widths using the mouse:

1. Point to the column border that needs adjusting.

2. When the pointer changes to ↔, hold down the left mouse button and drag the border to the left to make the column narrower or to the right to make the column wider.

3. Adjust the column widths attractively. Leave approximately 0.5" to .75" between the longest line and the border. Use the Horizontal Ruler as a guide.

4. The widths of the columns can be displayed by pointing to the column marker on the ruler, holding down the ALT key, and clicking the left mouse button.

To center table horizontally on the page:

TABLE TOOLS/LAYOUT/TABLE PROPERTIES/TABLE TAB/CENTER ALIGNMENT

1. Click in a table cell.

2. Click the Layout tab.

3. From the Table group, click the Table Properties button. The Table Properties dialog box displays.

4. From the Table tab, select Center Alignment.

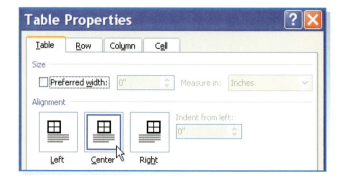

KEYBOARDING PRO DELUXE ⟩ See References/Word commands/Lesson 47

FORMATTING DEFAULTS

The defaults of *Word 2007* and *Word 2003* differ significantly.

Default	Word 2007	Word 2003
Body font and size	Calibri (sans serif) 11 point	Times New Roman (serif) 12 point
Heading font	Cambria (sans serif) varied size	Arial (sans serif) varied sizes
Title style	Cambria, 26 point, dark blue, left align	Arial, 16 point, bold, centered
Margins	1" left, right, top, and bottom	1.25" left and right; 1" top and bottom
Line spacing	1.15	1.0
Space after paragraph	10 point	0
Document theme	Office 	None

The new defaults—particularly the line spacing and the space after paragraph—produce documents that look different than traditional document formats. *Microsoft* emphasizes that the rationale for changing the defaults is to enhance both readability and the appearance of documents. The illustration on the left below shows how the date, letter address, and salutation of a letter would appear if traditional format guides were used with the *Word 2007* defaults. The illustration on the right shows how guides and defaults can be modified to produce an attractive letter format.

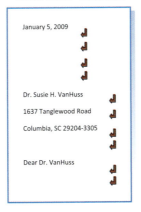

Word 2007 Defaults

Word 2007 Defaults Modified

FORMATTING DECISIONS

Decisions regarding document formats require consideration of four elements: (1) attractiveness of the format, (2) readability of the format, (3) effective use of space on the page, and (4) efficiency in producing the document. Both documents formatted with *Word 2007* defaults and *Word 2003* defaults can meet these criteria. Employed students may find that they are creating documents using *Word 2007* in one setting and *Word 2003* traditional formats in the other.

In this textbook, you will prepare *Word 2007* documents using both formats to ease the transition from the traditional format to the new one. By using *Word 2003* style—a *Word 2007* style that emulates the defaults of *Word 2003*—you will learn to use the new features and at the same time produce traditional document formats. You will also learn to produce *Word 2007* document formats so that you are prepared for offices that have already made the transition to the new defaults. Full-page model documents are illustrated in both styles. The Reference Manual also provides illustrations of *Word 2007* formats and formats from previous versions of *Word*.

LESSON 47

Enhance Table Appearance

WARMUP 47a

Key each line, striving for control. Repeat if desired.

alphabet	1	Dixie Vaughn acquired that prize job with a firm just like yours.
figures	2	By May 15 do this: Call Ext. 4390; order 472 clips and 168 pens.
easy/figures	3	The 29 girls kept 38 bushels of corn and 59 bushels of rich yams.
easy	4	The members paid half of the endowment, and their firm paid half.

| 1 | 2 | 3 | 4 | 5 | 6 | 7 | 8 | 9 | 10 | 11 | 12 | 13 |

SKILL BUILDING

47b Textbook Keying

1. Key the drill, concentrating on good keying techniques.
2. Repeat the drill if time permits.

1/2 fingers

5 Take the Paz exit; make a right turn; then the street veers left.

6 Stop by and see the amateur videos of Zoe at six o'clock tonight.

7 We made an excellent pizza with leftover bread, cheese, and beef.

Home row

8 Dallas shall ask Sal to sell fake flash fads; Sal sells all fads.

9 A small fast salad is all Kallas had; Dallas adds a dash of salt.

10 Dallas saw all flasks fall; alas Dad adds a fast fake hall flask.

Third row

11 We used thirty pails of yellow powder; Wesley threw the rest out.

12 I should go to the store with Paul to get eggs for the apple pie.

13 Did you see the request for Sy to take the test with your sister?

47c Timed Writing

1. Key a 3' timed writing, working for speed.
2. Key a 3' timed writing, working for control.

	gwam	1'	3'
Little things do contribute a lot to success in keying.	11	4	35
Take our work attitude, for example. It's a little thing; yet	24	8	40
it can make quite a lot of difference. Demonstrating patience	36	12	44
with a job or a problem, rather than pressing much too hard for a	50	17	48
desired payoff, often brings better results than we expected.	63	21	53
Other "little things," such as wrist and finger position, how we	76	25	57
sit, size and location of copy, and lights, have meaning for	88	29	61
any person who wants to key well.	95	32	63

1' | 1 | 2 | 3 | 4 | 5 | 6 | 7 | 8 | 9 | 10 | 11 | 12 | 13 |
3' | 1 | 2 | 3 | 4 |

Word Processing Essentials

LEARNING OUTCOMES

- Learn basic *Word 2007* commands.
- Create, save, and print documents.
- Apply text, paragraph, and page formats.
- Review documents and apply communication skills.
- Build keyboarding skills.

LESSON 26 — Learn Essential Functions

WARMUP 26a

Key each line, striving for control. Repeat if desired.

alphabet	1	Lorenz quietly exited just before the five, wet campers got back.
adjacent	2	I was sad that four people quit before our guys joined the choir.
direct	3	Brent must bring a great many golf umbrellas to sell to my group.
easy	4	Jane may go to visit the lake and fish with the girls. May I go?

SKILL BUILDING

26b Timed Writing
1. Key a 3' timed writing, working for speed.
2. Key a 3' timed writing, working for control.

all letters

	gwam	1'	3'
Many students find it quite difficult to juggle the things		12	4
they want to do with the things they ought to do. Too often the		25	8
things that they find the most tempting and desirable to do are just		39	13
distractions from doing things that need to be given priority.		51	17
The key is to set priorities and stick with them. Those who		12	21
organize their work and do the critical things first not only		25	25
accomplish more, they are the most likely to have sufficient time		38	30
to do the things that they enjoy doing as well.		47	33
Choosing friends wisely also helps you to stay on target.		12	37
Students who have friends with the same type of expectations as		25	41
they do usually help each other to meet their goals. They value		38	45
their time and try to use it well.		44	48

```
1' |  1  |  2  |  3  |  4  |  5  |  6  |  7  |  8  |  9  | 10  | 11  | 12  | 13  |
3' |        1        |        2        |        3        |        4        |
```

---

1. Center the main heading in uppercase and bold; tap ENTER. Key the secondary heading in bold and center it. Capitalize each word; tap ENTER.

2. Use the Insert Table dialog box to create the table shown below. Key the text in the table and center column heads.

3. Center the table vertically on the page.

4. Check and close. (*46-d4*)

OFFICIAL BIRDS AND FLOWERS
For Selected States

State	Official Bird	Official Flower
Alaska	Willow ptarmigan	Forget-me-not
Arkansas	Mockingbird	Apple blossom
California	California valley quail	Golden poppy
Connecticut	American robin	Mountain laurel
Delaware	Blue hen chicken	Peach blossom
Georgia	Brown thrasher	Cherokee rose
Idaho	Mountain bluebird	Syringe
Illinois	Cardinal	Native violet
Louisiana	Eastern brown pelican	Magnolia
Maryland	Baltimore oriole	Black-eyed Susan
Massachusetts	Chickadee	Mayflower
Nebraska	Western meadowlark	Goldenrod
New Jersey	Eastern goldfinch	Purple violet
New Mexico	Roadrunner	Yucca
North Carolina	Cardinal	Dogwood

WORD SCREEN

You are about to learn the leading word processing package available today. At the same time, you will continue to develop your keyboarding skills. You will use *Word*, an application of the *2007 Microsoft Office System*©, to create and format professional-looking documents. Most, if not all of you, will have completed the skill building activities on the previous page using *Keyboarding Pro DELUXE*.

Keyboarding Pro DELUXE users: If you are using *Keyboarding Pro DELUXE*, it will launch or open *Microsoft Word* automatically when you choose the first activity to be done in *Word*. See instructions on pages ix–xii.

Non-*Keyboarding Pro DELUXE* users: Start *Word* now.

1. Click the Start button at the bottom left corner of your screen and select *Word* from the programs listed.

2. You may also have an icon on your screen that you can double-click to launch *Word*.

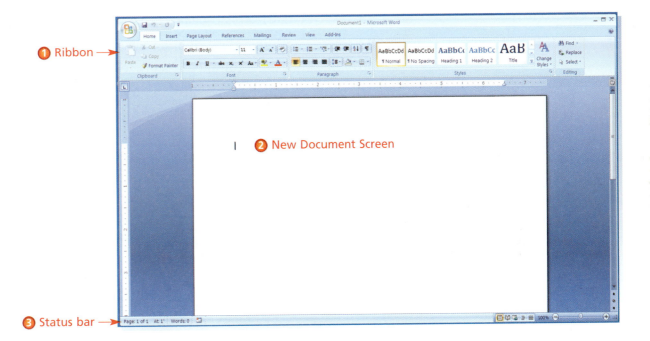

When you first use *Word*, you will note three distinct segments of the screen:

❶ The Ribbon containing the commands that you will use is located at the top of the screen.

❷ The New Document screen on which you will key your documents appears in the center of the screen.

❸ The status bar, which gives information about the position in the document and enables you to view the document in different formats, is located at the bottom of the screen.

Study the entire screen on your computer for a few minutes; then you will work with the various segments.

46-d2

Table with Formatting

1. Key the main heading using uppercase, center alignment, and bold; tap ENTER. Key the secondary heading using bold. Capitalize each word; tap ENTER. Change the alignment to left and turn bold off.
2. Create the table and key the information in the cells.
3. Select row 1. Bold and center-align the column headings. Center-align cells A2–A6. Right-align cells C2–C6.
4. Center the table vertically on the page.
5. Check and close. (*46-d2*)

PERSONAL COMPUTER ACCESSORIES

Inventory as of December 31, 20--

Stock Number	Description	Units Available
JGC2144	4mm Transporter	5,745,000
JGC9516	DLT/TK 20-pack Transporter	19,034,100
TMA3252	Mobile Base Storage System	3,972,155
CDS4971	Casa Multimedia Storage	9,734,250
LGT8920	Optical Keyboard and Mouse	10,457

46-d3

Table with Proofreaders' Marks

1. Create a three-column, four-row table. Key the text in the table.
2. Place the cursor in cell C4; tap the TAB key to create another blank row. Key the last row.
3. Center table vertically on the page. Check and close. (*46-d3*)

POMMERY SPRINGS PROJECT STATUS   *Center and Bold*

Job	Description	Date Completed
Road work	Building and grading	February 10, 20--
Drain	Adding french drain	February 25, 20--
Lot prep~aration~	Clearing and leveling	March 12, 20--
Pond	Adding silt fence	March 15, 20-- *add row*

KEY AND FORMAT TEXT AND PARAGRAPHS

In earlier lessons, you learned to key text using wordwrap. In this lesson and the next one, you will learn to format text and paragraphs.

- To begin a new paragraph, tap ENTER.
- To indent the first line of a paragraph to the first default tab, tap the TAB key.

 Insertion Point | To edit or format text, you must move the insertion point around with the mouse or use the arrow keys on the keyboard.

- To use the mouse, move the I-beam pointer to the desired position and click the left mouse button.

RIBBON BASICS

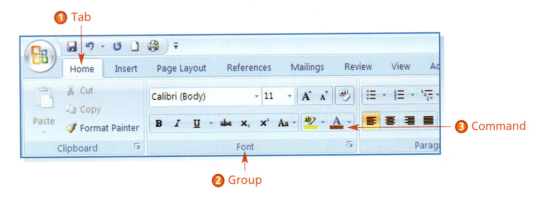

❶ Tab

❸ Command

❷ Group

You key text using the keyboard. You format text using the commands contained on the **Ribbon**. The Ribbon has three basic components:

❶ **Tabs**—located at the top of the Ribbon. Home, the first tab, has been selected.

Note that when you click a different tab, the options below the tab row change. Try clicking the Insert tab and the Page Layout tab. Note the types of activites that are included below each of these tabs. Click the Home tab again.

❷ **Groups**—contain a number of related items. The names are positioned at the bottom of the Ribbon below each group. The group shown above is the *Font* group.

On the Home tab, the groups are Clipboard, Font, Paragraph, Styles, and Editing. These functions are commonly used while you are keying, formatting, and editing text.

❸ **Commands**—the buttons, the boxes for keying information, and the menus that provide a choice of options. The command shown above is the *Font Color* command.

 **KEYBOARDING PRO DELUXE** ▸ See References/Word Commands/Lesson 26

SELECT TEXT

To apply Font commands, you must first select the text to which you want to apply the command and then click that command.

- Click at the beginning of the text and drag the mouse over the text to select it.
- Double-clicking within a word will select that word.

To apply Paragraph commands, you must click in the paragraph or select it. **Note:** Each time you tap ENTER, *Word* begins a new paragraph.

1. Center-align and key the main heading in bold; tap ENTER.
2. Change the alignment to left and turn bold off.
3. Create a three-column, four-row table.
4. Key the table shown below.
5. Select row 1; then bold and center-align the column headings. Row 1 is called the **header row** because it identifies the content in each column.
6. Check and close. (*46-drill2*)

COLLEGE SPORTS PROGRAM

Fall Events	Winter Events	Spring Events
Football	Basketball	Golf
Soccer	Gymnastics	Baseball
Volleyball	Swimming	Softball

APPLICATIONS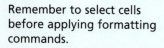

46-d1

Create Table

1. Key the main heading using center alignment, bold, and uppercase. Tap ENTER, change the alignment to left, and turn bold off.
2. Create the table shown below.
3. Select row 1. Bold and center-align the column headings. Center-align cells C2–C7.
4. Center the table vertically on the page (Page Layout/Page Setup dialog box launcher/Layout tab).
5. Check and close. (*46-d1*)

TIP

Remember to select cells before applying formatting commands.

KEY CONTACTS FOR BUILDING PROJECT

Contact	Title	Telephone Number
Lara G. Kim	Architect	420-555-0176
James C. Weatherwax	Contractor	317-555-0190
Kkatere Shadab	Site Supervisor	513-555-0164
Joanna B. Breckenridge	Interior Designer	624-555-0137
Loriana Gonzalez	Project Consultant	502-555-0126
Mei Liang Pong	Engineer	812-555-0171

1. Key your name in the New Document screen and tap ENTER.

2. Click the Home tab and hold the mouse over the items in the Font group to identify the command and note the short description of the function it performs. You will use some of these commands in the next drill.

3. Note that some of the commands such as *Font* and *Underline* have down arrows on the side of the command. Click the down arrow to see the menu of options that can be selected.

4. Click the Insert tab and the Page Layout tab and note the groups and commands that are located on these tabs.

5. Click the Home tab.

6. Leave the document open—keep it on your screen.

Note: If you need to leave this drill now, be sure to read the information on File Management on page 77 prior to exiting this drill and moving to the next activity. Otherwise, read the information that follows and continue with Drill 1 below.

HOME TAB COMMANDS

HOME TAB/FONT GROUP/FONT COMMANDS

The path (Home Tab/Font Group/Font Commands) including the tab, group, and commands is provided for most functions to assist you in locating them easily. To follow the path: Click the tab (Home); then look for the group label (Font) at the bottom of the ribbon, and select the command (Bold).

TIP

Click the down arrow next to the font and the font size commands to select a different font and size. Also click the down arrow to select double underline.

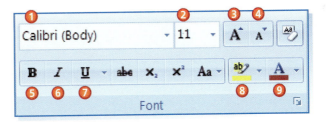

1 Font   2 Font Size   3 Grow the Font   4 Shrink the Font
5 Bold   6 Italic   7 Underline   8 Text Highlight Color   9 Font Color

1. In the open document below your name, key the phrases or sentences, including the information in parentheses shown below. Do not apply formats.

2. Select your name and highlight it in yellow.

3. Apply the formats shown in parentheses to each sentence or phrase. Remember to select the text before formatting it. If the command has a down arrow, click it to select the appropriate option.

4. Select Font Formats and click Shrink the Font twice; then click Grow the Font once.

5. Leave the document open—keep it on your screen.

Font Formats (Bold, Times New Roman, 16 point)

I read, *Learn to be Productive*, in the <u>Office Productivity Journal</u>. (Italic; then Underline)

The balance was <u>$45,750</u>; the loss was $12,398. (Double Underline; then red font color)

SELECTING PORTIONS OF A TABLE

TABLE TOOLS/LAYOUT/TABLE/SELECT

If you wish to apply a format such as bold, alignment, or italics to the table, you must first select the table. Likewise, to format a specific row, column, or cell, you must select the table parts and then apply the format.

The **Select** button, found in the Table group of the Layout tab under Table Tools, makes it easy for you to select portions of a table or the entire table. Click the insertion point in the cell of the table; then click the Select button and choose Select Cell to select only the cell the insertion point is in. Choosing Select Row or Select Column will highlight the entire row or column that contains the cell. Choose Select Table to highlight the entire table.

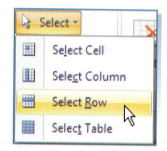

The mouse can also be used to select the entire table or portions of a table.

To select	Move the insertion point:
Entire table	Over the table and click the Table Move handle in the upper left of the table. (**Option:** Table Tools, Select, Select Table) To move the table, drag the Table Move handle to a new location.
Column	To the top of the column until a solid down arrow appears; click the left mouse button.
Row	To the left area just outside the table until the pointer turns to an open arrow (⇗), then click the left mouse button.

Note: You can also select rows and columns by selecting a cell, column, or row, and dragging across or down.

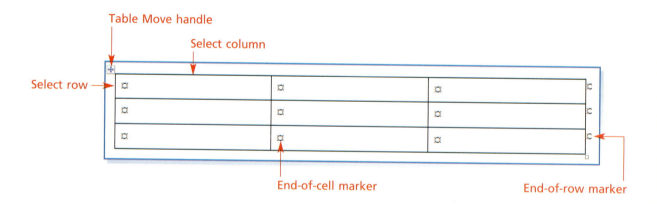

FILE MANAGEMENT

TIP

Read the information on file management carefully. The ability to manage files effectively is a very important career skill.

File management refers to saving documents in an organized manner so that they can be easily located and used again. Files may be managed by software or by the individual user. *Keyboarding Pro DELUXE* manages files automatically. It opens the appropriate document, saves, checks, and closes it. However, if you wish to use your word processing skills in other classes or in any situation other than your keyboarding class, you will have to learn how to manage your own files effectively.

An effective way to manage files is to create folders to store related documents. An important part of file management is naming files and folders effectively. For example, it is more effective to store all documents that relate to your English class in one folder and to your Economics class in a different folder than to store them all in one folder.

If you are not using *Keyboarding Pro DELUXE*, create a new folder for each module of the textbook. Documents for this module should be saved in a folder named *Module 3*. You are working in Lesson 26 on a document named Drill 1. Therefore a logical filename would be *26-drill1*. It is a short but easily identifiable name. You can store a file in a variety of locations, such as to a folder on your hard drive, a CD, a flash drive, a disk, a shared drive on a network, on the desktop, or to other removable storage media. Your instructor will indicate the location you should use for storing files in this class if you are not using *Keyboarding Pro DELUXE*.

If you are using *Keyboarding Pro DELUXE*, your software will save your file with the correct name. Note in the next activities that *Keyboarding Pro DELUXE* users follow different procedures for saving, closing, and opening documents than non-*Keyboarding Pro DELUXE* users.

OFFICE BUTTON

OFFICE BUTTON/COMMAND

TIP

The Office button is available from all tabs on the ribbon.

 The Office button located in the upper-left corner of the Ribbon provides you with all of the commands that you need to work with files. When you click the Office button, a menu drops down with the commands shown on the left and the most recently opened documents on the right.

Take a few minutes to review some of the options on the Office Button menu shown at the right. For example, you can create a new document, open an existing document, save a document, or print a document from this menu. Note that some of the options have arrows that display other functions. Click the arrow next to the Print icon and note the options.

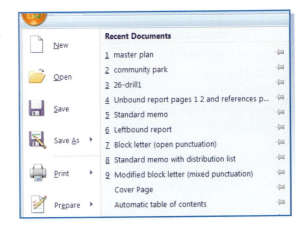

Note: The normal path (tab/group/command) is not used because the Office button is available for all tabs on the Ribbon. Remember to click the Office button any time you are working with files—New, Open, Close, Save, Save As, or Print.

TABLES TOOLS

When the insertion point is clicked in a table cell, additional tabs are added to the right of the Ribbon. A **Design** tab and a **Layout** tab are added under Table Tools. Click the Design tab to display features that allow you to change the appearance of the table. The Layout tab contains features that allow you to alter the table structure.

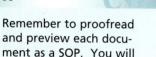

TIP

Remember to proofread and preview each document as a SOP. You will not be reminded to do this.

MOVE WITHIN A TABLE

The insertion point displays in cell A1 when a table is created. Tap the TAB key to move to the next cell, or simply use the mouse to click in a cell. Refer to the table below as you learn to key text in a table.

Tap or Press	Movement
TAB	To move to the next cell. If the insertion point is in the last cell, tapping TAB will add a new row.
SHIFT + TAB	To move to the previous cell.
ENTER	To increase the height of the row. If you tap ENTER by mistake, tap BACKSPACE to delete the line.

KEYBOARDING PRO DELUXE See References/Word commands/Lesson 46

DRILL 1   CREATE TABLE

1. Create a three-column, four-row table using the Table menu.

2. Turn on Show/Hide and notice the marker at the end of each cell and each row.

3. Use Print Layout View to see the Table Move handle and the Sizing handle.

4. Drag the Table Move handle down the page. This moves the table. Drag the handle back to the original position.

5. Close the table without saving.

6. Create a four-column, four-row table using the Insert Table command.

7. Move to cell C1. Move to cell B3.

8. Move to cell B1 and tap ENTER. Delete the ¶ to restore the size of the cell.

9. Move to cell D4 and tap TAB; this added a row to the bottom of the table. Close the table without saving it.

SAVE AND SAVE AS

OFFICE BUTTON/SAVE OR SAVE AS

You will use the Save and Save As commands on the Office Button menu to preserve your documents for future use. If you are saving a document for the first time, clicking either the Save or Save As button will display the Save As dialog box shown below.

To save a document:

1. Click the Office Button and then Save As to display the Save As dialog box.

2. In the Save As dialog box, click the arrow and select the location you wish to store your file. If you need to create a new folder, click the Create New Folder button on the right to display the New Folder dialog box.

3. Key the name of the folder in the Name box ❸ and click OK.

4. Key the name of the file in File name box ❹; leave the default Word Document in the Save as type box; and click Save ❺.

Once you have saved a document, you can just click the Save button and it will save the latest changes to the document in the same location with the same name. If you wish to make a copy of the document, click the Save As button and give the document a new name.

SAVE DOCUMENT USING KEYBOARDING PRO DELUXE

To save a document using *Keyboarding Pro DELUXE* without checking it, click the Back button. This option is normally used for work in progress.

To error-check a document and save it, click the Check button. Then review your results and close the window.

Note: For non-*Keyboarding Pro DELUXE* users, the filenames are shown in parentheses after all drills and documents.

DRILL 1 continued   SAVE DOCUMENT USING WORD

1. With Drill 1 open, click the Office button to display the File menu.

2. Click Save or Save As to display the Save As dialog box.

3. Select the location you wish to save the file.

4. Click the Create New Folder button and create a new folder named *Module 3*.

5. Key the filename **26-drill1** and click Save.

6. Leave the document open.

Several methods can be used to create a table. If you are creating a small table with just a few columns and rows, it may be easier to use the Table menu. If you are creating a more complex table, you will want to use the Insert Table command.

To create a table using the Table menu:

INSERT/TABLES/TABLE

1. Click the insertion point at the position where the table is to be inserted. Click the Insert tab to display the Tables group.
2. Click the Table button, and then under Insert Table, drag to select the number of columns and rows needed for the table.
3. Click the left mouse button to display the table in the document.

To create a table using the Insert Table command:

INSERT/TABLES/TABLE

1. Click the insertion point where the table is to be inserted.
2. In the Tables group on the Insert tab, click the Table button.
3. Click the Insert Table command ❶ to display the Insert Table dialog box.
4. Insert the number of columns by keying the number or using the spin buttons ❷.
5. Insert the number of rows by keying the number or using the spin buttons ❸; then click OK ❹. The table displays with the insertion point in the first cell, cell A1.
6. Key the text in cell A1; tap TAB to move to the next cell.

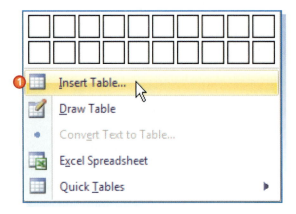

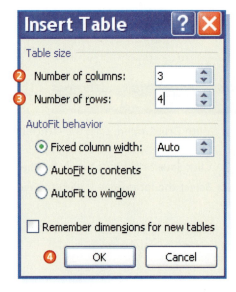

CLOSE DOCUMENT
OFFICE BUTTON/CLOSE

You can close a document and leave *Word* open, or you can close a document and exit *Word*. If you have only one document open, and you click the Close button at the top right side of the screen, you will close the document and exit *Word*. If you have more than one document open, the Close button will close the document only.

To close a document and leave *Word* open:

1. Click the Office button **1**.
2. Click the Close button **2** at the bottom of the menu.

NEW DOCUMENT
OFFICE BUTTON/NEW

 The New button on the Office Button menu displays the New Document dialog box. Note the options that are available.

To create a new *Word* document:

1. Click the Office button **1** to display the drop-down menu.
2. On the Office Button menu, click New **2** to display the New Document dialog box.
3. Click the Blank Document button **3**; then click the Create button at the bottom of the dialog box.

DRILLS 1 AND 2 — CHECK DOCUMENT AND OPEN NEW DOCUMENT USING KEYBOARDING PRO DELUXE

1. Check the document and review the report; close the window.
2. On the Lesson menu, select the next activity 26-drill 2 to open it.
3. Key your name at the top of the document and tap ENTER.
4. Key the document name **26-drill2** and tap ENTER.
5. Key the following sentence:

   This is a new document I have created.
6. Check and close the document.

DRILLS 1 AND 2 — CLOSE DOCUMENT AND OPEN NEW DOCUMENT (NON-KEYBOARDING PRO DELUXE USERS)

1. Proofread the open document for errors.
2. Save and close *26-drill1*.
3. Open a new document.
4. Key your name on the first line and tap ENTER.
5. Key the document name **26-drill2** and tap ENTER.
6. Key the following sentence:

   This is a new document I have created.
7. Check, save, and, close the document (*26-drill2* in your *Module 3* folder).

TABLES FEATURE

The Tables feature makes it easy to present data and graphics in a *Word* document. Aligning text, numbers, and graphics in a *Word* document can be tedious if you only use tabs and spaces. A table will help you align columns and rows of text and numbers with ease.

Tables: Columns and rows of data—either alphabetic, numeric, or both.

Column: Vertical list of information labeled alphabetically from left to right ❶.

Row: Horizontal list of information labeled numerically from top to bottom ❷.

Cell: An intersection of a column and a row ❸. Each cell has its own address consisting of the column letter and the row number (cell A1).

Use Show/Hide to display end-of-cell markers in each cell ❹ and end-of-row markers at the end of each row ❺. End-of-cell and end-of-row markers are useful when editing tables. Use Print Layout View to display the Table Move handle in the upper left of the table ❻. Drag the Table Move handle to move the table to a different location in the document. The Sizing handle in the lower right of the table can be used to make the table larger or smaller ❼.

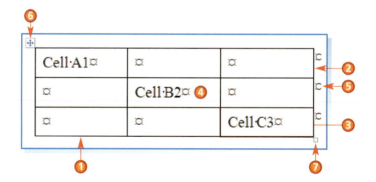

CREATE TABLES

INSERT/TABLES/TABLE

Tables are inserted into existing documents or new documents. Begin creating a table by clicking the Insert tab ❶ to display the Insert ribbon. Locate the Tables group ❷. The **Table button** ❸ contains options for creating various types of tables; you will use several of the options in this module.

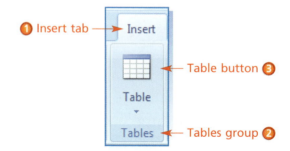

OPEN AN EXISTING DOCUMENT

OFFICE BUTTON/OPEN

 ❶ On some occasions, you will want to use documents that you have previously prepared and saved.

Keyboarding Pro DELUXE users: To open a document that you have previously prepared, simply select that activity from the Lesson menu. If you are returning to a document you have already begun, then choose Open existing document. Non-*Keyboarding Pro DELUXE* users always follow *Word* directions.

TIP

If you have recently used the document you are opening, it will be listed in the Recent Documents on the Office Button menu. You can double-click the filename to open it.

To open an existing document:

1. Click the Office button to display the menu.

2. Click the Open button ❶ to display the Open dialog box.

3. Select the location where you saved the file. Click on the appropriate folder ❷, select the filename ❸, and click Open ❹. You may also double-click the filename to open it.

-or-

If you have recently worked with the document, double-click it on the list of Recent Documents ❺.

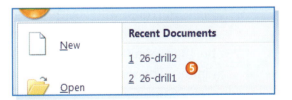

PRINT A DOCUMENT USING KEYBOARDING PRO DELUXE

Check the document; then print and close the checked document. If you wish to print a closed document, choose Print Document from the Document Options dialog box.

Table Essentials

LEARNING OUTCOMES

- Create tables.
- Change table structure.
- Format tables.
- Incorporate tables within documents.
- Build keying speed and accuracy.

LESSON 46 ▸ ## Create Tables

WARMUP 46a

Key each line, striving for control. Repeat if desired.

alphabet	1	Jim Ryan was able to liquefy frozen oxygen; he kept it very cold.
figures	2	Flight 483 left Troy at 9:57 a.m., arriving in Reno at 12:06 p.m.
direct reaches	3	My brother served as an umpire on that bright June day, no doubt.
easy	4	Ana's sorority works with vigor for the goals of the civic corps.

| 1 | 2 | 3 | 4 | 5 | 6 | 7 | 8 | 9 | 10 | 11 | 12 | 13 |

SKILL BUILDING

46b Timed Writing
1. Key a 3' timed writing, working for speed.
2. Key a 3' timed writing, working for control.

all letters

	gwam	3'
The most important element of a business is its clientele. It is	4	61
for this reason that most organizations adopt the slogan that the	9	65
customer is always right. The saying is not to be taken literally, but	13	70
in spirit.	14	71
Patrons will continuously use your business if you provide a	18	75
quality product and good customer service. The product you sell must	23	79
be high quality and long lasting. The product must perform as you	27	84
claim. The environment and surroundings must be safe and clean.	32	88
Customers expect you to be well groomed and neatly dressed.	36	92
They expect you to know your products and services and to be	40	96
dependable. When you tell a customer you will do something, you must	44	101
perform. Patrons expect you to help them willingly and quickly. Add	49	105
a personal touch by greeting clientele by name, but be cautious about	54	110
conducting business on a first-name basis.	56	113

3' | 1 | 2 | 3 | 4 |

PRINT AND PRINT PREVIEW

OFFICE BUTTON/PRINT

The menu from the Office button is used for previewing and printing documents as well as for saving documents. Hold the mouse over the arrow next to the Print button ❶ and note that the right side of the menu displays three options to preview or print your document.

Print ❷ displays the Print dialog box, which allows you to select the printer you want to use, the number of copies, and other options.

Quick Print ❸ prints one copy directly to the default printer.

Print Preview ❹ displays the document exactly like it will look printed. Once you have previewed a document, you must click the Close Print Preview button to return to your document. Note you can also Print from the Print Preview toolbar.

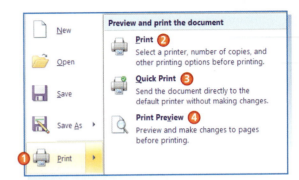

To print one copy of a document on the default printer:

1. On the Office Button menu, click the arrow next to Print ❶.

2. Select Quick Print ❸.

To preview a document:

1. On the Office Button menu, point to Print or click the arrow next to Print ❶.

2. Click Print Preview ❹ to display both the document as it will look printed and the Print Preview toolbar.

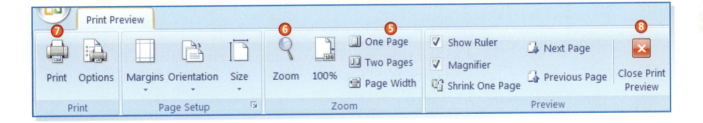

3. Note some of the options available:

    a. View one or two pages of a document ❺ at one time.

    b. Zoom ❻ in closer or out wider.

    c. Print ❼ from this toolbar.

    d. Close Print Preview ❽ to return to your document.

DRILL 2

PROOFREADING AND EDITING

1. Key the drill, making all necessary corrections.
2. Preview, check, and close. (*proofreading-drill2*)

First impressions does count, and you never get a second chance to make a good first impression. This statement applys too both documents and people. The minute you walk in to a room you are judged by you appearance, your facial expressions, and the way you present your self. As soon as a document is opened, it is judged by it's appearance and the way it is presented. First impressions are often lasting impressions therefore you should strive to make a positive first impression for yourself and for the documents you prepare. Learn to manage your image and the image of your documents.

DRILL 3

PROOFREADING FOR CONSISTENCY

 LINGER

1. Proofread the letter for consistency in usage, facts, and format (block letter style).
2. Verify information against the price list below. Make corrections. Use today's date for the letter and your name for the writer's.
3. Preview, check, and close. (*proofreading-drill3*)

COMPUTERS AND PRINTERS		
Product	**Manufacturer**	**Price**
Workstation 2010	Chimera	$2,779
550MHz processor, 19" monitor, 64GB RAM, 9.1GB hard drive, 7 x 24 dedicated workstation, 40X variable CD-ROM drive		
Amina Optima Notebook	Finn	2,199
1.86GHz processor, 17" XGA active matrix display, 2GB RAM, 100GB hard drive, latest Capstone Office Suite, combo 24x/10x/24x CD-RW and 8x DVD-ROM drives		
Winger Laser Printer	Primat	399
1200 dpi, 250-sheet input tray, 27 ppm		
Ink Jet Color Printer	Primat	299
9600 x 2400 dpi, 100-sheet input tray, 24 ppm, up to 16 million colors		
AZ Printer/Copier/Scanner	Ventura	499
1200 dpi, 150-sheet input tray, 22 ppm, scans directly to e-mail, integrated desktop software for organizing scanned documents, OCR software for text editing		

DRILL 3   PREVIEW AND PRINT DOCUMENT

1. Open Drill 1 (*26-drill1*); key **Drill 3** on the line below the last line of text.

2. Preview the document; then close Print Preview.

3. *Keyboarding Pro DELUXE* users: Use *Keyboarding Pro DELUXE* to print the document.

4. Click the Office button to display the menu again. Use Quick Print to print one copy of the document using the default printer.

5. Non *Keyboarding Pro DELUXE* users: Save the document with a new name and close it. Use the filename that is shown in parentheses. (*26-drill4*)

EXIT WORD

1. Display the Microsoft Office menu button and click the Exit *Word* button at the lower right side of the menu.

-or-

2. Click the Close button at the top right of the screen.

APPLICATIONS

26-d1

Create a New Document

1. Key your name on the first line and then key **26-d1** on the next line.

2. Key the following sentences using the *Word 2007* defaults; then apply the font formats as they appear in the sentences. Do not apply the formats until you have keyed all sentences. Tap ENTER after each sentence.

I have changed the font on this sentence to Times New Roman, 12-point type.

This sentence has Gray-25% highlighting.

Our loss this year was $63,946; last year our net profit was $175,820.

This sentence illustrates the use of **bold**, *italic*, and <u>single underline</u>.

Grow this sentence to 16 point; then shrink this part to 10 point.

3. Preview, proofread, and print the document.

4. Check and close. (*26-d1*)

5. Exit *Keyboarding Pro DELUXE* or *Word*.

Reminder: Non-*Keyboarding Pro DELUXE* users must open a document for each activity. After you have completed an activity, proofread, preview, print, save the document with the name provided in parentheses, and close the document.

PROOFREADING GUIDES

The final and important step in producing a document is proofreading. Error-free documents send the message the organization is detail-oriented and competent. Apply these procedures when producing any document.

1. Check spelling using the Spelling feature.

2. Proofread the document on the screen. Be alert for words that are spelled correctly but are misused, such as *you/your*, *in/on*, *of/on*, *the/then*, etc.

3. Check the document for necessary parts for correctness; be sure special features are present if needed—for example, in a letter, check for the enclosure or copy notation.

4. View the document on screen to check placement. Save and print.

These additional steps will make you a better proofreader:

5. Try to allow some time between writing a document and proofreading it.

6. If you are reading a document that has been keyed from a written draft, place the two documents next to each other and use guides to proofread the keyed document line by line against the original.

7. Proofread numbers aloud or with another person.

Proofreading for consistency is another important part of preparing documents. Consistency in style or tone, usage, facts, and format conveys an impression of care and attention to detail that reflects well on the writer and his or her organization. In contrast, lack of consistency gives an impression of carelessness and inattention to detail. Lack of consistency also makes documents more difficult to read and understand.

Proofreading statistical copy is extremely important. As you proofread, double-check numbers whenever possible. For example, verify dates against a calendar and check computations with a calculator. Remember these tips for proofreading numbers.

- Read numbers in groups. For example, the telephone number 618-555-0123 can be read in three parts: **six-one-eight**, **five five-five**, **zero-one-two-three**.

- Read numbers aloud.

- Proofread numbers with a partner.

DRILL 1

PROOFREADING

 PROOF-IT

1. Print the data file.

2. Use proofreaders' marks to mark corrections. The letter contains nine mistakes in formatting, capitalization, number use, spelling, and keying.

3. Revise the letter and format it correctly.

4. Preview, check, and close. (*proofreading-drill1*)

LESSON 27

Formatting Essentials

WARMUP 27a

Key each line, striving for control. Repeat if desired.

alphabet	1	Alex, a smart student, saw five zebras quickly jump a high fence.
figure	2	Kyoko mailed Invoices 73981 and 67358 on 4/15/2006 at 4:29 today.
double letters	3	Jarrett cheerfully killed millions of bugs near the pool at noon.
easy	4	Jane may go to visit the lake and fish with the girls? May I go?

NEW FUNCTIONS

27b

PARAGRAPH FORMATS

HOME/PARAGRAPH/COMMAND

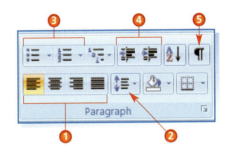

In Lesson 26, you worked with formats in the Font group on the Home tab. In this lesson you will work with some of the formats in the Paragraph group on the Home tab. Note that some of the commands are clustered together in this group.

➊ **Alignment commands**—Align Left, Center, Align Right, and Justify—specify how text lines up.

➋ **Line Spacing**—determines the amount of space between lines of text.

➌ **Bullets and Numbering**—formats for lists of information.

➍ **Decrease and Increase Indent**—moves all lines of a paragraph to the right or the left.

➎ **Show/Hide**—displays paragraph markings and other nonprinting characters.

Paragraph formats apply to an entire paragraph. Each time you tap ENTER, *Word* inserts a paragraph mark and starts a new paragraph. Thus, a paragraph may consist of a partial line or of several lines. You must be able to see where paragraphs begin and end to format them.

SHOW/HIDE

HOME/PARAGRAPH/SHOW/HIDE

 Turning on the Show/Hide button displays all nonprinting characters such as paragraph markers (¶) or spaces (..). The Show/Hide button appears highlighted when it is active. Nonprinting characters can be turned off by clicking the Show/Hide button again.

45-d2

1. Create a title page for the leftbound report prepared in *45-d1*. Use the Cover Page feature.
2. Key the following information:

   Document title: See title *45-d1*.

   Document subtitle: **For Design Department**

   Author name: **Student's Name, Information Technology Manager**
3. Continue to next document. (*45-d2*)

45-d3

Traditional Report

1. Rekey the report prepared in *45-d1*, stopping after the first bulleted list. Format in the traditional report format; double-space. Assume the report is an unbound report.
2. Indent the footnotes; change font to Times New Roman 12 point.
3. Single-space the bulleted items; double-space between the items.
4. Number the pages at the top right; do not print the page number on the first page. Check that no side headings appear at the bottom of the page alone.
5. Check the test and close. (*45-d3*)

CHECKPOINT

Congratulations! You have successfully completed the lessons in Module 5. To check your understanding and for more practice, complete the objective assessment and performance assessment located on the textbook website at www.collegekeyboarding.com.

ALIGNMENT

DISCOVER

Enhanced Tool Tips
Position the mouse pointer over a command to display the name of the function, a description of it, and the keyboard shortcut to apply (if available).

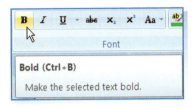

① **Align Text Left**—all lines begin at left margin.

② **Center**—all lines are centered.

③ **Align Text Right**—all lines are aligned at the right margin.

④ **Justify**—all lines are aligned at both the left and right margins.

To apply alignment formats:

1. Turn on Show/Hide.
2. Click in a single paragraph or select multiple paragraphs to which a format is to be applied.
3. Click the format to be applied.

③ Student's·Name¶

② PARAGRAPH·FORMATS¶

① Note·that·my·name·has·Align·Text·Right·format·applied·to·it.··The·title· has·Center·format·applied.··This·paragraph·uses·the·default·Align·Text· Left·format.¶

④ This·last·paragraph·is·formatted·using·Justify.··Justify·aligns·text·at·both· margins.··Additional·space·is·added·to·force·the·text·to·align·evenly·at· the·right·margin.··The·only·line·in·a·justified·paragraph·that·may·not·end· at·the·right·margin·is·the·last·line·of·the·paragraph.¶

DRILL 1	**ALIGN PARAGRAPHS**

1. Key your name and tap ENTER.
2. Click the Home tab and hold the mouse over each command in the Paragraph group to identify the command and note the description of the function it performs.
3. Some commands such as Line Spacing and Bullets have down arrows next to the command. Click the arrow to see the options that can be selected.

4. Key the document shown above. Your name replaces *Student's Name*.
5. Format the title in uppercase, bold, 14-point Cambria font.
6. Format the document with the alignments shown. The red numbers illustrate alignment styles. Do not key them.
7. Preview, check, and close. (*27-drill1*)

With an understanding of the copyright laws, users now realize that materials placed on a website may be copyrighted and are not available for downloading or copying and pasting into other documents. Sound advice is always to seek permission from the original copyright owner before using the material. Purchasing royalty-free content is another excellent way to avoid any question of copyright infringement.

Technology

Understanding the copyright laws and awareness of all types of copyrighted material are important as copyright owners fight against infringement. Interestingly, technology is and will continue to be a key player in the policing of copyright offenders. Weatherford shares the following ways technology is currently being used:

- Locking up data by disabling the printing function and removing the cut, copy, and paste functions
- Placing digital watermarks on an image that identify the source
- Requiring a password from the copyright owner for users to gain access to copyrighted material[2]

Summary

Awareness of copyright laws and the various copyright infringements—especially in light of possibilities available through the Internet—is very important in combating violations. Additionally, individuals must realize that technology will continue to be an effective tool in policing copyright violators.

Footnotes

[1]Allison Morgan, "Know the Copyright Law," *Digital Journal*, February 2008, p. 21.

[2]John E. Weatherford, "Technology Aids in Stopping Copyright Offender," *Hopper Business Journal*, Fall 2008, http://www.hbj.edu/technologyaids.htm (accessed December 26, 2008).

References

Morgan, Allison. "Know the Copyright Law." *Digital Journal*. February 2008, 20-25.

Weatherford, John E. "Technology Aids in Stopping Copyright Offenders." *Hopper Business Journal*. Fall 2008. http://www.hbj.edu/technologyaids.htm (accessed December 26, 2008).

BULLETS AND NUMBERING

HOME/PARAGRAPH/BULLETS AND NUMBERING

 Numbering is used for lists of items that are in sequence, whereas bullets are used for an unordered listing. Bullets can be converted to numbers by selecting the list and choosing numbers or vice versa. Different styles are available for both bullets and numbers.

To apply Bullets and Numbering:

1. Key the list.
2. Select the list and click either the Bullets or Numbering command.

To select a different format for Bullets and Numbering:

1. Click the down arrow on either the Bullets or the Numbering command to display the library of styles.
2. Select the desired style.

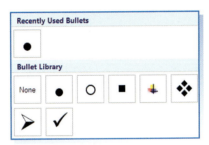

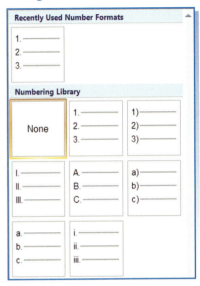

DRILL 2	APPLY BULLETS AND NUMBERING

1. Key the two lists shown below before applying formats; use default spacing.
2. Apply Square bullets to the first list below the heading *Favorite Puppies*.

3. Apply numbers to the list below the heading *Pet Nutrition*; select the first option from the Numbering Library.
4. Preview the document; check and close it. (*27-drill2*)

Favorite Puppies
Cairn Terrier
Cavalier King Charles Spaniel
Shih Tzu

Pet Nutrition
Consult your veternarian and select the proper type of food.
Monitor portions carefully.
Provide appropriate treats.

TIP

Remember to proofread and preview each document before you move to the next one.

1. Key the leftbound report shown below in the new report format, using *Word 2007* defaults.
2. Insert footnotes as shown in the report. Indent the long quotation appropriately.
3. Number the pages at the top right; do not print the page number on the first page.
4. Key the references on a separate reference page at the end of the report.
5. Continue to next document. (*45-d1*)

Copyright Law in the Internet Age

Copyright owners continue to face copyright challenges as technology advances more rapidly than ever before. History shows us that copyright infringements occur at the introduction of each new invention or emerging technology. Examples include the phonograph and tape recorder and mimeograph and copy machines. Today, the Internet age provides users the ease of copying and distributing electronic files via the Internet.

Copyright owners of content published on the Web, photographers who view their photographs on Web pages, and recording artists whose music is downloaded from the Internet are only a few examples of copyright issues resulting from the Internet age. Compounding the issue is that many Internet users may not be aware they are violating copyright law. The following list shows actions taken daily that are considered copyright infringements:

- Copying content from a Web page and pasting it into documents
- Reproducing multiple copies of a journal article that were printed from an online journal
- Distributing presentation handouts that contain cartoon characters or other graphics copied from a Web page
- Presenting originally designed electronic presentations that contain graphics, sound and video clips, and/or photographs copied from a Web page
- Duplicating and distributing copies of music downloaded from the Web

Copyright Laws

To avoid copyright infringement, the Internet user must be knowledgeable about copyright law. Two important laws include The Copyright Law of 1976 and the Digital Millennium Copyright Act, which was enacted in 1998 to update the copyright law for the digital age. Morgan explains that under the Copyright Law of 1976:

> Original works are protected by copyright at the very moment that they are first originated—printed, drawn, captured, or saved to a digital storage area. The copyright protection is automatic when the original work is first established in the real medium of expression.[1]

continued

LINE SPACING OPTIONS

HOME/PARAGRAPH/LINE SPACING

DISCOVER

SuperTooltips—provide an enhanced description of a function and help on how to use it.

Hold the mouse over the Line Spacing button in the Paragraph group to display a SuperTooltip; then hold the mouse over Format Painter in the Clipboard group.

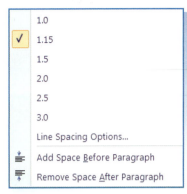

The default line spacing for *Word 2007* is 1.15. Note the options that are displayed by clicking the down arrow on the Line Spacing button. Previous versions used 1.0 as single spacing (SS) and 2.0 as double spacing (DS). The 1.15 default is treated the same as single-spacing; it just allows a little more space between lines of type. The default amount of space after each paragraph is 10 points. Note that you can remove space before or after a paragraph.

To change line spacing:

1. Position the insertion point in the paragraph whose spacing you wish to change.
2. Click the Line Spacing command and select the desired spacing.

Note the differences between 1.15 spacing ❶, 1.0 spacing ❷, and 2.0 spacing shown below ❸. Also note the amount of space (10 points) after paragraphs ❹.

❶ These first two paragraphs are keyed using the default spacing of 1.15. The extra space between the lines makes text easier to read.

10 points ❹

❶ Note that tapping enter to move to the next paragraph adds additional space between the paragraphs. The amount of space added is 10 points.

❷ Note in this paragraph and in the fourth paragraph shown below that the spacing has been changed to single spacing or 1.0 spacing.

❷ The lines of text are closer together. More text can be placed on one page when single spacing is used to format a document.

❸ The fifth and sixth paragraphs are keyed using double spacing or 2.0 spacing. When double spacing is used, paragraphs are indented.

10 points ❹

❸ The use of double spacing is likely to decline since the default provides enough space between the lines to enhance reading.

LESSON 45   Assessment

WARMUP 45a

Key each line, striving for control. Repeat if desired.

one-hand sentences

1 In regard to desert oil wastes, Jill referred only minimum cases.
2 Carra agrees you'll get a reward only as you join nonunion races.
3 Few beavers, as far as I'm aware, feast on cedar trees in Kokomo.
4 Johnny, after a few stewed eggs, ate a plump, pink onion at noon.
5 A plump, aged monk served a few million beggars a milky beverage.

| 1 | 2 | 3 | 4 | 5 | 6 | 7 | 8 | 9 | 10 | 11 | 12 | 13 |

SKILL BUILDING

45b   Timed Writing

1. Key a 1' timed writing on each paragraph; work to increase speed.
2. Key a 3' timed writing on both paragraphs.

all letters

gwam   1'   3'

	1'	3'
How is a hobby different from a business? A very common way	12	4
to describe the difference between the hobby and the business is	25	8
that the hobby is done for fun, and the business is done as work	38	13
which enables people to earn their living. Does that mean that	51	17
people do not have fun at work or that people do not work with their	65	22
hobbies? Many people would not agree with that description.	77	26
Some people begin work on a hobby just for fun, but then they	12	30
realize it has the potential to be a business. They soon find out	26	34
that others enjoy the hobby as well and would expect to pay for	39	39
the products or services the hobby requires. Many quite successful	52	43
businesses begin as hobbies. Some of them are small, and some grow	66	48
to be large operations.	72	49

1' | 1 | 2 | 3 | 4 | 5 | 6 | 7 | 8 | 9 | 10 | 11 | 12 | 13 |
3' | 1 | 2 | 3 | 4 |

APPLICATIONS

45c

Assessment

 Continue

 Check

With *Keyboarding Pro DELUXE*: When you complete a document, proofread it, check the spelling, and preview for placement. When you are completely satisfied, click the Continue button to move to the next document. Click the Check button when you are ready to error-check the test. Review and/or print the document analysis results.

Without *Keyboarding Pro DELUXE*: Key the documents in sequence. When time has been called, proofread all documents again and identify errors.

REMOVE SPACE AFTER PARAGRAPH

HOME/PARAGRAPH/LINE SPACING

 Sometimes it is desirable to remove the extra space after a paragraph to give copy a more traditional appearance. The spacing options provide an easy way to remove space after a paragraph.

TIP

Always display Show/Hide to format paragraphs.

To remove space after a paragraph:

1. Position the insertion point at the end of the paragraph you wish to remove the spacing after.
2. Click the Line Spacing command ❶ and then Remove Space After Paragraph ❷.

DRILL 3   **APPLY LINE SPACING**

1. Key the six paragraphs illustrated on the previous page; then format by applying the same line spacing and space after paragraph illustrated. The red numbers guide you to the proper alignment. Do not key the numbers.

2. Position the insertion point at the end of the second-to-last paragraph and remove the space after the paragraph.

3. Preview the document and check and close it. (*27-drill3*)

CLIPBOARD GROUP

HOME/CLIPBOARD/CUT, PASTE, OR COPY

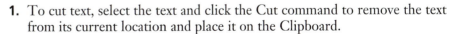 The Clipboard group on the Home tab provides very useful editing functions. The Clipboard is a feature used to store multiple items that have been cut or copied so that they can be used in other locations. You will work with the Clipboard more extensively in later lessons. An overview of the four editing commands follows.

Cut—removes the selected text from its current location.

Paste—positions the text that was cut in another location.

Copy—makes an additional copy of the selected text.

Format Painter—enables you to copy the format of one paragraph to another.

To cut, paste, and copy text:

1. To cut text, select the text and click the Cut command to remove the text from its current location and place it on the Clipboard.

2. To paste the text, place the insertion point where the text is to be pasted and click the Paste command.

3. To copy text, select the text to be copied and click the Copy command to leave it in its current position and make a copy of it.

4. Position the insertion point where the text is to be pasted and click the Paste command.

44-d3
Reference Page

Hunter McWhirter, Vice President, has requested that you format a reference page using the traditional format for a report needed for a meeting today.

1. In a new blank document, change to *Word 2003* style and change font to Times New Roman. Key the references shown below in appropriate hanging indent format.
2. Format the title appropriately in the traditional format. Change left margin for a leftbound report.
3. Check and close. (*44-d3*)

References

Duran, Delane. *New Markets for the 21st Century*. 7th ed. Boston: Serendipity Press, 2008.

Grantham, Connor. gconnor@mail.com "My Concerns About the Market." August 8, 2008, e-mail to Alexandra Sarnowska (accessed August 12, 2008).

Townsel, Gabriel. "World Events and the Market." *Marketplace Today*. Fall 2008. http://www.mt.com/worldevents.htm (accessed October 23, 2008).

Westberry, Anna Maria and Margarita Cruz. "How to Invest in Today's Markets." *Market World*. March 20, 2008, 103-108.

44-d4
Edit Leftbound Report

1. Open *44-d2*. Read this report carefully for content.
2. In the first paragraph of the *Delivering Presentations* section, tap ENTER before the last sentence that begins "The speaker must be energetic and must project the voice." Move your insertion point to the end of that sentence.
3. Search the Internet for information about using the voice effectively when delivering an oral presentation.
4. Compose a short paragraph that adds more meaningful information to this paragraph. Be sure to paraphrase your research. If you choose to lift words, phrases, or entire sentences, key quotation marks around the direct lift. If you quote more than four lines, indent the quotation.
5. Insert a footnote at the end of the paragraph. Use the three examples below to assist you in formatting your footnote correctly.
6. Check and close the document. (*44-d4*)

Website

[1]Lori Guo-Patterson, "Top Ten Athletes," *The Sports Journal*, Spring 2008, http://www.tsj.edu/athletes/topten.htm (accessed June 25, 2008).

Website (No Author)

[1]"Delivery Skills," The Speech Clinic, February 2008, http://www.speechclinic/delivery.htm (accessed December 1, 2009).

Online Journal, Magazine, or Newspaper

[1]Missy Watson, "Technology Helps," *Hopper Business Journal*, Fall 2008, http://www.hbj.edu/technologyhelps.htm (accessed May 26, 2009).

DRILL 4   CUT, COPY, AND PASTE

1. In a new document, key your name and tap ENTER.
2. Key the document name **27-drill4**, and tap ENTER.
3. Key only the first and second sentences below.
4. Select *quickly* in the first sentence and cut it; then click between *graphics* and *by* and paste it.

5. Select the text in the second sentence and click Copy. Click at the end of the sentence and tap ENTER; then click Paste.
6. Edit the third sentence, which you have just copied, to add the text shown in the third sentence shown below.
7. Check the document and close it. (*27-drill4*)

The Cut and Paste functions enable you to quickly move text, pictures, or other graphics by cutting from one location and pasting in another location.

The Copy function enables you to duplicate text, pictures, or other graphics in another location.

The Copy function enables you to duplicate text, pictures, or other graphics in another location in the same document or in a different document.

FORMAT PAINTER

HOME/CLIPBOARD/FORMAT PAINTER

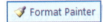 The Format Painter can be used to copy a format from one paragraph to another paragraph or to multiple paragraphs.

To copy a paragraph format to a single paragraph:

1. Click in the paragraph that has the desired format.
2. Click the Format Painter.
3. Click in the paragraph to copy the desired format.

To copy a paragraph format to multiple paragraphs:

1. Double-click the Format Painter to keep it turned on.
2. Click in the paragraphs to copy the desired format to each paragraph.
3. Click Format Painter to turn it off or tap ESC.

DRILL 5   FORMAT PAINTER

1. In a new document, key your name, and tap ENTER.
2. Key the document name **27-drill5**, and tap ENTER twice.
3. Key the title, **SERENDIPITY**, and tap ENTER.
4. Turn on Show/Hide (Home/Paragraph/Show/Hide) and key the paragraphs on the following page; tap ENTER after each paragraph.
5. Click your name and right-align it. Click Format Painter once; then click the document name.
6. Click the second paragraph below the title, apply double line spacing (2.0), Times New Roman, 12-point font, and tap TAB to indent the paragraph.

7. With the insertion point in paragraph 2, click Format Painter once; then click paragraph 1.
8. With the insertion point still in paragraph 1, double-click Format Painter; then click paragraph 3.
9. Click paragraph 4 and then turn off Format Painter.
10. Remove the extra space after the first three paragraphs.
11. Preview, check, and close the document. (*27-drill5*)

27-

Editing
Formats

LESS

WARM

Key each
control.

SKIL

44b T
1. Key e
   tratin
   keyin
   ENTER
   3-line
2. Repe:

TIP

Keep F
as you
row ar
row.

44c T
1. Key a
   work
2. Key a
   work

43-d1

Continued

Summary

Effective speakers understand the importance of knowing the audience and developing a clear purpose in the beginning and maintaining that focus throughout the research, composition, and delivery of the presentation. The speaker's task will be much easier, and the audience will benefit as well.

Footnotes

[1]Samantha Vilella and Nathan T. Gunach, *Effective Presentations* (Indianapolis: Manchester Press, 2008), p. 38.

[2]Isabella Carrabbua, "The Purpose of the Purpose: A Clear Focus," *Contemporary Writers' Digest*, December 2008, p. 141.

43-d2

Title Page

1. Create a title page for the leftbound report prepared in *43-d1*. Use the Cover Page feature.
2. Key the following information:

   Document title: See *43-d1*.

   Document subtitle: **For Stoltman & Langston Associates, LLC**

   Author name: **John E. Swartsfager, Chief Training Officer**
3. Check and close the document. (*43-d2*).

43-d3

Leftbound Report

1. Open *38-d2* and format the document as a leftbound report.
2. Insert page numbers. Do not print the page number on the first page.
3. Add the last paragraph shown below.
4. Check and close the document. (*43-d3*)

Summary

Remember to plan your page layout with the three basic elements of effective page design. Always include sufficient white space to give an uncluttered appearance. Learn to add bold when emphasis is needed, and do consider your audience when choosing typestyles. Finally, use typestyles to add variety to your layout, but remember, no more than two typestyles in a document.

Ribbon Essentials

WARMUP 28a

Key each line, striving for control. Repeat if desired.

alphabet	1	Beatriz joked quietly and played with five or six cute young men.
figure	2	I fed 28 men, 30 women, 19 girls, 25 boys, 17 babies, and 4 dogs.
one hand	3	Jimmy saw him carve a great pumpkin; John deserved better awards.
balanced hand	4	Jamale Rodney, a neighbor, and Sydney may go to the lake by auto.

SKILL BUILDING

28b Textbook Keying

Key each line once, concentrating on using good keying techniques; tap ENTER twice after each 2-line group.

one hand	5	A few treats were served as reserve seats were set up on a stage.
	6	In my opinion, a few trees on a hilly acre created a vast estate.
balanced hand	7	Pam and Jake did go to visit the big island and may fish for cod.
	8	Ken may visit the men he met at the ancient chapel on the island.
1/2 fingers	9	Kimberly tried to grab the bar, but she missed and hurt her hand.
	10	My name is Frankie, but I prefer to be called Fran by my friends.
3/4 fingers	11	Zola and Polly saw us play polo at Maxwell Plaza; we won a prize.
	12	Zack quickly swam past all six boys at a zoo pool on Saxony Land.

28c Timed Writing

1. Key a 3' timed writing, working for speed.
2. Key a 3' timed writing, working for control.

all letters

	gwam	1'	3'
Learning new software can be fun, but it often requires much		12	4
hard work. However, if you are willing to work hard, in a short period		26	9
of time, you can learn important skills.		35	12
If you accept change easily, you are more likely to learn new		12	16
things quickly. A person who avoids change has just about the		25	20
same chance of learning new software as a lazy person.		36	24
Working smart might be just as important as working hard.		12	28
Help is easy to use if you will take the time to explore the resources		26	33
that are provided in your software.		33	35

43-d1

Leftbound Report with Footnotes

1. Key the leftbound report shown below and on the next page. Format the title and side headings with the appropriate style.
2. Insert the two footnotes as marked in the report.
3. Key the items in the bulleted list and then apply the bullets.
4. Indent the long quotation 0.5" from the left margin.
5. Insert page numbers appropriately.
6. Check and close the document. (*43-d1*)

Planning a Successful Presentation

Presenters realize the need to prepare for a successful presentation. Two areas of extensive preparation are the development of a thorough audience analysis and a well-defined presentation purpose.

Audience Analysis

The presenter must conduct a thorough audience analysis before developing the presentation. The profile of the audience includes the following demographics.

- Age and gender
- Education
- Ethnic group
- Marital status
- Geographic location
- Group membership

Interviews with program planners and organization leaders will provide insight into the needs, desires, and expectations of the audience. This information makes the difference in preparing a presentation that is well received by the audience.

Purpose of the Presentation

After analyzing the audience profile, the presenter has a clear focus on the needs of the audience and then writes a well-defined purpose of the presentation. Isabella Carrabbua, a well-known writer, states:

Long Quotation —
With a clear focus, the presenter confidently conducts research and organizes a presentation that is on target. The presenter remembers to state the purpose in the introduction of the presentation to assist the audience in understanding the well-defined direction of the presentation. In the conclusion of the presentation, the speaker often will remind the audience of the purpose.

KEYBOARDING PRO DELUXE ▶ See References/Word commands/Lesson 43

continued

NEW FUNCTIONS

28d

DATE AND TIME

INSERT/TEXT/DATE & TIME

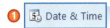 One of the most frequently used commands on the Insert tab is the Date & Time command. Most business documents are dated.

TIP

Remember to proofread and preview each document as a SOP. You will not be reminded to do this.

To insert the date and/or time:

1. Position the insertion point where you wish to insert the date or time.

2. On the Insert menu in the Text group, click the Date & Time command ❶ to display the Date and Time dialog box.

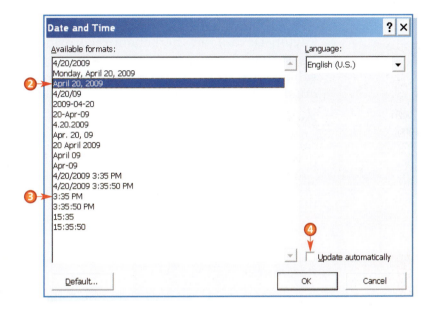

3. Select the desired date format (April 20, 2009) ❷ or time format (3:35 PM) ❸. In this textbook, assume mm/dd/yyyy format (April 20, 2009) is the default format for the date. Use this default unless the directions specify to use a different format.

4. Leave Update automatically ❹ blank unless you want it to update each time the document is opened. Click OK.

DRILL 1   INSERT DATE AND TIME

1. In a new document, key your name and right-align it; then tap ENTER.

2. Insert the date in the month/day/year format highlighted above and tap ENTER. Note that the date is right aligned.

3. Insert the time in hour/minute format. Tap ENTER.

4. Key the text shown below. Left-align the text.

5. Check the document and close it. *(28-drill1)*

The date shown above illustrates common business format. The time format also illustrates common business format; however, some businesses prefer to use lowercase (p.m.) for time format. The 4/20/2009 3:35 PM format is often used in tables or with statistical material.

DRILL 1 — FOOTNOTES

1. Key the paragraph in Drill 2. Insert the three footnotes. Tap ENTER once between each footnote.
2. Key all three sources on a separate Reference page in proper reference format.
3. Select the title *References* and apply the Title style.
4. Check and close the document. (*43-drill1*)

DRILL 2 — DELETE FOOTNOTES

1. Return to the document you just saved and closed (*43-drill1*).
2. Delete the second footnote.
3. Update the Reference page.
4. Check and close the document. (*43-drill2*)

Payton Devaul set the school record for points in a game—50[1]. He holds six statewide records. This makes him one of the top ten athletes in the school's history.[2] He expects to receive a basketball scholarship at an outstanding university.[3]

Footnotes

[1]Marshall Baker, *High School Athletic Records* (Seattle: Sports Press, 2007), p. 41.

[2]Lori Guo-Patterson, "Top Ten Athletes," *The Sports Journal*, Spring 2008, http://www.tsj.edu/athletes/topten.htm (accessed June 25, 2008).

[3]Payton Devaul, pdevaul@mail.com "Basketball Scholarship," January 9, 2008, e-mail to Kirk Stennis (accessed April 15, 2008).

References

Baker, Marshall. *High School Athletic Records*. Seattle: Sports Press, 2007.

Guo-Patterson, Lori. "Top Ten High School Athletes." *The Sports Journal*. Spring 2008. http://www.tsj.edu/athletes/topten.htm (accessed June 25, 2008).

Devaul, Payton, pdevaul@mail.com "Basketball Scholarship." January 9, 2008, e-mail to Kirk Stennis (accessed April 15, 2008).

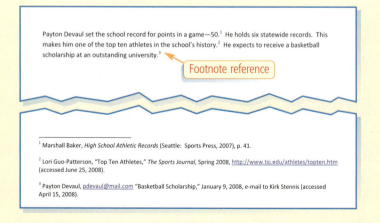

Payton Devaul set the school record for points in a game—50.[1] He holds six statewide records. This makes him one of the top ten athletes in the school's history.[2] He expects to receive a basketball scholarship at an outstanding university.[3]

Footnote reference

[1] Marshall Baker, *High School Athletic Records* (Seattle: Sports Press, 2007), p. 41.

[2] Lori Guo-Patterson, "Top Ten Athletes," *The Sports Journal*, Spring 2008, http://www.tsj.edu/athletes/topten.htm (accessed June 25, 2008).

[3] Payton Devaul, pdevaul@mail.com "Basketball Scholarship," January 9, 2008, e-mail to Kirk Stennis (accessed April 15, 2008).

2"

Title Style

References

Baker, Marshall. *High School Athletic Records*. Seattle: Sports Press, 2007.

Devaul, Payton, pdevaul@mail.com "Basketball Scholarship." January 9, 2008, e-mail to Kirk Stennis (accessed April 15, 2008).

Guo-Patterson, Lori. "Top Ten Athletes." *The Sports Journal*. Spring 2008. http://www.tsj.edu/athletes/topten.htm (accessed June 25, 2008).

Hanging indent

MARGINS

PAGE LAYOUT/PAGE SETUP/MARGINS

 Margins are the distance between the edge of the paper and the print. The default margins for *Word 2007* are 1" at the top, bottom, right, and left. Note that the default margins are called Normal. If you want to fit more information on a page, you might select Narrow margins. Or if you have a limited amount of information, you might select Wide margins. You could select Office 2003 Default or set a custom style to format leftbound reports.

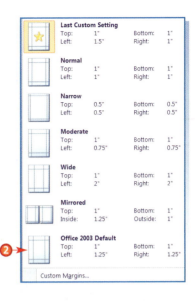

To change margins:

1. From the Page Layout tab in the Page Setup Group, click the down arrow on the Margins command ① to display the gallery of margins options.
2. Click the desired margins option ②.

DRILL 2 — CHANGE MARGINS

1. Open *28-drill1*. In *Keyboarding Pro DELUXE*, select Drill 2 from the Lesson menu; *28-drill1* will open automatically. Click Margins and then click Narrow. Note how the appearance of the document changes.

2. Click Wide margins and note the difference in appearance.

3. Click Office 2003 default. Note that 1.25" side margins make very little difference in document appearance than the 1.0" side margins of *Word 2007*.

4. Check and close. (*28-drill2*)

INDENT

PAGE LAYOUT/PARAGRAPH/INDENT

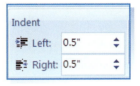 The Indent command indents all lines in the paragraph to the same point. Text can be indented from both the left and right sides. Remember that the TAB key only indents the first line.

To indent text:

1. Click the Indent command.
2. Click the up arrows on both the left and right side to increase them to .5".

DRILL 3 — INDENT TEXT

1. In a new document, key your name on the first line and right-align it.

2. Insert the date on the line below using the default format (mm/dd/yyyy).

3. Tap ENTER twice and key the title, **EFFECTIVE FORMATTING**. Center it and tap ENTER.

4. Apply Justify and key all text shown on the next page. Do not make any other format changes until all text has been keyed.

5. Apply Times New Roman, bold, 14-point font to the title.

6. Click in the second paragraph and indent it .5" on both the left and right sides.

7. Check and close. (*28-drill3*)

NEW FUNCTIONS

43d

FOOTNOTES

REFERENCES/FOOTNOTES/INSERT FOOTNOTE

Insert Footnote

References cited in a report are often indicated within the text by a superscript number (...story.[1]) and a corresponding footnote with full information at the bottom of the same page where the reference was cited.

Word automatically numbers footnotes sequentially with Arabic numerals (1, 2, 3), positions them at the left margin, and applies 10-point type. A footnote is positioned the same as the paragraph of the report. In a single-spaced or 1.15 line spacing report, the paragraphs and the footnotes are not indented. However, if the report is double-spaced and paragraphs indented, tap the TAB key to indent the footnote 0.5" from the left margin.

A footnote divider line is automatically added above the first footnote on each page. Tap the ENTER key once to add one blank line between footnotes.

To insert and edit footnotes:

REFERENCES/FOOTNOTES/INSERT FOOTNOTE

1. Switch to Print Layout view if not in Print Layout View ①.

2. Position the insertion point in the document where the footnote reference is to be inserted ②.

3. Click the References tab ③.

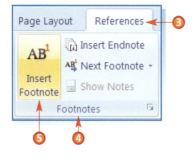

4. Choose the Footnotes group ④.

5. Click Insert Footnote ⑤.

6. The reference number and the insertion point appear at the bottom of the page. Key the footnote ⑥.

7. Click anywhere above the footnote divider line to return to the document ⑦.

To edit a footnote, click in the footnote at the bottom of the page and make the revision. To delete a footnote, select the reference number in the text and tap DELETE.

Good formatting produces a document with a professional image and helps to make a good first impression. However, appearance is only one of many reasons to format documents effectively. My instructor said:

Indent   Effective formatting improves the readability of a document. It also adds structure and makes the document easier to understand. In addition, the format can be used to indicate which ideas are more important than other ideas.   Indent

My textbook makes many of the same points that my instructor made. It emphasizes that formatting documents appropriately is an important part of communicating effectively. Although the default formats of *Word 2003* and those of *Word 2007* are quite different, you can format documents effectively using the defaults of either software version.

RULER

Some commands are easier to use if the Vertical and Horizontal Rulers are displayed. If your ruler is not displayed, click the View Ruler button at the top of the scroll bars on the top right side of the screen. The Ruler will display. The Ruler can be displayed from any of the Command tabs at the top of the ribbon (Home, Insert, Page Layout, etc.). The numbers on the Horizontal Ruler indicate the distance in inches from the left margin.

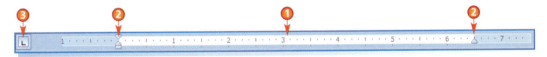

❶ Line of writing—the white area of the Ruler.

❷ Indent markers—the markers at each end of the line of writing.

❸ Tab alignment marker—the *L* at the left side of the rule is the Left tab alignment marker. Clicking the Tab Alignment marker will cause the tab to change to other types of tabs.

In the last drill, you indented text from both the right and left sides by using the Indent command. You can also indent text by dragging the markers at each end of the line of writing.

Note that the Indent markers on the line of writing shown on the Ruler below have moved in .5" on each side.

 KEYBOARDING PRO DELUXE See References/Word commands/Lesson 28

WARMUP 43a

Key each line, striving for control. Repeat if desired.

alphabet 1 Melva Bragg required exactly a dozen jackets for the winter trip.

figures 2 The 1903 copy of my book had 5 parts, 48 chapters, and 672 pages.

direct reach 3 Olga, the French goalie, defended well against the frazzled team.

easy 4 Rodney and a neighbor may go to the dock with us to work for Ken.

| 1 | 2 | 3 | 4 | 5 | 6 | 7 | 8 | 9 | 10 | 11 | 12 | 13 |

SKILL BUILDING

43b Timed Writing
1. Key a 1' timed writing on each paragraph; work to increase speed.
2. Key a 3' timed writing on both paragraphs.

all letters

	gwam	1'	3'

Did you know there are only small differences among a role model, 13 | 5 | 51

mentor, and sponsor? A role model is one who provides an excellent 27 | 9 | 56

example for others to follow. A mentor is one who gives good advice 40 | 14 | 60

when you have job questions. A sponsor is a person who will support 54 | 19 | 65

you for a job or a new job responsibility. 63 | 22 | 68

One person may fill all three roles, or several people may serve as 15 | 26 | 73

role models, mentors, or sponsors. These persons usually have higher 29 | 31 | 77

ranks than you do, which means they will be able to get information 43 | 36 | 82

that you and your zealous peers may not have. Often a mentor will 56 | 40 | 87

share information with you that will help you to make good decisions 70 | 45 | 91

about your career. 74 | 46 | 93

| 1' | 1 | 2 | 3 | 4 | 5 | 6 | 7 | 8 | 9 | 10 | 11 | 12 | 13 |
| 3' | | 1 | | | 2 | | | 3 | | | 4 | | |

COMMUNICATION

43c Proofread Report

RESOURCES

1. In the open document, proofread the report for consistency. First, print the report and mark any errors you locate on the printed copy. As an editor, you will want to use the proofreaders' marks shown on page 55 to mark the corrections. In the upper-right corner, write the following: **Your Name, Editor**.

2. Exchange reports with a classmate. Then make the corrections indicated on your classmate's edited report. If you do not agree with his/her edits, discuss the questioned items and reach an agreement. Make the final edits.

3. At the end of the corrected report, key the following:

   a. Corrections made by: **Your Name**

   b. 1st Editor: **Your Classmate's Name**

4. Check and close. (*43c*)

5. Submit the report you marked in step 1 and the report you corrected in step 2. (Team Goal: Correct all errors.)

TABS

Document tabs can be set and cleared on the Horizontal Ruler. The small gray lines below each half-inch position are the default tab stops. The Tab Alignment button at the left edge of the Ruler indicates the type of tab. Tabs can be set in a document to align text vertically.

Word has five types of tabs.

 ❶ Left Tab	Aligns text at the left.
❷ Center Tab	Aligns text evenly on both sides of the tab stop.
❸ Right Tab	Aligns text at the right.
Decimal Tab	Aligns numbers at the decimal point.
Bar Tab	Aligns text to the right of a vertical bar.

Alignment button →

To set a tab: Click the Alignment button, select desired type, and then click Horizontal Ruler where you want to set the tab.

To delete a tab: Click the tab marker on the Ruler, and drag it straight down.

To move a tab: Click the tab marker on the Ruler, and drag it to the new location.

DRILL 4 — SET AND MOVE TABS

1. On the Horizontal Ruler, set a left tab at 1", a center tab at 3.25", and a right tab at 5.5". (See ruler above.)

2. Key the first three lines of the drill below. Tap TAB at the beginning of each line. Tap ENTER twice after the third line.

3. Drag the left tab to 1.5" and the right tab to 5". Key the last three lines; note they will not align with the first three lines as shown in the illustration.

4. Check and close. (*28-drill4*)

	Left Tab 1"	Center Tab 3.25"	Right Tab 5.5"
(Tap TAB)	Largest player	324	Offensive tackle
	Average	255.5	Team
	Smallest player	165	Punter

	Left Tab 1.5"	Center Tab 3.25"	Right Tab 5"
Reset Tabs (Tap TAB)	Tallest player	6'6"	Tight end
	Average	6'	Team
	Shortest player	5'10"	Running back

Guidelines for Business Dress

Companies are employing image consultants to teach employees what is appropriate business casual and to plan the best business attire to project the corporate image. Erica Gilreath (2008), the author of *Casual Dress*, a guidebook on business casual, provides excellent advice on how to dress casually and still command the power needed for business success. She presents the following advice to professionals:

- Do not wear any clothing that is designed for recreational or sports activities, e.g., cargo pants or pants with elastic waist.

- Invest the time in pressing khakis and shirts or pay the price for professional dry cleaning. Wrinkled clothing does not enhance one's credibility.

- Do not wear sneakers.

- Be sure clothing fits properly. Avoid baggy clothes or clothes that are too tight.

In summary, energetic employees working to climb the corporate ladder will need to plan their dress carefully. If business casual is appropriate, it is best to consult the experts on business casual to ensure a professional image.

References

Gilreath, Erica. "Dressing Casually with Power." http://www.casualdress.com (accessed March 23, 2008).

Monaghan, Margaret. "Business Dress Codes May Be Shifting." *Business Executive.* April 2008, 34-35.

Sutphin, Rachel. "Your Business Wardrobe Decisions Are Important Decisions." *Business Management Journal.* January 2007, 10-12.

Tartt, Kelsey. "Companies Support Business Casual Dress." *Management Success.* June 2005, 23-25.

1. Prepare a title page for the unbound report completed in *42-d2*. Use the Cover Page feature to create the title page. Choose the Alphabet style from the Built-In category of the Cover Page gallery.

2. Key the following information:

   Document title: Refer to title of *42-d2*.

   Document subtitle: **For All Employees**

   Author name: **Your name, Image Consultant**

3. Check and close. (*42-d3*)

28-d1

Heading, Date, Tabs

1. Tap ENTER three times; then key the title. Insert the date on the next line as a subheading using day/month/date/year format.
2. Tap ENTER and key the first paragraph using Times New Roman, 12-point font.
3. Set a left tab at 1", a center tab at 3.25", and a right tab at 5.5".
4. Key the remainder of the document.
5. Format the title and the date as indicated.
6. Check and close. (28-d1)

Arial, 14 point bold center ————————————→ Preseason Starting Lineup

Times New Roman 12 point bold, center ————————————→ *Current Date*

The head coach named the preseason starting lineup today. She said that the positions were very competitive and might not be the same when the season started.

Power forward	6'1"	Shawna Kulchar
Small forward	6'	Larissa Perovic
Center	6'3"	Olga Gortman
Shooting guard	5'10"	Tonisha Burgess
Point guard	5'9"	Sara Penn

28-d2

Heading, Indent, Date

1. Tap ENTER three times; then key the entire document shown below.
2. Indent the second paragraph .5" from the left and right sides.
3. Insert the date and time right-aligned on the line below the last paragraph; use 00/00/0000 00:00 PM format.
4. Check and close. (28-d2)

Weekly Report (Cambria, 16-point bold)

The head football coach spoke with reporters at his weekly news conference. He was asked about the summer workout program and seemed to be very frustrated with some of his student-athletes. The coach said:

> Summer workouts are voluntary programs, and it is against the rules to require student-athletes to participate. However, the workouts are a good way to judge the commitment level of your players. Some of our players are very committed and are very likely to get playing time. Others are lazy, and it is doubtful they will be ready to play when the season begins.

In response to a reporter's question, he indicated only about a dozen of the 85 scholarship players did not show up regularly. The goal of the program is to improve conditioning and lessen the likelihood of injuries.

42-d1

Reference Page

1. Open *41-d1*.
2. Position the insertion point at the end of the report. Insert a manual page break to begin a new page. Key **References** approximately 2" from the top of the page; apply the Title style.
3. Key the references in hanging indent style. (**Hint:** Try the shortcut, CTRL + T.)
4. Check and close. (*42-d1*)

Millsaps, John. *Communicating in Business*. 3rd ed. Philadelphia: Dyess and Dubose Business Press, 2008, 12-14.

Quattlebaum, Sarah E. "Formatting Electronic References." *Computer Weekly*. December 2008, 155-159.

42-d2

Leftbound Report

1. Key the following leftbound report; indent the long quotation 0.5" from the left margin.
2. Number the pages at the top right; suppress the page number on the first page.
3. Key the references on a Reference page at the end of the report.
4. Check for side headings left alone at the bottom of the page.
5. Check and close. (*42-d2*)

TIP

Reminder: Use the Plain Number 3 format for page numbers in a header as the default.

Trends for Business Dress

Casual dress in the workplace has become widely accepted. According to a national study conducted by Schoenholtz & Associates, a majority of the companies surveyed allowed employees to dress casually one day a week, usually Fridays (Tartt, 2005, 23). The trend continued to climb as shown by the 2006 survey by Schoenholtz & Associates. Fifty-eight percent of office workers surveyed were allowed to dress casually for work every day, and 92 percent of the offices allowed employees to dress casually occasionally (Sutphin, 2007, 10).

Decline in Trend

The trend to dress casually may be shifting, states Susan Monaghan (2008, 34):

Although a large number of companies are allowing casual attire every day or only on Fridays, a current survey revealed a decline of 10 percent in 2008 when compared to the same survey conducted in 2007. Some experts predict the new trend for business dress codes will be a dress up day every week.

What accounts for this decline in companies permitting casual dress? Several reasons may include:

1. Confusion of what business casual is with employees slipping into dressing too casually (work jeans, faded tee-shirts, old sneakers, and improperly fitting clothing).

2. Casual dress does not portray the adopted corporate image of the company.

3. Employees are realizing that promotion decisions are affected by a professional appearance.

continued

LESSON 29 | Editing Essentials

WARMUP 29a

Key each line, striving for control. Repeat if desired.

alphabet 1 JoQuin and Zola packed five large boxes for their weekly meeting.
fig/symbol 2 I bought 48 crabs, 50# of shrimp, and 26 fish ($1,397 @ 10% off).
double letters 3 All planning committees have four dinner meetings with key staff.
easy 4 Bud got the tub of big worms to go to the dock to fish with them.

SKILL BUILDING

29b Textbook Keying
Key each line once, concentrating on using good keying techniques. Tap ENTER twice after each 3-line group.

Direct reach words, phrases, and sentences

5 hung deck jump cent slope decide hunt serve polo brave cedar pump
6 no way | in tune | many times | jump in | funny times | gold plated | in sync
7 June and Cecil browsed in craft shops and found many funny gifts.

Adjacent reach words, phrases, and sentences

8 were pop safe sad quick column tree drew opinion excite guy point
9 we are | boil over | are we | few rewards | short trek | where are we going
10 Bert said he tries to shop where we can buy gas, oil, and treats.

29c Textbook Keying
Key each line once, striving for fluency.

11 Ken may go to the big lake to fish for sockeye and dig for clams.
12 Jan may go with us to visit the ancient chapel on the big island.
13 Their goal is to fix the bicycle or dismantle it to fit in a box.
14 A cow roams the cornfield, and fox, quail, and duck also roam it.
15 A neighbor bid by proxy for eighty bushels of corn and rye blend.

NEW FUNCTIONS

29d

NAVIGATE AND VIEW A DOCUMENT

The document window displays only a portion of a page at one time. The keyboard, mouse, and scroll bars can be used to move quickly through a document to view it.

Keyboard options—press CTRL + HOME to go to the beginning of a document and CTRL + END to move to the end of the document. The Page Up and Page Dn keys can also be used to move through a document.

Mouse—use the scroll bars to move through the document. Scrolling does not change the position of the insertion point; it only changes your view of the document. You must click in the text to change the position of the insertion point.

1. Key the text below.
2. Place the insertion point after the first set of goals. Insert a manual page break.
3. Continue keying page 2.

4. Use the Page Number command to insert a number at the top of the page. Use Plain Number 3 as the default style. Do not print number on the first page.
5. Check and close. (*42-drill4*)

Goal 1: Membership Development

Objective: To increase membership.

Indent ──▶ **Plan**

     A. Review and evaluate membership benefits.
     B. Study avenues for additional membership benefits.

◀── **Insert page break.**

Goal 2: Staff Development

Objective: To enhance performance and motivation of staff.

Indent ──▶ **Plan**

     A. Review and evaluate previous staff development programs.
     B. Survey staff to determine needs.
     C. Implement relevant staff development programs.

DOCUMENT DESIGN

REFERENCE PAGE

References cited in the report are listed at the end of the report in alphabetical order by authors' last names. The reference list may be titled References or Bibliography; apply the Title style to the reference page title.

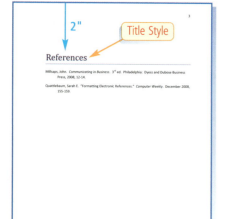

2" Title Style

References

Millsaps, John. *Communicating in Business.* 3rd ed. Philadelphia: Dyess and Dubose Business Press, 2008, 12-14.

Quattlebaum, Sarah E. "Formatting Electronic References." *Computer Weekly.* December 2008, 155-159.

Become familiar with the three types of references listed below:

1. A book reference includes the name of the author (last name first), work (italicized), city of publication, publisher, and copyright date.

2. A magazine reference shows the name of the author (last name first), article (in quotation marks), magazine title (italicized), date of publication, and page references.

3. A reference retrieved electronically includes the author (inverted), article (in quotation marks), publication (italicized), publication information, Internet address, and date the document was retrieved or accessed (in parentheses).

Begin the list of references on a new page by inserting a manual page break at the end of the report. Begin the title of the reference page at approximately 2" from the top of the page (same as the first page of the report). Number the reference page at the top right of the page. References are keyed in the hanging indent format; tap ENTER once between references.

SCROLL BAR AND VIEWS

The vertical and horizontal scroll bars are located on the lower-right side of the screen.

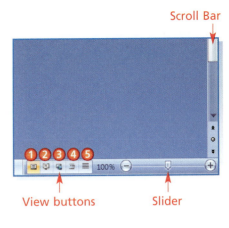
Scroll Bar

To move through a document:

- Click above or below the scroll bar. -or-
- Click the bar and drag it to the desired position. -or-
- Click the up and down arrows.

View buttons   Slider

Slider—used to zoom in and out on a document. Note that the Slider is positioned in the center of the bar, which shows text at 100% of its actual size.

To view smaller or larger versions of text:

1. To view a larger version of a segment of text, move the Slider toward the right or the positive (+) side. The text will be larger, but you see a smaller segment of it.

2. To see more of the document at one time, move the Slider toward the left or the negative (–) side. If you move the Slider to about 50%, you can probably see two full pages of a document.

Views—display document in different formats. The view that is selected when you save and close a document will be the view that displays when that document is opened again. Views can be accessed by clicking the view on the status bar or the View tab.

1. **Print Layout**—this shows the document as it will look when it is printed.

2. **Full Screen Reading**—this view uses the full screen to display the document. To return to the Normal view, click Close ❻ at the top right side of the screen.

3. **Web Layout**—shows the document as it will appear on the Web.

4. **Master Document Tools**—displays the document in outline format.

5. **Draft**—displays the document without graphics and formatting.

KEYBOARDING PRO DELUXE ▸ See References/Word commands/Lesson 29

DRILL 1   NAVIGATING AND VIEWING A DOCUMENT

1. In *27-d1*, move to the last line of the document; select the document name, and replace it with *29-drill1*.

2. Use the keyboard to move up and down through the document. Press CTRL + END to move to the end of the document; then press CTRL + HOME to go to the beginning of it.

3. Use the mouse, the scroll bar, and the up and down arrows to move in the document.

4. Move the Slider to the left to 50% and view the document; then move it to 200% and view the document.

5. Move the Slider back to the center at 100%.

6. Click each View button and check the document in that view; leave the document in Print Layout view.

7. Check and close. (*29-drill1*).

Godo, Eiko and Krystol McCurdy. *The Style Manual.* 6th ed. Boston: Blackwell and Johnson Publishers, 2008.

Osaji, Allison. "Know the Credibility of Electronic Citations." *Graduate Education Journal.* November 2008, 93-97.

Raybon, Charles R. "Software Helps Writers Apply Correct Style." *Writing Style Journal.* Fall 2008. http://www.writers.com/softwareandstyle.htm (accessed November 10, 2008).

Walters, Daniel S. dswalters2@umt.edu "Final Report Available on Intranet." August 11, 2008, e-mail to Stephen P. Cobb (accessed September 14, 2008).

DRILL 2 — FORMAT TEXT WITH HANGING INDENT — REFERENCES

1. In the open document, select the references and format them with a hanging indent. (**Hint:** Try the shortcut.)

2. Check and close. *(42-drill2)*

DRILL 3 — FORMAT TEXT WITH HANGING INDENT — GLOSSARY

1. In the open document, select all the glossary entries, and format them with a hanging indent.

2. Check and close. *(42-drill3)*

MANUAL PAGE BREAK

INSERT/PAGES/PAGE BREAK

When a page is filled with copy, the software automatically inserts a soft page break, which is indicated with a dotted line across the page when you are in Draft View. You may need to begin a new page, however, before the page is filled. To begin a new page, you must insert a manual page break.

To insert a manual page break:

1. From the Insert tab in the Pages group, click Page Break ❶.

2. The insertion point moves to the next page; the status line at the bottom of the screen indicates this change.

   (**Shortcut:** CTRL + ENTER)

A manual page break will not move as text is inserted or deleted. To remove a manual page break, position the insertion point at the beginning of the page after the page break and tap the BACKSPACE key.

 KEYBOARDING PRO DELUXE See References/Word commands/Lesson 42

SPELLING AND GRAMMAR OPTIONS

Three options are available for detecting errors in your documents.

axtual (spelling or keying)

It are to late. (Grammar and contextual)

1. Color-coded squiggly lines appear in your text as you key. Red indicates spelling or keying errors, green indicates grammar errors, and blue indicates contextual errors such as using *to* for *two* or *too*. Correct these errors as you key.

2. The Grammar and Spelling status is shown in the status bar at the bottom of the screen. The pen shows it is still checking. The ✗ indicates the document has errors. The ✓ indicates the document is error free.

ABC ✓

Spelling & Grammar

3. On the Review tab click Spelling & Grammar to display the Spelling and Grammar dialog box. You can either click Ignore Once or Change to correct the error. This feature is generally used to check the entire document at once. Note that many errors you make keying are corrected automatically by a function called AutoCorrect.

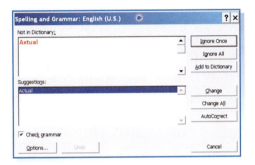

HELP

Help is installed on your computer when *Office 2007* is installed and more extensive help can also be accessed from *Office Online*.

To access *Word* Help:

1. Tap the **F1** key.

   -or-

2. Click the **Help** button ❶ at the top right of the screen.

3. In the *Word* Help search box ❷, key the topic on which you need help.

4. To access Help if you are not connected to the Internet, click the down arrow on Search ❸ and click Word Help under Content from this computer ❹.

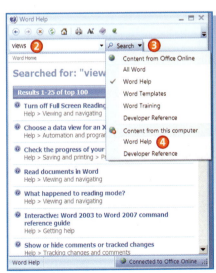

LESSON 42 | Report with Reference Page

WARMUP 42a

Key each line, striving for control. Repeat if desired.

alphabet	1	Two exit signs jut quietly above the beams of a razed skyscraper.
figures	2	Send 345 of the 789 sets now; send the others on August 1 and 26.
direct reach	3	I obtain many junk pieces dumped by Marvyn at my service centers.
easy	4	Enrique may fish for cod by the dock; he also may risk a penalty.

| 1 | 2 | 3 | 4 | 5 | 6 | 7 | 8 | 9 | 10 | 11 | 12 | 13 |

SKILL BUILDING

42b Timed Writing

1. Key a 1' timed writing on each paragraph; work to increase speed.
2. Key a 3' timed writing on all paragraphs.

LA

all letters

	gwam	1'	3'
Does a relationship exist between confidence and success? If		12	4	42
you think it does, you will find that many people agree with you.		26	9	46
However, it is very hard to judge just how strong the bond is.		38	13	50
When people are confident they can do a job, they are very		12	17	54
likely to continue working on that task until they complete it		24	21	58
correctly. If they are not confident, they give up much quicker.		38	25	63
People who are confident they can do something tend to enjoy		12	29	67
doing it more than those who lack confidence. They realize that		25	34	71
they do better work when they are happy with what they do.		37	37	75

| 1' | 1 | 2 | 3 | 4 | 5 | 6 | 7 | 8 | 9 | 10 | 11 | 12 | 13 |
| 3' | | 1 | | | 2 | | | 3 | | | 4 | | |

NEW FUNCTIONS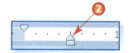

42c

HANGING INDENT

Hanging indent places the first line of a paragraph at the left margin and indents all other lines to the first tab. It is commonly used to format bibliography entries, glossaries, and lists. Hanging indent can be applied before text is keyed or after.

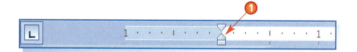

To create a hanging indent:

1. From the Horizontal Ruler, click the hanging indent marker ❶.
2. Drag the Hanging Indent marker ❷ to the position where the indent is to begin.
3. Key the paragraph. The second and subsequent lines are indented beginning at the marker. (**Shortcut:** CTRL + T, then key the paragraph; or select the paragraphs to be formatted as hanging indents and press CTRL + T.)

DRILL 1   HANGING INDENT

1. Drag the Hanging Indent marker to 0.5" to the right; then key the references on the following page.

2. Turn Hanging Indent off by dragging the Hanging Indent marker back to the left margin.

3. Check and close the document. (*42-drill1*)

1. Key the paragraphs, filling in the information indicated.
2. Print the document; proofread it and mark any corrections needed using proofreaders' marks.

3. Correct the document. *(29-drill2)*

Review proofreaders' marks in Lesson 23, page 55.

My name is (*student's name*). I am a (*class level*) at (*school*) located on (*street*) in (*city, state*). In addition to (*name of this course*), I am also enrolled in (*names of other courses; modify sentence if you are not enrolled in any other courses*). My instructor in this course is (*title and name*).

The reason I enrolled in this course is (*complete sentence*). What I like most about this course is (*complete sentence*). What I like least about this course is (*complete sentence*).

1. Key the nine sentences (tap ENTER after each sentence) and the following paragraph shown below. Make the edits indicated by the proofreaders' marks. Use Help if needed.

2. Proofread and correct any errors.
3. Use Spelling and Grammar.
4. Check and close. *(29-drill3)*

DISCOVER

Insert/Delete—to insert text, click in the document at the point you wish to insert text and key the text.

To delete text, select the text and tap the DELETE key.

Do you assess you**r** writing skills as average, great, or mediocre?

You should also ask your instructor ~~about~~ *to assess* your writing skills.

Your instructor ~~will know~~ *may teach you* how to ~~greatly~~ improve your writing skills.

Do you ~~always~~ *take the time to* edit and proofread carefully things that you write?

A few people who do not bother to edit the**i**r work are good writers.

Learning to edit effective*ly* may be just as important as writing well.

Another question to ask *answer* is: how important are writing skills?

G**r**eat writing skills are needed to be successful in ~~most~~ *many* careers.

You can improve your writing skills **by** making it a priorit*e*y *to do so*.

Judge your writing ~~only~~ *after* if you have proofread and edited your work.

stet Take the time to *carefully* evaluate your completed work. Is the copy forma**t**ted attractively? Does it read ~~good~~ *well*? **h**ave your corrected all grammar and spelling errors**?** If your work does not impress you, it will not impress any one else.

journals, e-mail messages, and other sources. Use the style manuals and other electronic resources made available to assist writers in this important task.

With the availability and volume of excellent electronic resources, writers are including a number of electronic citations along with printed journals, books, and newspapers. Sarah Quattlebaum (2008, 159) writes:

> Electronic citations may include online journal articles or abstracts, articles on CD-ROM, e-mail messages, discussion list messages, etc. To format references for documents retrieved electronically, include the author (if given), date of publication, title of article, name of publication, URL, and date document was retrieved from the Internet.

Summary

Experienced writers understand the importance of selecting credible resources, documenting references in the report, and applying the exact reference style required for the report. Learning to document your references accurately is an important step toward becoming an experienced writer.

29-d1

Rough Draft

1. Key the document below, making all edits indicated by the proofreaders' marks on the copy. Use the editing tools you have learned in this module. Use Help if needed.

2. Add the title, **STANDARD OPERATING PROCEDURES** and subtitle, **Document Production**; apply Cambria bold font to both; use 14 point for the title and 12 point for the subtitle.

3. Proofread; check spelling and grammar; correct errors; check and close. (*29-d1*)

Following standard operating procedures designed for this *lc* Keyboarding *lc* Course will enhance productivity and eliminate the need to repeat directions for each activity. These procedures will also ensure that documents are prepared in a consistent manner, and managed *the files are* appropriately.

Use Cambria, 11 point Bold → Procedures for *Keyboarding Pro DELUXE* Users

Change bullet format to round

- Select an activity to open a new *word* document or a data file.

- Use the Back and Check buttons to easily manage your files.

Use Cambria, 11 point Bold → Procedures for Non-*Keyboarding Pro DELUXE* Users

Change bullet format to round

- Prepare a folder for each module with the name of the module to store all documents for that module.

- Save each document with the lesson number and drill or application name (*29-drill1* or *29-d1*).

- Open a data file as soon as you see a CD icon plus *a* filename (*fitness*) and save it immediately with the drill or application name in which it is used.

Use Cambria, 11 point Bold → Procedures for Both *Keyboarding Pro DELUXE* and Non-*Keyboarding Pro DELUXE* Users

Change numbers to bullets

1. Preview, proofread, and print each document as soon as you complete it.

2. Prepare an envelope when you key a letter. *for each letter*

3. Add your reference initials at the bottom of each letter or memo that does not have your name as the signature.

4. Add an Enclosure or Attachment notation if the document contains one. *refers to materials being enclosed or attached*

Documentation in Report Writing

Preparing a thorough and convincing report requires excellent research, organization, and composition skills as well as extensive knowledge of documenting referenced materials. The purpose of this report is to present the importance of documenting a report with credible references and the techniques for creating accurate citations.

Documenting with References

For a report to be credible and accepted by its readers, a thorough review of related literature is essential. This background information is an important part of the report and provides believability of the writer and of the report. When sharing this literature in the body of the report, the writer understands the following basic principles of report documentation:

1½"

1"

- All ideas of others must be cited so that credit is given appropriately.
- The reader will need to be able to locate the material using the information included in the reference citation.
- Format rules apply to ideas stated as direct quotations and ideas that are paraphrased.
- Use the citations and bibliographic features of contemporary word processing software to assist to apply manuscript styles appropriately.
- A thorough list of references adds integrity to the report and to its author.

Good writers learn quickly how to evaluate the many printed and electronic references that have been located to support the theme of their reports. Those references judged acceptable are then cited in the report. Writer John Millsaps (2008, 12) shares this simple advice:

Indented Long Quotation →

Today writers can locate a vast number of references in very little time. Electronic databases and Internet Web pages are very easy to locate and provide a multitude of information. The novice writer will be quick to include all these references in a report without verifying their credibility. Just as writers verify the value of printed sources, experienced writers check electronic sources as well.

Using a Style Manual

Three popular style manuals are the *MLA Handbook*, *The Chicago Manual of Style*, and the *Publication Manual of the American Psychological Association*. After selecting a style, carefully study the acceptable formats for citing books, magazines, newspapers, brochures, online

WARMUP 30a

Key each line, striving for control. Repeat if desired.

alphabet 1 Gay expected to solve the jigsaw puzzle more quickly than before.

figures 2 Jane opened Rooms 16, 20, and 39 and locked Rooms 48, 53, and 57.

shift 3 Ted and I spent April in San Juan and May in St. Paul, Minnesota.

easy 4 The island is the shape of a big sleigh. Jamal got clams for us.

SKILL BUILDING

30b Timed Writing
Key two 3' timed writings.

all letters

	gwam	3'

I have an interesting story or two that will transport you to   4 | 53

faraway places, to meet people you have never known, to see   8 | 57

things you have never seen, to experience things available only to   13 | 61

a select few. I can help you master appropriate skills you desire   17 | 66

and need; I can inspire you, excite you, instruct you, challenge   22 | 70

you, and entertain you. I answer your questions. I work with you   26 | 75

to realize a talent, to express a thought, and to determine just who   31 | 79

and what you really are and want to be. I help you to understand   35 | 84

words, to write, and to read. I help you to discover the mysteries   40 | 88

of the past and the secrets of the future. I am your library. I hope   44 | 93

I shall see you regularly. You are very likely to find me online.   49 | 97

3' | 1 | 2 | 3 | 4 |

APPLICATIONS

30c

Assessment

Continue

Check

With *Keyboarding Pro DELUXE*: When you complete a document, proofread it, check the spelling, and preview for placement. When you are completely satisfied, click the Continue button to move to the next document. Click the Check button when you are ready to error-check the test. Review and/or print the document analysis results.

Without *Keyboarding Pro DELUXE*: Key the documents in sequence. When time has been called, proofread all documents again and identify errors.

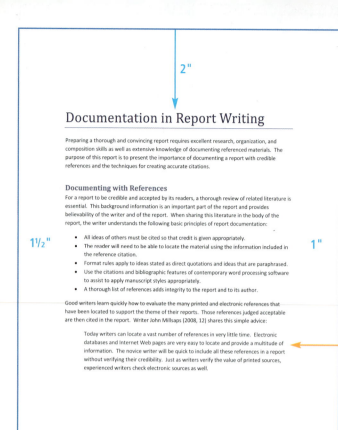

2"

Documentation in Report Writing

Preparing a thorough and convincing report requires excellent research, organization, and composition skills as well as extensive knowledge of documenting referenced materials. The purpose of this report is to present the importance of documenting a report with credible references and the techniques for creating accurate citations.

Documenting with References

For a report to be credible and accepted by its readers, a thorough review of related literature is essential. This background information is an important part of the report and provides believability of the writer and of the report. When sharing this literature in the body of the report, the writer understands the following basic principles of report documentation:

1½" **1"**

- All ideas of others must be cited so that credit is given appropriately.
- The reader will need to be able to locate the material using the information included in the reference citation.
- Format rules apply to ideas stated as direct quotations and ideas that are paraphrased.
- Use the citations and bibliographic features of contemporary word processing software to assist to apply manuscript styles appropriately.
- A thorough list of references adds integrity to the report and to its author.

Good writers learn quickly how to evaluate the many printed and electronic references that have been located to support the theme of their reports. Those references judged acceptable are then cited in the report. Writer John Millsaps (2008, 12) shares this simple advice:

> Today writers can locate a vast number of references in very little time. Electronic databases and Internet Web pages are very easy to locate and provide a multitude of information. The novice writer will be quick to include all these references in a report without verifying their credibility. Just as writers verify the value of printed sources, experienced writers check electronic sources as well.

Indented Long Quotation

LEFTBOUND REPORT

The binding on a report usually takes about 0.5" of space. Therefore, when a report is bound on the left, use a 1.5" left margin for all pages.

The same right, top, and bottom margins are used for both unbound and leftbound reports. Refer to the full-page model of the first page of a leftbound report on page 164. The second and subsequent pages would begin at 1" from the top of the page.

APPLICATIONS

41-d1

Leftbound Report with Long Quotation

1. Key the model leftbound report on pages 164–165. Use a 1.5" left margin.
2. Tap ENTER to position the title at about 2".
3. Indent the long quotations 0.5" from the left margin.
4. Insert page number to display in the upper-right corner; suppress page number on the first page.
5. Check for side headings alone at the bottom of the page.
6. Check and close. (*41-d1*)

41-d2

Cover Page

1. Prepare a cover page for *41-d1*. Use the Cover Page feature to create the title page. Choose the Alphabet style from the Built-In category of the Cover Page gallery.
2. Enter the following information:

   Document title: Refer to title of *41-d1*

   Document subtitle: **For Keyboarding Students**

   Author Name: Your name
3. Check and close. (*41-d2*).

30-d1
Rough Draft

TIP

Remember to proofread and preview each document before you move to the next one.

1. Tap ENTER three times; use double spacing and Wide margins.
2. Key the title, **YOU ARE WHAT YOU EAT** and apply Arial 14-point bold format, and center-align. Use Times New Roman 12-point font for the remainder of the document.
3. Key the document, making all edits indicated by the proofreaders' marks.
4. Set a right-align tab at 4"; key your name below the last line of the document; insert the date using standard business format directly below your name.
5. Remove the extra spacing after paragraphs including your name.
6. Proofread; use spelling and grammar; correct all errors; continue with next document. (30-d1)

A speaker said, "you are what you eat". the speaker didnot mean to imply that fast food make fast people, or that an hearty meal makes a person heart, or even that good food manes a person good? On the other hand, though, a healthfull diet does indeed make person healthier; and good health effects many things including performance, energy level, and attitude. Learning what to include in a healthful diet is the 1st step. The 2nd step is developing the discipline to apply that knowledge. The results are wellworth the effort. IN fact, good health may be one of the most often over looked treasures within human existance.

30-d2
Tabs

1. Tap ENTER three times. Key title centered; apply Cambria 16 point, bold font. Insert date directly below; apply Cambria 12 point, bold font.
2. Format remainder of document using default Calibri 11 point. Bold the headings *Name* and *Description*. Set a left tab at .5" and a right tab at 6.0". See tip at left.
3. Check the test and close. (30-d2)

TIP

You may have to undo the automatic capitals in the Name column. Point to the initial letter until the AutoCorrect Options button appears, click the button, and then choose the Undo option you see.

Internet Groups on Campus

Current date

Name	Description
webdes	Web page design topics
biz	Business administration majors
bioeng	Biomedical engineers
sprtmg	Sports management
marband	Marching band

CHECKPOINT →

Congratulations! You have successfully completed the lessons in Module 3. To check your understanding and for more practice, complete the objective assessment and performance assessment located on the textbook website at http://www.collegekeyboarding.com.

The thrust to use e-mail almost exclusively is causing a tremendous challenge for both e-mail recipients and companies.

Indent

With the convenience of electronic mail resulting in its widespread use, many users are forsaking other forms of communication—face-to-face, telephone (including voice mail), and printed documents. Now companies are challenged to create clear e-mail policies and to implement employee training on effective use of e-mail. (Ashford, 2008, 2)

Communication experts have identified problems that may occur as a result of misusing e-mail. Two important problems include information overload (too many messages) and inappropriate form of communication.

DOCUMENT DESIGN

REPORT DOCUMENTATION

Reports must include the sources of all information used in the report. Documentation gives credit for published material, whether electronic or printed, that is quoted or closely paraphrased by the writer. The writer may document sources by using footnotes, endnotes, or internal citations. In this module, you will use internal citations and footnotes.

At the end of the report, the writer provides the reader with a complete alphabetical listing of all references. This allows the interested reader to locate the original source. You will learn to format a reference list in Lesson 42.

INTERNAL CITATIONS

Internal citations are an easy and practical method of documentation. The last name of the author(s), the publication date, and the page numbers(s) of the cited material are shown in parentheses within the body of the report (Crawford, 2008, 134). This information cues a reader to the name Crawford in the reference list included at the end of the report. When the author's name is used in the text to introduce the quotation, only the year of publication and the page numbers appear in parentheses: "Crawford (2008, 134) said that…."

Short, direct quotations of three lines or fewer are enclosed within quotation marks. Long quotations of four lines or more are indented 0.5" from the left margin.

If a portion of the text that is referenced is omitted, use an ellipsis (…) to show the omission. An ellipsis is three periods, each preceded and followed by a space. If a period occurs at the end of a sentence, include the period or punctuation.

According to Estes (2008, 29), "Successful businesses have long known the importance of good verbal communication."

Short Quotation

Probably no successful enterprise exists that does not rely for its success upon the ability of its members to communicate:

Make no mistake, both written and verbal communication are the stuff upon which success is built in all types of organizations…. Both forms deserve careful study by any business that wants to grow. Successful businesspeople must read, write, speak, and listen with skill. Often professional development in these areas is needed. (Schaefer, 2008, 28)

Long Quotation

KEYBOARDING PRO DELUXE › SKILL BUILDING/ACCURACY EMPHASIS

1. Select the Skill Building tab, Accuracy Emphasis, and then Assessment 1.

2. Key the timing from the screen for 3'; work for control.

3. Complete Lesson A or the first lesson you have not completed in either Speed Emphasis or Accuracy Emphasis as suggested by the software.

4. Your results will be summarized in the Skill Building Report.

 KEYBOARDING PRO DELUXE › TIMED WRITINGS

Writing 23

1. Key a 1' writing on each paragraph. (Remember to change the source in the Timed Writing Settings dialog box.) Compare your *gwam* on the two paragraphs.

2. Key additional 1' writings on the slower paragraph.

	gwam	1'	3'
There are many qualities which cause good employees to stand		12	6
out in a group. In the first place, they keep their minds on the		25	13
task at hand. Also, they often think about the work they do and		38	19
how it relates to the total efforts of the project. They keep		52	26
their eyes, ears, and minds open to new ideas.		60	30
Second, good workers may be classed as those who work at a		13	6
steady pace. Far too many people work by bits and pieces. They		25	13
begin one thing, but then they allow themselves to be easily taken		39	19
away from the work at hand. A lot of people are good starters,		52	26
but many less of them are also good finishers.		60	30

1. Key the paragraph below and preview the document.

2. Position the insertion point at the beginning of sentence 4. Tap ENTER.

3. With the insertion point in paragraph 2, change the top and side margins to 2". Preview the document.

4. At the end of sentence 4, tap ENTER. Key and complete this sentence with the better response, (a) or (b).

   The margin command affects the appearance of the (a) entire document (b) paragraph containing the insertion point.

5. Check and close. (*41-drill1*)

6. Change the left, right, and top margins to 1.5". Apply margin settings to the whole document.

7. Check and close. (*41-drill2*)

Attractive document layout begins with margins set an equal distance from the left and right edges of the paper. When margins are equal, the document appears balanced. One exception to the equal-margin rule is in the formatting of reports bound at the left. To ensure the appearance of equal left and right margins in a leftbound report, you must add extra space to the left margin to allow for the binding.

INDENT

HOME/PARAGRAPH/INCREASE INDENT

 When a writer paraphrases or quotes material longer than three lines from another source, the quote must be set off from the rest of the report. Quoted material is set off by indenting it 0.5" from the left margin.

The Indent feature moves all lines of a paragraph to the next tab. In contrast, TAB moves only the first line of a paragraph to the next tab. Indent is a paragraph command. The Indent feature enables you to indent text from either the left or right margin or from both margins. You may apply an indent to text as you key or to text that has already been keyed.

Increase Indent

Decrease Indent

To indent text from the left margin:

1. From the Home tab in the Paragraph group, click the Increase Indent button ❶.

2. Key the paragraph and tap ENTER.

To decrease the left indent, click the Decrease Indent button.

 KEYBOARDING PRO DELUXE See References/Word commands/Lesson 41

DRILL 3   INDENT

1. Key the copy that follows on the next page.

2. To indent from the left margin, click Increase Indent.

3. For paragraph 3, click Decrease Indent.

4. Check and close. (*41-drill3*)

LESSON B

1. Select the Skill Building tab and choose either Speed Emphasis or Accuracy Emphasis as recommended in Assessment 1. Complete Lesson B.
2. Your results will be summarized in the Skill Building Report.

 SKILL BUILDING/TECHNIQUE BUILDER

DRILL 11

BALANCED-HAND COMBINATIONS
Key each line once, working for fluency. DS between groups.

1 to today stocks into ti times sitting until ur urges further tour
2 en entire trend dozen or order support editor nd and mandate land
3 he healthy check ache th these brother both an annual change plan
4 nt into continue want of office softer roof is issue poison basis

5 My brother urged the editor to have an annual health check today.
6 The manager will support the change to order our stock annually.
7 The time for the land tour will not change until further notice.
8 Did the letter mention her position or performance in the office?

 TIMED WRITINGS

1. Key a 1' writing on each paragraph. Compare your *gwam*.
2. Key additional 1' writings on the slower paragraph.

Writing 24

gwam 1' | 3'

Most of us, at some time, have had a valid reason to complain— 12 | 6
about a defective product, poor service, or perhaps being tired of 26 | 13
talking to voice mail. Many of us feel that complaining, however, 39 | 20
to a firm is an exercise in futility and don't bother to express 52 | 26
our dissatisfaction. We just write it off to experience and 64 | 32
continue to be ripped off. 70 | 35

Today, more than at anytime in the past consumers are taking some 12 | 6
steps to let their feelings be known—and with a great amount of 25 | 13
success. As a result, firms are becoming more responsive to 38 | 19
the needs of the consumer. complaints from customers alert firms 51 | 26
to produce or service defect and there by cause action to be taken 65 | 33
for their benefit. 70 | 35

1' | 1 | 2 | 3 | 4 | 5 | 6 | 7 | 8 | 9 | 10 | 11 | 12 | 13 |
3' | 1 | 2 | 3 | 4 |

LESSON 41

Leftbound Report with Long Quotations

WARMUP 41a

Key each line, striving for control. Repeat if desired.

alphabet	1	Jacki might analyze the data by answering five complex questions.
figures	2	Memo 67 asks if the report on Bill 35-48 is due on the 19th or the 20th.
shift	3	Plum trees on a hilly acre, in my opinion, create no vast estate.
easy	4	Did the foal buck? And did it cut the right elbow of the cowhand?

SKILL BUILDING

41b Textbook Keying

1. Key each line once, concentrating on using good keying techniques; tap ENTER twice after each 3-line group.
2. Repeat if time permits.

	5 you yes yelp year yield yellow yule yours symbol pray grassy money
y/t	6 to at tent triek treat trestle tribute thirty match matter clutter
	7 Timothy printed a symbol, yacht, and yellowjacket for Mr. Forsyst.
	8 got get giggle gargle gargoyle gangway engage eagle magic peg piggy
g/h	9 he she her head harp hay heavy hearth homograph hyena high height
	10 Gail Hughes, a researcher, charted the height and weight of Hugh.

| 1 | 2 | 3 | 4 | 5 | 6 | 7 | 8 | 9 | 10 | 11 | 12 | 13 |

REVIEW FUNCTIONS

41c

MARGINS

PAGE LAYOUT/PAGE SETUP/MARGINS

Margins are the distance between the edge of the paper and the print. The default settings are 1" side margins and 1" top and bottom margins. Default margins stay in effect until you change them.

To set margins not listed in the gallery:

1. From the Page Layout tab, in the Page Setup group, click Margins and then click Custom Margins ❶. The Page Setup dialog box displays.

2. From the Margins tab ❷, click the up or down arrows to increase or decrease the default settings ❸.

3. Apply margins to the Whole document ❹ unless directed otherwise.

4. Click OK.

LESSON C

SKILL BUILDING/ACCURACY EMPHASIS

Select the Skill Building tab, the appropriate emphasis, and then Lesson C. Your results will be summarized in the Skill Building Report.

SKILL BUILDING/TECHNIQUE BUILDER

DRILL 12

BALANCED-HAND
Key each line once for fluency; DS between groups.

1 an anyone brand spans th their father eighth he head sheets niche
2 en enters depends been nd end handle fund or original sport color
3 ur urban turns assure to took factory photo ti titles satin still
4 ic ice bicycle chic it item position profit ng angle danger doing

5 I want the info in the file on the profits from the chic bicycle.
6 The original of the color photo she took of the factory is there.
7 Assure them that anyone can turn onto the road to the urban area.
8 The color of the title sheet depends on the photos and the funds.

TIMED WRITINGS

1. Take a 1' writing on each paragraph.
2. Take a 3' writing on both paragraphs.

Writing 25

	gwam	1'	3'
Practicing basic health rules will result in good body condition.		14	5
Proper diet is a way to achieve good health. Eat a variety of foods each		28	9
day, including some fruit, vegetables, cereal products, and foods rich		42	14
in protein, to be sure that you keep a balance. Another part of a good		57	19
health plan is physical activity, such as running.		67	22
Running has become popular in this country. A long run is a big		13	27
challenge to many males and females to determine just how far they		26	31
can go in a given time, or the time they require to cover a measured		40	36
distance. Long runs of fifty or one hundred miles are on measured		53	40
courses with refreshments available every few miles. Daily training is		67	45
necessary in order to maximize endurance.		76	48

```
1' |  1 |  2 |  3 |  4 |  5 |  6 |  7 |  8 |  9 | 10 | 11 | 12 | 13 |
3' |       1      |       2      |       3      |       4      |
```

40-d1

Continued

Writers also take advantage of the online thesaurus for choosing the most appropriate word and the spelling and grammar features to ensure spelling and grammar correctness. Additionally, electronic desk references and style manuals are just a click away.

Finally, all the report needs is the title page. Effective writers know that it pays dividends to create a custom title page that truly reflects the quality of the report that it covers. Use page borders and shading as well as graphics to create an attractive title page.

Two simple steps followed in a systematic order will assist you in your goal to learn to win at writing. Knowing the approach is the first step; the second step is to practice, practice, practice.

40-d2

Title Page

1. Create a title page for the unbound report prepared in *40-d1*. Use the Cover Page feature.

2. Key the following information:

   Document title: **Learn to Win at Writing**

   Document subtitle: **For XYZ Employees**

   Author name: **Jennifer Schoenholtz, Office Manager**

3. Check and close. (*40-d2*)

LESSON D

SKILL BUILDING/ACCURACY EMPHASIS

Select the Skill Building tab; choose the appropriate emphasis and then Lesson D.

SKILL BUILDING/TECHNIQUE BUILDER

DRILL 13

ADJACENT KEY REVIEW
Key each line once; strive for accuracy. DS between groups.

1 nm many enmity solemn kl inkling weekly pickle oi oil invoice join
2 iu stadium medium genius lk milk talk walks uy buy buyer soliloquy
3 mn alumni hymn number column sd Thursday wisdom df mindful handful
4 me mention comment same fo found perform info le letter flew files

5 The buyer sent his weekly invoices for oil to the group on Thursday.
6 Mindful of the alumni, the choirs sang a hymn prior to my soliloquy.
7 An inmate, a fogger, and a genius joined the weekly talks on Monday.
8 They were to join in the talk shows to assess regions of the Yukon.

TIMED WRITINGS

1. Take a 1' writing on each paragraph.
2. Take a 3' writing on both paragraphs.

Writing 26

gwam 1' | 3'

	1'	3'
All people, in spite of their eating habits, have two major needs	13	4
that must be met by their food. They need food that provides a	26	9
source of energy, and they need food that will fill the skeletal and	40	13
operating needs of their bodies. Carbohydrates, fats, and protein	53	18
form a major portion of the diet. Vitamins and minerals are also	66	22
necessary for excellent health.	72	24
Carbohydrates make up a major source of our energy needs.	12	28
Fats also serve as a source of energy and act as defense against	25	32
cold and trauma. Proteins are changed to amino acids, which are	38	37
the building units of the body. These, in turn, are utilized to make	52	41
most body tissue. Minerals are required to control many body	64	45
functions, and vitamins are used for normal growth and aid against	77	50
disease.	84	52

```
1' | 1 | 2 | 3 | 4 | 5 | 6 | 7 | 8 | 9 | 10 | 11 | 12 | 13 |
3' |    1    |    2    |    3    |    4    |
```

DISCOVER

Insert file—Position insertion point where file is to be inserted. On the Insert tab, click Object in the Text group. Select Create from File; choose the desired file; click Insert; and click OK.

1. Key the unbound report that follows. Position the title at approximately 2".
2. Insert the data file *writing* below the second paragraph. (**Note:** Be sure to position the insertion point where you want the text to appear before inserting the file.)
3. Format the first side heading *Research* correctly. Check the remaining three side headings for proper format.
4. Revise the side headings to make them parallel (gramatically consistent).
5. Insert page numbers; do not print the page number on page 1.
6. Preview the document to verify page numbers and that side headings are not left alone at the bottom of the page.
7. Check and close the document. (*40-d1*)

Learn to Win at Writing

Being able to communicate effectively continues to be one of the most demanded work skills. Today's high demand for clear, concise, and logical communication makes it impossible for an employee to excuse himself or herself from writing by saying, "I'm just not a writer," or "I can't write."

Realizing you need to improve your writing skills is the first step to enhancing them. Then you must apply a systemized approach to writing as detailed in this report.

Insert the data file writing here.

The effective writer understands the importance of using technology to create an attractive document that adheres to correct style rules. Review the list below to determine your use of technology in the report writing process.

- Number preliminary pages of the report with small Roman numerals at the bottom center of the page.
- Number the report with Arabic numbers in the upper-right corner.
- Create attractive headers or footers that contain helpful information for the reader.
- Suppress headers, footers, and page numbering on the title page and on the first page of the report.
- Invoke the Widow/Orphan control feature to ensure that no lines display alone at the bottom or top of a page.
- Use the Keep with next command to keep side headings from appearing alone at the bottom of the page.
- Format references using the hanging indent feature.
- Use typographic or special symbols to enhance the report.

continued

LESSON E

 **KEYBOARDING PRO DELUXE**

SKILL BUILDING/ACCURACY EMPHASIS

Select the Skill Building tab; choose the appropriate emphasis and then Lesson E.

 **KEYBOARDING PRO DELUXE**

SKILL BUILDING/TECHNIQUE BUILDER

DRILL 14

WORD BEGINNINGS
Key each line once, working for accuracy. DS between groups.

br
1 bright brown bramble bread breath breezes brought brother broiler
2 In February my brother brought brown bread and beans from Boston.

exe
3 exercises exert executives exemplify exemption executed exemplary
4 They exert extreme effort executing exercises in exemplary style.

bt
5 doubt subtle obtains obtrusion subtracts indebtedness undoubtedly
6 Extreme debt will cause more than subtle doubt among my creditors.

ny
7 tiny funny company nymph penny nylon many anyone phony any brainy
8 Anyone as brainy and funny as Penny is an asset to their company.

KEYBOARDING PRO DELUXE

TIMED WRITINGS

1. Take a 1' writing on each paragraph.
2. Take a 3' writing on both paragraphs.

Writing 27

	gwam	1'	3'
Many people believe that an ounce of prevention is worth a pound		13	4
of cure. Care of your heart can help you prevent serious physical		26	9
problems. The human heart is the most important pump ever		38	13
developed. It constantly pushes blood through the body tissues. But		51	17
the layers of muscle that make up the heart must be kept in proper		65	22
working order. Exercise can help this muscle to remain in good		77	26
condition.		80	27
Another important way of keeping a healthy heart is just to avoid		13	31
habits which are considered detrimental to the body. Food that is high		27	36
in cholesterol is not a good choice. Also, use of tobacco has quite a		41	40
bad effect on the function of the heart. You can minimize your chances		56	45
of heart trouble by avoiding these bad health habits.		66	49

1' | 1 | 2 | 3 | 4 | 5 | 6 | 7 | 8 | 9 | 10 | 11 | 12 | 13 |
3' | 1 | 2 | 3 | 4 |

To use Keep with next:

1. Select the side heading and at least two lines of the paragraph that follows it.
2. On the Home tab, in the Paragraph group, click the Paragraph Dialog Box Launcher. The Paragraph dialog box displays.
3. From the Line and Page Breaks tab , select Keep with next ②.
4. Click OK. The side heading moves to the next page.

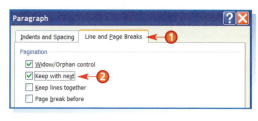

 **KEYBOARDING PRO DELUXE** See References/Word commands/Lesson 40

DRILL 3 | PAGE BREAKS AND PAGE NUMBERS | KEEP WITH NEXT

1. Add page numbers positioned at the top of page at the right. Use Plain Number 3 as the default style. Do not print a page number on the first page.
2. Select the side heading at the bottom of the page along with the entire address and the first line with a time note.
3. Apply the Keep with next command so the side heading moves to page 2.
4. Preview to verify that the page number appears on page 2 only and that the side heading appears on page 2.
5. Check and close. (40-drill3)

DOCUMENT DESIGN

MULTIPLE-PAGE REPORT

In Lesson 38 you learned to format a one-page unbound report. Because reports are often longer than one page, you will learn in Lesson 40 to format a multiple-page report. When a multiple-page report is created, page numbers are required on all pages except the first. Study the illustration below noting specifically the position of page numbers. Review the callouts as well to reinforce your understanding of report formats.

To format a multiple-page report:

1. Insert page numbers at the upper-right corner in the header position (0.5").
2. Suppress the page number on the first page.
3. Protect side headings that may be separated from the related paragraph with the Keep with next feature. **Note:** The Keep with next feature is turned on automatically when styles are applied to a side heading.

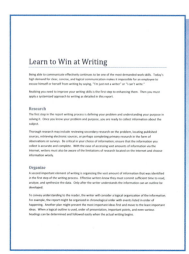

Business Correspondence Essentials

LEARNING OUTCOMES

- Format memos and e-mail.
- Format letters in block letter and modified block style using new *Word 2007* format and traditional format.
- Create envelopes.
- Modify tabs.
- Improve keying speed and accuracy.

LESSON 31

Memos and E-mail

WARMUP 31a

Key each line, striving for control. Repeat if desired.

alphabet	1	I quickly explained to two managers the grave hazards of the job.
figures	2	All channels—16, 25, 30, and 74—reported the score was 19 to 8.
shift	3	Maxi and Kay Pascal expect to be in breezy South Mexico in April.
easy	4	Did the man fight a duel, or did he go to a chapel to sign a vow?

| 1 | 2 | 3 | 4 | 5 | 6 | 7 | 8 | 9 | 10 | 11 | 12 | 13 |

SKILL BUILDING

31b Timed Writing
1. Key a 3' timed writing, working for speed.
2. Key a 3' timed writing, working for control.

all letters

	gwam	3'
Hard work is required for job success. Set high goals and	4	43
devote time to the exact things that will help you succeed. Work	8	47
hard each day and realize you must be willing to make sacrifices.	13	51
Avoid being like the loser who says, "It may be possible, but	17	55
it's too difficult." Take on the attitude of the winner who says,	21	59
"It may be difficult, but it's possible." Count on working hard.	26	64
Also, seek mentors to pilot you in your long road to success.	30	69
They will encourage you and will challenge you to reach for higher	34	73
dreams even when you are very happy with where you are.	39	77

| 1' | 1 | 2 | 3 | 4 | 5 | 6 | 7 | 8 | 9 | 10 | 11 | 12 | 13 |
| 3' | | 1 | | | 2 | | | 3 | | | 4 | | |

NEW FUNCTIONS

40d

PAGE NUMBERS

INSERT/HEADER AND FOOTER/PAGE NUMBER

The Page Number command automatically inserts the correct page number on each page. Page numbers may be positioned automatically in the header position (0.5" at top of page) or in the footer position (bottom of the page). To prevent the number from printing on the first page, you will modify the layout.

TIP

Use the Plain Number 3 format for page numbers in a header as the default.

To insert page numbers:

1. On the Insert tab, in the Header and Footer group, click the down arrow on the Page Number button ①.

2. Click Top of Page ②. A gallery of page number styles displays ③.

3. Click the down scroll arrow to browse the various styles ④. Click Plain Number 3 from the gallery ⑤. The page number displays in the header position at the top right.

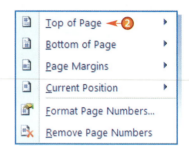

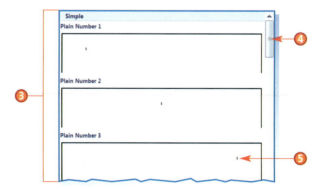

To remove the page number from the first page:

DESIGN/OPTIONS/DIFFERENT FIRST PAGE

On the Design tab, from the Options group, click Different First Page ⑥. The page number does not display on the first page.

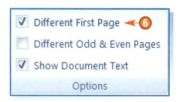

LINE AND PAGE BREAKS

HOME/PARAGRAPH/DIALOG BOX LAUNCHER

Pagination or breaking pages at the appropriate location can easily be controlled using two features: Widow/Orphan control and Keep with next.

Widow/Orphan control prevents a single line of a paragraph from printing at the bottom or top of a page. A check mark displays in this option box indicating that Widow/Orphan control is "on" (the default).

Keep with next prevents a page break from occurring between two paragraphs. Use this feature to keep a side heading from being left alone at the bottom of a page.

NEW FUNCTIONS

31c

VERTICAL PAGE POSITION

When formatting documents, the user must decide on the vertical page position of the document. The default top margin for *Word 2007* is 1". Often users will simply tap the ENTER key to move the document lower on the page. Later in this module you will learn the Center Page command to center a document vertically on the page.

Two methods are often used to determine the vertical position of text.

VERTICAL RULER

The Vertical Ruler is displayed at the far left of the screen. If your ruler is not displayed, click the View Ruler button at the top of the scroll bars on the top right side of the screen. The ruler will display.

The blue area at the top of the ruler is the 1" top margin. The white area or the writing area begins at 0" and extends 9". The blue area at the bottom of the rule is the 1" bottom margin. To begin a document at approximately 2", you would tap ENTER three times until the insertion point is positioned at about the 1" marker on the Vertical Ruler.

STATUS LINE

Refer to the status line located at the bottom of the screen. The vertical page position does not display by default in *Word 2007*. To display it, right-click on the status line and click Vertical Page Position. The vertical page position now appears at the bottom left side on the status line.

| Page: 1 of 1   At: 2" |

DRILL 1   VERTICAL PAGE POSITION

1. In a new document, display the vertical page position on the status line.
2. Tap the ENTER key three times to position the insertion point at about 1" on the ruler bar.

3. Insert the current date.
4. Check that the date prints approximately 2" from the top of the page.
5. Check and close. *(31-drill1)*

REMOVE SPACE AFTER PARAGRAPH

HOME/LINE SPACING

By this point you realize that *Word 2007* automatically adds extra white space (10 points) after the ENTER key is tapped. The white space between paragraphs is greater than the white spacing between the lines within the paragraph. The extra white space between paragraphs makes the text easier to read and saves the user time in only tapping the ENTER key once between paragraphs ❶.

However, on some occasions, it is necessary to remove the space added after a paragraph ❷. Remember that your software defines a paragraph when the ENTER key is tapped. The document design in Module 4 for interoffice memos and business letters will include several instances when the extra spacing adds unnecessary white space and consumes too many lines. Study the two examples shown below.

❶ Default Spacing

Daniel J. Lippincott

Business Manager

❷ Extra Spacing Removed

Daniel J. Lippincott
Business Manager

LESSON 40 | Multiple-Page Report

WARMUP 40a

Key each line, striving for control. Repeat if desired.

alphabet	1	Jayne Cox puzzled over workbooks that were required for geometry.
figures	2	Edit pages 308 and 415 in Book A; pages 17, 29, and 60 in Book B.
shift	3	THE LAKES TODAY, published in Akron, Ohio, comes in June or July.
easy	4	The town may blame Keith for the auditory problems in the chapel.

SKILL BUILDING

40b Textbook Keying

1. Key each line once, concentrating on using good keying techniques; tap ENTER twice after each 4-line group.
2. Repeat the drill if time permits.

n/u	5	nun nut unbolt null unable nudge under nurture thunder numb shunt
	6	Uncle Hunter runs with me to hide under the bed when it thunders.
c/e	7	ecru cell echo ceil check cedar pecan celery secret receive price
	8	Once Cecilia checked prices for acceptable and special offerings.
b/r	9	brag barb brown carbon brain marble break herb brace gerbil brick
	10	Bradley will try to break the unbroken brown brood mare bareback.
n/y	11	many bunny irony grainy granny sunny phony rainy runny zany funny
	12	Aunt Nanny says rainy days are for funny movies and many candies.

COMMUNICATION

40c Proofreading

In Lesson 38 you learned the unbound report format. Check your understanding of the unbound report by completing Drills 1 and 2 below. Refer to pages 147–148 if you have questions.

DRILL 1 | FORMAT KNOWLEDGE

Key each line at the right, choosing the correct choice shown in parentheses. Use the numbering feature to number each statement. Check and close. (*40-drill1*)

1. The title that appears on the first page of a report is keyed approximately (1", 2") from the top of the page.
2. The title is keyed at the (center, left margin.)
3. The title is formatted using the (Heading 1, Title) style; the font size of the title is (14 point, 26 point).
4. Side headings are keyed at the (center, left margin); the font size of side headings is (12 point, 14 point).
5. Side margins of an unbound report are (default or 1", 1.5").

DRILL 2 | PROOFREAD FOR CONSISTENCY ASSOCIATIONS & ASSOCIATIONSKEY

1. Open **associationskey** from the data files and print; close this file.
2. Open **associations** and print. Proofread this report and mark any formats that are not consistent with the solution printed in step 1. Use the proofreaders' marks shown on page 55 to mark all corrections.
3. Correct the errors you marked. Print.
4. Submit the edited copy and the final copy to your instructor.
5. Check and close. (*40-drill2*)

TIP

Remember to proofread and preview each document for placement. You will not be reminded to do this.

KEYBOARDING PRO DELUXE   See References/Word commands/Lesson 31

To remove space after paragraph:

1. Select the desired lines. Remember you are removing space after a paragraph (or when the ENTER key is tapped).
2. From the Home tab, on the Paragraph group, click the down arrow by the Line Spacing button. Select Remove Space After Paragraph.

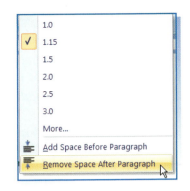

DRILL 2 — REMOVE SPACE AFTER PARAGRAPH

1. Key the following lines:

Distribution List:
    Allen Bejahan
    Janet James
    Terry Johnson
    Ray Lightfoot

2. Select the first four lines. ❶
3. Apply the Line Spacing option to remove space after paragraph.
4. Check and close. (*31-drill2*)

COMMUNICATION

31d

PROOFREAD AND FINALIZE A DOCUMENT

Before documents are complete, they must be proofread carefully for accuracy. Error-free documents send the message that you are detail oriented and capable. Apply these procedures when processing all documents:

1. Use Spelling and Grammar to check spelling when you have completed the document.
2. Proofread the document on screen to be sure that it makes sense.
3. Preview the document, and check the overall appearance.
4. Save the document, and then print it.
5. Compare the document to the source copy (textbook), and check that text has not been omitted or added. Revise, save, and print if necessary.

DRILL 3 — DATA FILES AND PROOFREAD A DOCUMENT PROOFREAD

1. The CD ROM in the back of your book contains extra files you will use in this course. These files, known as data files, are organized by module. A CD icon appears with the drill or application heading when a data file is used, and the data filename appears as well.
2. Non *Keyboarding Pro DELUXE* Users: Ask your instructor how to access these files, or install the files on the hard drive following the instructions on the CD-ROM.

When the files are installed, locate the data path or folder where these files are stored. *Keyboarding Pro DELUXE* users: The data file will open automatically when you access the activity.

3. Open the data file *proofread*.
4. Apply steps 1-4 of the proofreading procedures discussed in **31d** above.
5. Apply step 5; the source copy is the paragraph shown above in **31d**.
6. Check and close. (*31-drill3*)

---

1. Create a cover page using the Cover Page feature. Select the Alphabet style in the Built-In category.
2. Click *[Type the document title]* and key **Updates for Document Processing**.
3. Key **Word 2007** as the document subtitle.
4. Key **Jun Yoshino** as the author name.
5. Click *[Pick the date]*, select the down arrow, and select a date.
6. Check and close the document. (*39-drill2*)

APPLICATIONS

39-d1
Unbound Report

1. Key the unbound report that follows. Position the title at approximately 2".
2. Add bullets to the three items.
3. Check and close. (*39-d1*)

Credible and Acceptable Reporting

Although its contents are of ultimate importance, a finished report's look is of almost equal importance. If it is to achieve the goal for which it was written, every report, whether it serves a business or academic purpose, should be acceptable from every point of view.

Citations, for Example

No matter which format is used for citations, a good writer knows citations are inserted for the reader's benefit; therefore, anything the writer does to ease their use will be appreciated and will work on the writer's behalf. Standard procedures, such as those stated below, make readers comfortable.

- Italicize titles of complete publications.
- Use quotation marks with parts of publications.
- Months and certain locational words may be abbreviated.

And the Final Report

The final report should have an attractive, easy-to-read look. The report should meet the criteria for spacing, citations, and binding that have been established for its preparation. Such criteria are set up by institutional decree, by generally accepted standards, or by subject demands. A writer should discover limits within which he or she must write and observe those limits with care.

In Conclusion

Giving the report a professional appearance calls for skill and patience from a writer. First impressions count when preparing reports. Poorly presented materials are not read, or at least not read with an agreeable attitude.

39-d2
Cover Page

1. Create a cover page using the Cover Page feature. Select the Alphabet style from the Built-In category of cover pages.
2. Key the report title from *39-d1* as the document title. Key **For All Management Employees** as the document subtitle.
3. Key **Dana Olmstead, Division Manager** as the author's name and title.
4. Check and close the document. (*39-d2*).

In Module 3 you learned a variety of basic word processing functions. Now you are ready to apply these skills in formatting business documents. Two formatting approaches will be introduced in this textbook—the new document approach for *Word 2007* users and the traditional document approach for *Word 2003* users. Why are two document formatting approaches needed? The answer is simple—the defaults of *Word 2003* and *Word 2007* are vastly different. Our goal is to prepare you for the entry into industry—whether your employer supports the traditional defaults of *Word 2003* or the new defaults of *Word 2007*. As industry transitions to the new interface, the *Word 2007* document formats will be widely used and accepted. In instances where the formatting differences are minor, the new document approach for *Word 2007* users will be taught. For example, memos will be formatted with the new document approach. In Module 4 you will learn both approaches to formatting letters.

MEMORANDUMS

Messages sent to employees within an organization are called **memorandums** (memos for short). Memos may be printed on plain paper or on letterhead. Often a memo is sent electronically. It can either be in the form of an e-mail or as an attachment to an e-mail. Memos were designed to be documents that stayed within a company. However, e-mail is changing the role of memos. Study the full-page illustration of a memo on the following page.

To format a memo:

1. Tap ENTER three times to position the first line of the heading at about 2".
2. Format the memo headings in bold and uppercase. Turn off bold and uppercase, and tap TAB once or twice after each heading to align the information. Generally, courtesy titles (Mr., Ms., etc.) are not used; however, if the memo is formal, the receiver's name may include a title.
3. Use the 1.15 default line spacing. Tap ENTER once after each paragraph.
4. Add reference initials one line below the body if the memo is keyed by someone other than the sender. Do not include initials when keying your own memo.
5. Items clipped or stapled to the memo are noted as attachments; items included in an envelope are enclosures. Key these notations one line below the reference initials.

To format a distribution list:

When memos are sent to more than one person, list their names after TO. Generally the names are listed in alphabetical order; some organizations, however, list the names in order of rank. For readability, key the names on separate lines. When sending the memo to many people, refer to a distribution list at the end of the memo. Example: *TO: Task Force Members—Distribution Below*. Indent the names on the distribution list to the first tab. Remove the extra spacing between the list of names.

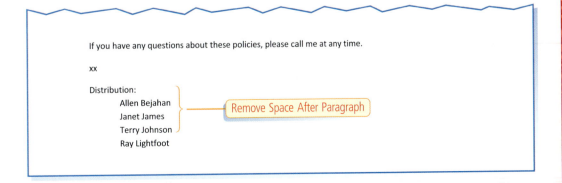

If you have any questions about these policies, please call me at any time.

xx

Distribution:
　　Allen Bejahan
　　Janet James　　　　　Remove Space After Paragraph
　　Terry Johnson
　　Ray Lightfoot

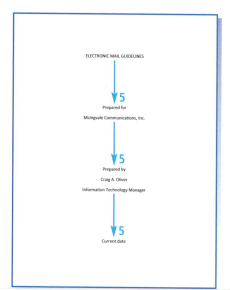

Traditional Title Page

COVER PAGE

INSERT/PAGES/COVER PAGE

Reports often include a cover or title page that identifies the report to the reader. As the name implies, the cover page is positioned on top of the report and provides an attractive cover for it. Traditionally a title page includes the title of the report, the name and title of the individual or the organization for which the report was prepared, the name and title of the writer, and the date the report was completed. The illustration at the left shows the traditional title page. Each line is center aligned. Allow nearly equal space between parts of the page (tap ENTER about five times).

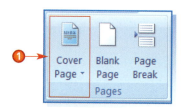

Word offers the Cover Page feature, which inserts a fully formatted cover page. You may choose from a variety of attractively formatted covers. Study the illustration of a cover page created using the Cover Page feature below. Remember, this only illustrates one specific style; you have many others from which to choose.

To create a cover page:

1. From the Insert tab in the Pages group, click Cover Page ❶. A gallery of cover pages displays.
2. Click the scroll arrows to determine the desired style ❷.
3. Select the desired style ❸. The cover page opens as a *Word* document.
4. Select *Type the document title* ❹ and key the report title. Repeat for all other items located in the template. **Note:** A blank page follows the cover page for keying the report.

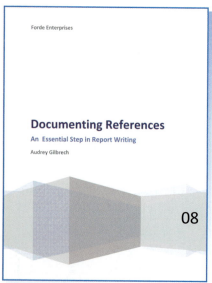

Cover Page, *Word 2007*

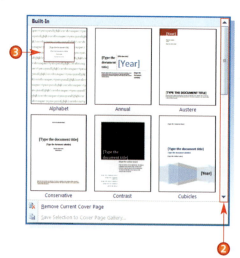

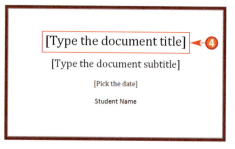

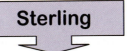

Sterling

1195 Singing Cactus Avenue
Tucson, AZ 85701-0947

(Tap ENTER three times) → 2"

TO: Students ↓ 1

FROM: Roger C. Westfield ↓ 1

DATE: Insert current date ↓ 1

SUBJECT: A New Perspective on Memos ↓ 1

Your instructor has asked that I prepare a memo for you describing the changing role of memos and the importance of formatting memos effectively. Sterling uses its logo and company name on the top of its memos. First, you will learn to prepare memos on plain paper. Later you will learn to use templates for them. A template is a stored document format that would contain the company logo and name as well as the memo headings. ↓ 1

The format does not differ regardless of whether plain paper or a template is used. The headings are positioned about 2" from the top of the paper, and default side margins are used. Headings are keyed in uppercase and bold; tap the Enter key once after each heading. The body is single-spaced with a blank line between each paragraph. Notations such as reference initials, enclosures, or copies are keyed one blank line below the body. Some companies adopt slightly different styles; however, this style is very commonly used. ↓ 1

Often a memo is sent electronically. It can either be in the form of an e-mail or as an attachment to an e-mail. Memos were designed to be documents that stayed within a company. However, e-mail is changing the role of memos. E-mails, even though they are formatted as memos, are frequently sent outside of companies. Some companies use e-mail to deliver a document but attach a letter or a memo to it. ↓ 1

xx

Memo Format

BULLETS AND NUMBERING

HOME/PARAGRAPH/BULLETS OR NUMBERING

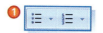 Numbered and bulleted lists are commonly used to emphasize information in reports, newspapers, magazine articles, and overhead presentations. Use numbered items if the list requires a sequence of steps or points. Use bullets or symbols if the list contains an unordered listing. *Word* automatically inserts the next number in a sequence if you manually key a number. *Word* also automatically removes the extra space after the paragraph in a bulleted or numbered list. Note the spacing in the illustrations shown below.

- Word processing
- Spreadsheet
- Database
- Presentation
- Desktop publishing

1. Preheat oven to 350°.
2. Cream butter and sugar; add eggs.
3. Add flour.

To create bullets or numbers:

1. Key the list without bullets or numbers. Then select the list to be bulleted or numbered.
2. From the Home tab in the Paragraph group, click the Bullets or Numbering button ❶.
3. To add or remove bullets or numbers, click the Bullets or Numbering button.
4. To convert bullets to numbers or vice versa, select the items to change and click either the Bullets or Numbering button.

DRILL 1   BULLETS

1. Key the text below as a single list; do not key the bullets.
2. Apply bullets to the list by selecting the text to be bulleted and clicking the Bullets button.
3. Convert the bullets to numbers. Select the bulleted items and click the Numbering button.
4. Add **Roll Call** as the second item.
5. Delete the number before *Next Meeting*.
6. Check and close. (*39-drill1*)

- Call to Order
- Reading and Approval of the Minutes
- Announcements
- Treasurer's Report

- Membership Committee Report
- Unfinished Business
- New Business
- Adjournment
- Next Meeting: November 3, 20--

ELECTRONIC MAIL (E-MAIL)

Electronic mail (or e-mail) is a message sent by one computer user to another computer user. E-mail was originally designed as an informal, personal way of communicating. However, it is now used extensively in business. For business use, e-mail should not be casual or informal.

Business writers compose e-mail messages in two ways. First, the writer may compose the entire communication (or message) in the body of the e-mail. Second, the writer may compose a brief e-mail message and then attach electronic documents to it. Distribution of electronic documents via e-mail is a common business practice; these electronic documents include many types of document formats, e.g., memos, letters, reports, contracts, worksheets, and presentations. It is important for the business writer to recognize the importance of attractive and acceptable formats of all documents, including e-mail messages.

Using e-mail requires an e-mail program, an e-mail address, and access to the Internet. If you cannot meet these requirements, format all e-mail in this text as memos.

Address e-mail carefully. Key and check the address of the recipient **1** and always supply a subject line **2**. Also, key the e-mail address of anyone who should receive a copy of the e-mail **3**.

Format the body **4** of an e-mail single-spaced; double-space between paragraphs. Do not indent paragraphs. Limit the use of bold, italics, and uppercase. For business use, avoid abbreviations and emoticons (e.g., BTW for *by the way* or :-) for *wink*).

Attach electronic documents **5** to an e-mail message using the attachment feature **6** of the e-mail program. The attached file can then be opened and edited by the recipient.

Unbound Report with Title Page

WARMUP 39a

Key each line, striving for control. Repeat if desired.

alphabet 1 The explorer questioned Jack's amazing story about the lava flow.

figure/sym 2 I cashed Cartek & Bunter's $2,679 check (Check #3480) on June 15.

1st/2nd fingers 3 Hugh tried to go with Katrina, but he did not have time to do so.

easy 4 The eighty firms may pay for a formal audit of their field works.

| 1 | 2 | 3 | 4 | 5 | 6 | 7 | 8 | 9 | 10 | 11 | 12 | 13 |

SKILL BUILDING

39b Textbook Keying

1. Key each line once, concentrating on using good keying techniques; tap ENTER twice after each 3-line group.
2. Repeat the drill if time permits.

TIP

Keep hands and arms still as you reach up to the third row and down to the first row.

t 5 it cat pat to top thin at tilt jolt tuft mitt flat test tent felt

r 6 fur bur try roar soar ram trap rare ripe true rear tort corral

t/r 7 The track star was triumphant in both the third and fourth heats.

m 8 me mine memo mimic named clam month maximum mummy summer remember

n 9 no snow ton none nine ninety noun mini mind minnow kennel evening

m/n 10 Men and women in management roles maximize time during commuting.

o 11 of one odd coil book oink cool polo crop soap yoyo option noodle

i 12 in it if did idea bike fix site with fill ilium indigo initiative

o/i 13 To know if you rock while giving a speech, stand on a foil sheet.

a 14 an as am is ask arm pass task team haze value salsa manage animal

s 15 so as sip spy must shape class shawl sister system second synergy

a/s 16 Assistants must find names and addresses for a class action suit.

e 17 he we me she they seal feel green there energy desire screensaver

i 18 is it in icon kite site tired unit limit feline service invisible

e/i 19 Initial triage services are limited to solely emergency patients.

39c Timed Writing

Key two 1' timed writings; work to increase speed.

all letters

	gwam	1'
The value of an education has been discussed many times with a		13
great deal of zest. The value of an education is often assessed in		26
terms of costs and benefits to the taxpayer. It is also judged in		39
terms of changes in the ones taking part in this process. Acquiring		53
gains in knowledge, skill, and attitudes is often thought to be a vital		67
part of a good education.		72

1' | 1 | 2 | 3 | 4 | 5 | 6 | 7 | 8 | 9 | 10 | 11 | 12 | 13 |

31-d1
Memo

— DISCOVER

1. Read the memo illustrated on page 115 carefully. Key this memo; do not key the memo letterhead. Begin the heading at approximately 2".
2. Use the Date and Time feature to insert the current date.
3. If the first letter of your reference initials is automatically capitalized, point to the initial until the AutoCorrect Options button appears. Click the button; then choose Undo Automatic Capitalization.
4. Proofread the memo carefully and make any changes that are necessary.
5. Check and close. (*31-d1*)

31-d2
Memo with Distribution List

1. Key the memo with a distribution list shown below. Remove the space after the paragraph when formatting the distribution list at the bottom of the memo.
2. Check and close. (*31-d2*)

TO: Manufacturing Team—Distribution Below

FROM: Mei-Ling Yee, Administrative Assistant

DATE: April 14, 2008

SUBJECT: Enrichment Seminars

As was stated by Robert Beloz in the January newsletter, *Focus for the New Year*, Foscari & Associates will be offering a series of enrichment seminars for its employees in the year ahead. If you have suggestions for seminars that would be beneficial to your team, please let me know.

We are proud to announce our first seminar offering, *First Aid and CPR*, on May 16 and 17. The seminar will be offered from 1 p.m. to 5 p.m. in the Staff Lounge. Participants will be awarded CPR certificates from the American Heart Association upon successful completion of this eight-hour course. If you are interested in taking this seminar, please call me at ext. 702 or send me an e-mail message by April 25.

You will want to mark your calendar today for this important seminar.

xx

Distribution:
    Eddie Barnett
    Steve Lewis
    Dinah Rice

31-d3
E-mail

Follow these directions for completing all e-mail applications in this text:

Without Internet access: Complete all documents as memos.

With an e-mail address: Complete the documents in your software and send them.

With Internet acccess but no e-mail address: Your instructor will assist you in setting up a free e-mail account and address.

1. Prepare an e-mail to your instructor using the subject line **CPR Certification Required**. Attach the file *31-d2* to the e-mail.
2. Print and send the e-mail or key it as a memo. Check and close. (*31-d3*)

Please review the attached memo from Mei-Ling Yee announcing the date for the *First Aid and CPR* seminar. All team members not certified in CPR are required to attend this seminar.

Choosing a typeface   167

Typeface refers to the style of printing on the page.   178

Matching the style or "feeling" of the type with the purpose   190

of the finished product is very important. For example,   202

you would not want to use a gothic or "old style" typeface   215

to promote a modern, high-tech product. Consider the bold-   227

ness or lightness of the style, the readability factor, and   233

the decorativeness or simplicity. Mixing more than three   251

different typefaces on a page should also be avoided. Vary   271

the type sizes to give the effect of different type styles.   275

Bold and italics can also be added for emphasis and vari-   286

ety, especially when only one type style is being used.   297

Adding White Space

Desktop publishing experts claim a novice is easily recognized by a dense
document filled with text and graphics and very little white space. This document
appears busy, difficult, and unappealing to the eye of the reader. To add white
space to a document, use left alignment, which leaves a ragged right edge. Adjust
paragraph spacing before and after a paragraph to modify white space. Finally,
increase margins around the page as well as between columns to create a more
attractive document.

WORKPLACE SUCCESS

Integrity

© PHOTODISC RED/GETTY IMAGES

Integrity is synonymous to the word *honesty* and is confronted by employees in the
workplace daily. Think about these rather common situations where integrity is
clearly a choice:

- Arriving at work ten minutes late and then drinking coffee and chatting with
  co-workers for ten more minutes

- Talking with relatives and friends throughout the day

- Leaving work early regularly for personal reasons

- Presenting a report to the supervisor as original work without crediting the
  proper individuals for thoughts and ideas in the report

- Presenting a report that was completed at the last minute and that includes
  facts and figures that have not been verified as accurate

Module 5 presents appropriate standards for citing references used in a report. As a
student, practice integrity in documenting sources. Avoid what may be considered
the easy way—copying text from the Internet and pasting it in a *Word* document.
In all situations, ask the question, "Am I being honest?"

31-d4

Memo with Distribution List

1. Key the memo below. Remove the space after the paragraph when formatting the distribution list at the bottom of the memo.
2. Check and close. (*31-d4*)

TIP

Key a dash as two hyphens, with no space before or after it. *Word* usually converts this to a solid line called an em-dash.

TO: Safety Officers—Distribution Below | FROM: Louis Cross | DATE: May 10, 2008 | SUBJECT: Safety Seminar

Mark your calendar for the *Safety Practices and Accident Prevention* seminar scheduled for June 2, 2008, from 9:00 a.m. to 4:30 p.m. The seminar will be held at the Kellogg Center.

New OSHA regulations will be presented at this seminar, so it is extremely important for you as a safety officer to be in attendance. The seminar will be conducted by OSHA employees and professors from the local university.

xx

Distribution:
    Lori Baker, Production
    George Markell, Maintenance
    Henry Otter, Human Resources

31-d5

E-mail

1. Prepare the e-mail below to your instructor; copy a classmate. Attach the file *31-d1*.
2. Print and send the e-mail or key it as a memo. Check and close. (*31-d5*)

Subject: Preparing E-mails

The guides that Sterling Design Consultants prepared for memos are good advice for preparing business e-mails as well. I have attached a copy of the memo from Mr. Westfield for your review.

Be sure to proofread and edit e-mails carefully. Making e-mails error free is as important as making any other document error free.

31-d6

Memo or E-mail

1. Determine your instructor's preferred method of communication for receiving the information below. If the preference is a memo, key as a memo. If the preference is e-mail, prepare the information as an e-mail.
2. Key the appropriate information in the memo heading. Use **Contact Information** as the subject of the memo.
3. Key your contact information where indicated.
4. Print and send the e-mail. Check and close. (*31-d6*)

The contact information that you requested for your keyboarding class database is shown below:

Name: ———————⟶ Tap the TAB key twice so the contact information will be aligned.

Address:

Home Phone:

Cell Phone:

E-mail Address:

38-d1

Unbound Report

1. Key the model report on the previous page. Tap ENTER three times to position the title at about 2". Use default side margins. **Hint:** To stop the word *e-mail* at the end of the first paragraph from breaking onto two lines, use a nonbreaking hyphen. (Use the keyboard shortcut SHIFT + CTRL + _.) Use Help if necessary.

2. Capitalize the first letter of all main words in the title; tap ENTER once after the heading. Then select the heading and apply the Title style.

3. Select the side heading and apply the Heading 1 style. Tap ENTER once after the side heading.

4. Check and close. (38-d1)

38-d2

Edit Unbound Report

 EDIT

1. In the open report, position the title at approximately 2". Apply Title style.

2. Correct the capitalization of the side headings; apply Heading 1 style.

3. Make other edits shown in the report. Refer to proofreaders' marks on page 55.

4. Key and format the side heading *Adding White Space*; then key the last paragraph of the report.

5. Check and close. (38-d2)

	words
Who Can Design a Better Brochure?	7
Producing a brochure with a professional appearance	17
requires careful creativity and planning. Not every one is	29
an accomplished paste-up artist who is capable of creating	41
a complex piece of printed art, but most skilled computer	50
users can create an attractive layout for a basic brochure.	62
Working with blocks	66
Work with copy and illustration in blocks. Type body	76
or text copy, leaving plenty of space for illustrations and	87
headlines. The blocks should then be arranged in a orderly	99
and eye-appealing manner.	101
Using a small a small size type is not recommended.	112
In most cases, use a font that is 11 point or larger to	122
make the document easy to read. Copy that is arranged in	133
more than one column is more attractive. Try not to key	143
copy across the full width of a page. Preferably break the	147
page into smaller columns of copy and intersperse with	160
illustrations.	163

Block Letter Format

WARMUP 32a

Key each line, striving for control. Repeat if desired.

alphabet	1	Extra awards given by my employer amazed Jo, the file clerk.
figures	2	I will be on vacation June 4-7, October 3, 5, 8, and December 6-9.
shift	3	Sue, May, Al, Tom, and Jo will meet us at the Pick and Save store.
easy	4	Ask the girl to copy the letter for all the workers in the office.

| 1 | 2 | 3 | 4 | 5 | 6 | 7 | 8 | 9 | 10 | 11 | 12 | 13 |

NEW FUNCTIONS

32b

AUTOMATIC CURRENT DATE

The automatic current date is another easy way to enter the current date.

1. Key the first four characters of the current month. The current month will display.

2. Tap the ENTER key to accept the date.

3. Tap the SPACEBAR to display the remainder of the current date.

DRILL 1 — AUTOMATIC DATE

1. In a new blank document, key the first four characters of the current month, e.g., Octo for October.

2. Tap the ENTER key and then the SPACEBAR.

3. Check and close. (*32-drill1*)

DIALOG BOX LAUNCHER

HOME/FONT GROUP/DIALOG BOX LAUNCHER

In some cases, more options than the ones displayed in a specific group may be needed. To access these options, click the Dialog Box Launcher ➊, the small diagonal arrow in the lower-right corner of the group. For example, when you click the Dialog Box Launcher for the Font group, the Font dialog box displays ➋.

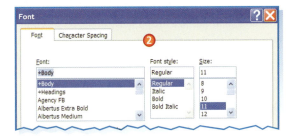

DRILL 2 — EXPLORE DIALOG BOX LAUNCHER

1. Open a new blank document.

2. On the Home tab, in the Font group, click the Dialog Box Launcher. Click Cancel to close the dialog box. Repeat step 2 for the Paragraph and Styles groups.

3. On the Page Layout tab, in the Page Setup group, click the Dialog Box Launcher.

4. On the References tab, in the Footnotes group, click the Dialog Box Launcher. Close the dialog box and the exercise.

2"

Title →

Electronic Mail Guidelines Title Style

Electronic mail, a widely used communication channel, clearly has three major advantages—time effectiveness, distance effectiveness, and cost effectiveness. To reap full benefit from this popular and convenient communication medium, follow the basic guidelines regarding the creation and use of e-mail.

Side Heading →

E-mail Composition   Heading 1 Style

Although perceived as informal documents, e-mail messages are business records. Therefore, follow these effective communication guidelines. Write clear, concise sentences, avoiding clichés, redundancies, and wordiness. Break the message into logical paragraphs, sequencing in an appropriate order. White space is important in e-mail messages as well as printed documents, so be sure to add extra space between paragraphs.

1"

Spell-check e-mail messages carefully, and verify punctuation and content accuracy. Do limit e-mail messages to one idea per message, and preferably limit to one screen. To ensure your e-mail message is opened, always include a subject line that clearly defines the e-mail message.

1"

E-mail Practices

Although many people are using e-mail, some do not use it as their preferred method of communication and may check it infrequently. To accomplish tasks more effectively, be aware of individuals' preferred channels of communication and use those channels. Understand that your preferred channel of communication is not always that of the person to whom you must communicate.

Consider an e-mail message the property of the sender, and forward only with permission. Some senders include a note in the signature line that reminds recipients not to forward e-mail without getting permission.

CENTER PAGE

PAGE LAYOUT/PAGE SETUP/DIALOG BOX LAUNCHER

The Center Page command centers a document vertically on the page. Should extra hard returns (¶) appear at the beginning or end of a document, these are also considered to be part of the document. Be careful to delete extra hard returns before centering a page.

To center a page vertically:

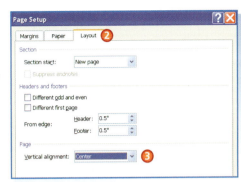

1. Position the insertion point on the page to be centered.
2. From the Page Layout tab on the Page Setup group, click the Dialog Box Launcher ❶. The Page Setup dialog box displays.
3. Click the Layout tab ❷.
4. Click the Vertical alignment down arrow. Select Center ❸.
5. Click OK.

KEYBOARDING PRO DELUXE See References/Word commands/Lesson 32

DRILL 3   CENTER PAGE

1. Key your first and last name in a new document and center-align it.
2. Center the page. Verify that your name now displays at about 4.5" on the Vertical Ruler. Allowing for the 1" top margin, your name would print at about 5.5" or the exact center of an 8½" x 11" sheet of paper.
3. Check and close the document. (*32-drill3*)

DOCUMENT DESIGN

32c

BUSINESS LETTERS

Business letters are used to communicate with persons outside of the business. Business letters carry two messages: the tone and content, and the appearance of the document. Appearance is important because it creates the critical first impression. Stationery, use of standard letter parts, and placement should convey that the writer is intelligent, informed, and detail minded.

STATIONERY

Letters should be printed on high-quality (about 24-pound) letterhead stationery. Standard size for letterhead is 8½" × 11". Envelopes should match the letterhead in quality and color.

DOCUMENT DESIGN

38d
Report Format Guides

UNBOUND REPORT FORMAT

Reports prepared without binders are called unbound reports. Unbound reports may be attached with a staple or paper clip in the upper-left corner. Study the illustration below to learn to format a one-page unbound report. A full-page model of another report is shown on the following page.

2"

Trends for Business Dress

Casual dress in the workplace has become widely accepted. According to a national study conducted by Schoen Associates, a majority of the companies surveyed allowed employees to dress casually one day a week, usually Fridays. Fifty-eight percent of office workers surveyed were allowed to dress casually for work every day, and 92 percent of the offices allowed employees to dress casually occasionally.

Decline in Trend
The trend to dress casually may be shifting, however. Although a large number of companies are allowing casual attire every day or only on Fridays, a current survey revealed a decline of 10 percent in 2007 when compared to the same survey conducted in 2006. Some experts predict the new trend for business dress codes will be a dressup day every week. What accounts for this decline in companies permitting casual dress? Several reasons may include:

1. Confusion about what business casual is, with employees slipping into dressing too casually (work jeans, faded tee-shirts, old sneakers, and improperly fitting clothing).
2. Casual dress does not portray the adopted corporate image of the company.
3. Employees are realizing that promotion decisions are affected by a professional appearance.

Guidelines for Business Dress
Companies are employing image consultants to teach employees what is appropriate business casual and to plan the best business attire to project the corporate image. Erica Gilreath, the author of *Casual Dress*, a guidebook on business casual, provides excellent advice on how to dress casually and still command the power needed for business success. She offers the following advice to professionals:

- Do not wear any clothing that is designed for recreational or sports activities, e.g., cargo pants or pants with elastic waist.
- Invest the time in pressing khakis and shirts or pay for professional dry cleaning. Wrinkled clothing does not enhance one's credibility.
- Do not wear sneakers.
- Be sure clothing fits properly. Avoid baggy clothes or clothes that are too tight.

In summary, energetic employees working to climb the corporate ladder will need to plan their dress carefully. If business casual is appropriate, it is best to consult the experts on business casual to ensure a professional image.

Margins: Use the preset default top, side, and bottom margins.

Font size: Use the 11-point default font size.

Spacing: Use the default 1.15 line spacing for all reports.

Title:

- Position at about 2". (Tap ENTER three times.)
- Capitalize the first letter of all main words.
- Tap ENTER once after heading.
- Apply the Title style; this style is 26-point Cambria font with a bottom border.

Side heading:

- Key side headings at the left margin.
- Capitalize the first letter of all main words.
- Apply Heading 1 style; this style is 14-point Cambria font.
- Tap ENTER once after heading.

Enumerated items:

- Use the default .25" indentation for numbers and bullets.
- Tap ENTER once after each item.

Page numbers:

- First page is not numbered.
- Second and succeeding pages are numbered in the upper-right corner in the header position (0.5").

BUSINESS LETTER FORMATS IN TRANSITION

With *Word 2007* and its new defaults, it is likely that two letter formats will be used until the transition of all users to the new interface. Study the two letters below to note the appearance of the letter keyed in *Word 2007* with its defaults and a letter keyed in the traditional format with *Word 2003* defaults.

E-Market, Group
10 East Rivercenter Boulevard
Covington, KY 41016-8765

Current date

Mr. Eric Seymour
Professional Office Consultants
1782 Laurel Canyon Road
Sunnyvale, CA 94085-9087

Dear Mr. Seymour

Have you heard your friends and colleagues talk about obtaining real-time stock quotes, real-time account balances and positions, NASDAQ Level II quotes, or extended-hours trading? If so, then they are among the many serious investors who have opened an account with E-Market Firm.

We are confident that the best decisions are informed decisions that are made in a very timely manner. E-Market Firm has an online help desk that provides information for all levels of investors, from beginners to the experienced serious trader. You can learn basic tactics for investing in the stock market, avoiding common mistakes, and picking up some advanced strategies.

To stay on top of the market and your investments, please visit our online investing website at http:www.emarketfirm.com to learn more about our banking and brokerage services and to access our online help desk. E-Market Firm is the premier site for online investing.

Sincerely

Emily Zumwalt
Marketing Manager

xx

New Business Letter Format

E-Market, Group
10 East Rivercenter Boulevard
Covington, KY 41016-8765

Current date

Mr. Eric Seymour
Professional Office Consultants
1782 Laurel Canyon Road
Sunnyvale, CA 94085-9087

Dear Mr. Seymour

Have you heard your friends and colleagues talk about obtaining real-time stock quotes, real-time account balances and positions, NASDAQ Level II quotes, or extended-hours trading? If so, then they are among the many serious investors who have opened an account with E-Market Firm.

We are confident that the best decisions are informed decisions that are made in a very timely manner. E-Market Firm has an online help desk that provides information for all levels of investors, from beginners to the experienced serious trader. You can learn basic tactics for investing in the stock market, avoiding common mistakes, and picking up some advanced strategies.

To stay on top of the market and your investments, please visit our online investing website at http://www.emarketfirm.com to learn more about our banking and brokerage services and to access our online help desk. E-Market Firm is the premier site for online investing.

Sincerely

Emily Zumwalt
Marketing Manager

xx

Traditional Business Letter Format

DOCUMENT DESIGN

NEW FUNCTIONS

38c

STYLES

HOME/STYLES/QUICK STYLES

The **Styles** feature enables you to apply a group of formats automatically to a document. A new *Word* document opens with approximately 18 styles attached to it. These styles include Normal, Heading 1, Heading 2, Heading 3, Heading 4, and Title. Normal is the default style of 11-point Calibri, left alignment, 1.15 spacing, and no indent. Text that you key is formatted in the Normal style unless you apply another style.

Styles include both character and paragraph styles. The attributes listed in the Font group on the Home ribbon and on the Font dialog box make up the text formats. **Text formats** apply to a single character or characters that are selected. To apply character styles using the Font group, select the characters to be formatted and apply the desired font.

Paragraph styles include both the character style and other formats that affect paragraph appearance such as line spacing, bullets, numbering, and tab stops.

To apply paragraph styles:

1. Select the text to which you want to apply a style.
2. On the Home tab in the Styles group ❶, choose a desired style shown in the Quick Styles gallery ❷.
3. If the desired tab does not display, click the More button ❸ to expand the Quick Styles gallery.
4. Select the desired style from the expanded list of styles ❹.

> **TIP**
>
> Remember to proofread and preview each document as a SOP. You will not be reminded to do this.

KEYBOARDING PRO DELUXE ▸ See References/Word commands/Lesson 38

DRILL 1	STYLES	SCHEDULE

1. In the open document, select the title on the first line. Apply the Title style. Click the More button to select this style.
2. Select the subtitle on the second line. Apply the Subtitle style.

3. Select *Monday*; apply the Heading 1 style. **Hint:** Click the scroll buttons to the right of the Styles buttons to move in the styles list.
4. Repeat step 3 for the remaining days of the week and the heading *Extracurricular Activities*.
5. Check and close. (*38-drill1*)

LETTER PARTS AND BLOCK LETTER FORMAT

Businesspeople expect to see standard letter parts arranged in the proper sequence. Letters consist of three main parts: the opening lines to the receiver (letter address and salutation), the body or message, and the writer's closing lines. Standard letter parts and the required spacing using the defaults of *Word 2007* are explained below and illustrated on the following page.

Block letter style is a typical business letter format in which all letter parts are keyed at the left margin. For most letters, use open punctuation, which requires no punctuation after the salutation or the complimentary closing.

Block Letter Style with Open Punctuation

Letterhead: Preprinted stationery that includes the company name, logo, address, and other optional information such as telephone number and fax number.

Dateline: Date the letter is prepared. Position at about 2" (tap ENTER three times) or use the Center Page command. Be sure to begin at least 0.5" below the letterhead.

Letter address: Complete address of the letter recipient. Begin two lines below the date (tap ENTER twice).

Generally include receiver's name, company name, street address, city, state (one space after state), and ZIP Code. Include a personal title, e.g., Mr., Ms., Dr. Remove the added space between the lines of the letter address.

Salutation (or greeting): Begin one line below the letter address (tap ENTER once). Include courtesy title with person's name, e.g., Dear Mr. Smith. Use *Ladies and Gentlemen* when addressing a company.

Body: Begin one line below the salutation.

Use the 1.15 default line spacing; tap ENTER once between paragraphs. **Complimentary closing:** Begin one line below the body. Capitalize only the first letter of the closing.

Writer's name and title: Begin two lines below the complimentary closing (tap ENTER twice).

Include a personal title to designate gender only when the writer's name is not gender specific, such as Pat or Chris, or when initials are used, such J. A. Moe.

Key the title on the first line with the name or separately on the second line, whichever gives better balance. Use a comma to separate name and title if on one line. If two lines are used, remove the added space between the two lines.

Reference initials: Begin one line below the writer's name and title. Key reference initials, e.g., **xx** in lowercase. Replace *xx* with your initials.

Report Essentials

LEARNING OUTCOMES

- Format two-page reports using *Word 2007* format and traditional format.
- Format reference pages and title pages.
- Indent long quotations and bibliography entries appropriately.
- Insert page numbers.
- Apply styles.
- Apply bullets and numbers.
- Insert and edit footnotes.

LESSON 38 — Unbound Report

WARMUP 38a

Key each line, striving for control. Repeat if desired.

alphabet	1	Dave Cagney alphabetized items for next week's quarterly journal.
figures	2	Close Rooms 4, 18, and 20 from 3 until 9 on July 7; open Room 56.
up reaches	3	Toy & Wurt's note for $635 (see our page 78) was paid October 29.
easy	4	The auditor is due by eight, and he may lend a hand to the panel.

| 1 | 2 | 3 | 4 | 5 | 6 | 7 | 8 | 9 | 10 | 11 | 12 | 13 |

SKILL BUILDING

38b Timed Writing

1. Key a 1' timed writing on each paragraph; work to increase speed.
2. Key a 3' timed writing on both paragraphs.

all letters

	gwam	1'	3'
Have simple things such as saying please, may I help you, and		12	4
thank you gone out of style? We begin to wonder when we observe		25	8
front-line workers interact with customers today. Often their bad		39	13
attitudes shout that the customer is a bother and not important. But		52	17
we know there would be no business without the customer. So what		66	22
can be done to prove to customers that they really are king?		79	26
First, require that all your staff train in good customer		12	30
service. Here they must come to realize that their jobs exist for		25	35
the customer. Also, be sure workers feel that they can talk to		38	39
their bosses about any problem. You do not want workers to talk		51	43
about lack of breaks or schedules in front of customers. Clients		64	48
must always feel that they are kings and should never be ignored.		77	52

| 1' | 1 | 2 | 3 | 4 | 5 | 6 | 7 | 8 | 9 | 10 | 11 | 12 | 13 |
| 3' | | 1 | | 2 | | | 3 | | | 4 | | |

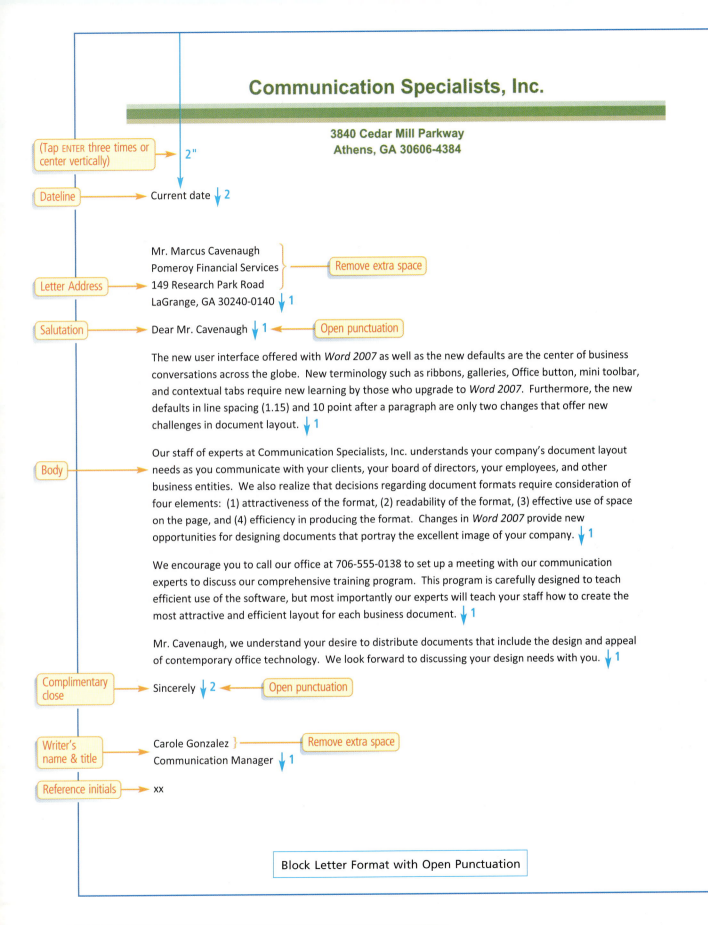

Communication Specialists, Inc.

3840 Cedar Mill Parkway
Athens, GA 30606-4384

(Tap ENTER three times or center vertically) → 2"

Dateline → Current date ↓ 2

Letter Address → Mr. Marcus Cavenaugh
Pomeroy Financial Services } Remove extra space
149 Research Park Road
LaGrange, GA 30240-0140 ↓ 1

Salutation → Dear Mr. Cavenaugh ↓ 1 ← Open punctuation

The new user interface offered with *Word 2007* as well as the new defaults are the center of business conversations across the globe. New terminology such as ribbons, galleries, Office button, mini toolbar, and contextual tabs require new learning by those who upgrade to *Word 2007*. Furthermore, the new defaults in line spacing (1.15) and 10 point after a paragraph are only two changes that offer new challenges in document layout. ↓ 1

Body → Our staff of experts at Communication Specialists, Inc. understands your company's document layout needs as you communicate with your clients, your board of directors, your employees, and other business entities. We also realize that decisions regarding document formats require consideration of four elements: (1) attractiveness of the format, (2) readability of the format, (3) effective use of space on the page, and (4) efficiency in producing the format. Changes in *Word 2007* provide new opportunities for designing documents that portray the excellent image of your company. ↓ 1

We encourage you to call our office at 706-555-0138 to set up a meeting with our communication experts to discuss our comprehensive training program. This program is carefully designed to teach efficient use of the software, but most importantly our experts will teach your staff how to create the most attractive and efficient layout for each business document. ↓ 1

Mr. Cavenaugh, we understand your desire to distribute documents that include the design and appeal of contemporary office technology. We look forward to discussing your design needs with you. ↓ 1

Complimentary close → Sincerely ↓ 2 ← Open punctuation

Writer's name & title → Carole Gonzalez } Remove extra space
Communication Manager ↓ 1

Reference initials → xx

Block Letter Format with Open Punctuation

DRILL 1

CAPITALIZATION

1. Review the rules and examples on the previous page.
2. Key the sentences, correcting all capitalization errors. Use the Numbering command to number each item.
3. Check and close. (*capitalize-drill1*)

1. according to one study, the largest ethnic minority group online is hispanics.
2. the american author mark twain said, "always do right; this will gratify some people and astonish the rest."
3. the grand canyon was formed by the colorado river cutting into the high-plateau region of northwestern arizona.
4. the president of russia is elected by popular vote.
5. the hubble space telescope is a cooperative project of the european space agency and the national aeronautics and space administration.
6. the train left north station at 6:45 this morning.
7. the trademark cyberprivacy prevention act would make it illegal for individuals to purchase domains solely for resale and profit.
8. consumers spent $7 billion online between november 1 and december 31, 2008, compared to $3.1 billion for the same period in 2007.
9. new students should attend an orientation session on wednesday, august 15, at 8 a.m. in room 252 of the perry building.
10. the summer book list includes *where the red fern grows* and *the mystery of the missing baseball.*

DRILL 2

CAPITALIZATION

CAPITALIZE2

1. Follow the specific directions provided in the data file. Remember to use the correct proof-readers' marks:

    Capitalize   sincerely

    lc Lowercase   My Dear Sir

2. Check and close. (*capitalize-drill2*)
3. Submit the rough draft and final copy to your instructor.

DRILL 3

CAPITALIZATION OF LETTER PARTS

1. Key the letter parts, using correct capitalization. Tap ENTER once after each item.
2. Check and close. (*capitalize-drill3*)

1. dear mr. petroilli
2. ladies and gentlemen
3. dear senator kuknais
4. very sincerely yours
5. dear reverend Schmidt
6. very truly yours
7. cordially yours
8. dear mr. fong and miss landow
9. respectfully yours
10. sincerely
11. dear mr. and mrs. Green
12. dear service manager

DRILL 4

CAPITALIZATION

CAPITALIZE4

1. This file includes a field for selecting the correct answer. You will simply select the correct answer. Follow the specific directions provided in the data file.
2. Check and close. (*capitalize-drill4*)

32-d1

Block Letter

1. Key the model letter on page 123 in block format with open punctuation. Assume you are using letterhead stationery.

2. Tap ENTER to position the dateline at about 2". Insert the current date using the Automatic Date feature.

3. Include your reference initials. If the first letter of your initials is automatically capitalized, point to the initial until the AutoCorrect Options button appears, click the button, and then choose Undo Automatic Capitalization.

4. Follow the proofreading procedures outlined in Lesson 31. Be sure to remove the added space in the letter address and between the writer's name and title. Use Show/Hide to view paragraph markers to confirm that you have correct spacing between letter parts.

5. Check and close. (*32-d1*)

32-d2

Block Letter

1. Key the letter below in block format with open punctuation. Insert the date using the automatic date.

2. Add your reference initials in lowercase letters. Remove extra space in the letter address and the writer's name and title.

3. Check and close. (*32-d2*)

Current date

Ms. Alice Ottoman
Premiere Properties, Inc.
52 Ocean Drive
Newport Beach, CA 92660-8293

Dear Ms. Ottoman

Is your website growing your real estate market as well as you would like? Internet Solutions invites you to take a look at our advanced strategies for marketing your properties on the World Wide Web. For example, we can create 360-degree panoramic pictures for your website. You can give your clients a virtual spin of the living room, kitchen, and every room in the house.

Call today for a demonstration of this remarkable technology and talk with our designers about other innovative website marketing strategies. Give your clients a better visual understanding of the property layout and more valuable information for decision making—something your competition does not have.

Sincerely

LeeAnn Rodgers
Marketing Manager

xx

CAPITALIZATION GUIDES

CAPITALIZE:

1. **First word of a sentence and of a direct quotation.**

   We were tolerating instead of managing diversity.
   The speaker said, "We must value diversity, not merely recognize it."

2. **Proper nouns**—specific persons, places, or things.

   Common nouns: continent, river, car, street
   Proper nouns: Asia, Mississippi, Buick, State Street
   Exception: Capitalize a title of high distinction even when it does not refer to a specific person (e.g., President of the United States).

3. **Derivatives** of proper nouns and capitalize **geographical** names.

   Derivatives: American history, German food, English accent, Ohio Valley
   Proper nouns: Tampa, Florida, Mount Rushmore

4. **A personal or professional title** when it precedes the name; capitalize a title of high distinction without a name.

   Title: Lieutenant Kahn, Mayor Walsh, Doctor Welby
   High distinction: the President of the United States

5. **Days of the week, months of the year, holidays, periods of history, and historic events.**

   Monday, June 8, Labor Day, Renaissance

6. **Specific parts of the country** but not compass points that show direction.

   Midwest   the South   northwest of town   the Middle East

7. **Family relationships** when used with a person's name.

   Aunt Carol   my mother   Uncle Mark

8. **A noun preceding a figure** except for common nouns such as line, page, and sentence.

   Unit 1   Section 2   page 2   verse 7   line 2

9. **First and main words of side headings, titles of books, and works of art.**
   Do not capitalize words of four or fewer letters that are conjunctions, prepositions, or articles.

   Computers in the News   Raiders of the Lost Ark

10. **Names of organizations and specific departments** within the writer's organization.

    Girl Scouts   our Sales Department

11. **The salutation of a letter and the first word of the complimentary closing.**

    Dear Mr. Bush   Ladies and Gentlemen: Sincerely yours,
    Very cordially yours,

32-d3

Block Letter and Center Page

1. Open *32-d2*.
2. Replace the letter address with the one below, using proper format.

   Ms. Andrea Virzi, J. P. Personnel Services, 2351 West Ravina Drive, Atlanta, GA 30346-9105.
3. Supply the correct salutation. Turn on Show/Hide (¶). Delete the hard returns above the dateline. Center the page vertically; preview to check placement. Note that a short letter looks more attractive centered vertically than positioned at 2.0".
4. Check and close. (*32-d3*)

32-d4

Block Letter and Center Page

1. Read the *Workplace Success* feature shown below.
2. In a new blank document, compose a letter to your instructor responding to this feature article. Follow the outline below to compose your letter.

   ¶1 Inform your teacher that you have read the feature article on organizational skills. Include a personal reaction to the information in the article.

   ¶2 Discuss your rating on the eight items listed below.

   ¶3 Discuss one organizational skill that you will work on this week. Explain your plan of action to improve this skill. **Note:** You may list something that is not included in the feature article.
3. Format the letter as a block letter with open punctuation in the new document format used by *Word 2007* users. Align the page at vertical center. Turn on Show/Hide (¶) to check that no hard returns are entered before the date or at the end of the letter. Refer to the model letter on page 123 to ensure all letter parts are used appropriately. Use your name as the writer's name; use *Student* as the writer's title. Reference initials are not needed since you are the writer of the message.
4. Check and close. (*32-d4*)

WORKPLACE SUCCESS

Organizational Skills

© RON CHAPPLE/THINKSTOCK IMAGES/JUPITERIMAGES

Well-organized employees accomplish daily tasks in a timely manner, avoid stress, and impress their employers and coworkers. Following simple daily time management practices reaps benefits and often even a promotion. How would you rate yourself on the following time management practices?

1. Prioritize tasks to be done each day and the amount of time needed to complete each task. Assign tasks to a specific time on the calendar.
2. Set designated times to answer e-mail and return phone calls.
3. Place calendar/planner on desk in location for easy access to add notes and see priority items.
4. Record notes, phone numbers, addresses in calendar and not on post-it notes.
5. Place phone, notepad, and pen on desk for easy reach.
6. Keep reference books in a designated location—not on the desk.
7. File any materials for which you no longer need immediate access.
8. Prepare folders for pending items, projects, and reading, and file those materials away instead of keeping them piled on the desktop.

37-d1
Memo with Distribution List

1. Key the memo to **Continuing Education Committee—Distribution List Below**. The memo is from **Alberto Valenzuela**. The date is April 3, 20--. The subject line is **May Seminar**.
2. The distribution list is as follows: John Patterson, Facilities Manager; Shawna Thompson, Regional Manager; Ed Vandenberg, Advertising Manager.
3. Continue to next document. (*37-d1*)

> **TIP**
>
> Remember to proofread and preview each document for placement before you move to the next one.

	gwam
I have invited Lynda A. Brewer, Ph.D., Earlham	33
College, Richmond, Indiana, to be our seminar	42
leader on Friday afternoon, May 10.	50
Dr. Brewer, a well-known psychologist who has	59
spent a lot of time researching and writing in the	69
field of ergonomics, will address "Stress Management."	80
Please make arrangements for rooms, speaker accom-	90
modations, staff notification, and refreshments.	100
I will send you Dr. Brewer's vita for use in pre-	110
paring news releases.	114
closing lines	139

37-d2
Block Letter

1. Key the letter below in the block letter style using *Word 2007* defaults; use open punctuation. Add an appropriate salutation. Send a copy of the letter to **Olivia Cavenaugh**. Center the letter vertically on the page.
2. Add an envelope to the document.
3. Continue to next document. (*37-d2*).

	words
Current date	Mr. John J. Long, Sales Manager	The Record Store	9822	11
Trevor Avenue	Anaheim, CA 92805-5885	22

With your letter came our turn to be perplexed, and we apologize. When we had our refund coupons printed, we had just completed a total redesign program for our product boxes. We had detachable logos put on the outside of the boxes, which could be peeled off and placed on a coupon. | 36 / 51 / 65 / 79

We had not anticipated that our distributors would use back inventories with our promotion. The cassettes you sold were not packaged in our new boxes; therefore, there were no logos on them. | 94 / 108 / 118

I'm sorry you or your customers were inconvenienced. In the future, simply ask your customers to send us their sales slips, and we will honor them with refunds until your supply of older containers is depleted. | 131 / 146 / 160

Sincerely yours | Bruna Wertz | Sales and Promotions Dept. | xx | 173

37-d3
Modified Block Letter/Traditional Format

1. Key *37-d2* above in the traditional modified block letter format with mixed punctuation.
2. Check the test and close. (*37-d3*)

CHECKPOINT ➡

Congratulations! You have successfully completed the lessons in Module 4. To check your understanding and for more practice, complete the objective assessment and performance assessment located on the textbook website at www.collegekeyboarding.com.

LESSON 33 — Block Letter with Envelope

WARMUP 33a

Key each line, striving for control. Repeat if desired.

1st finger

1 My 456 heavy brown jugs have nothing in them; fill them by May 7.
2 The 57 bins are numbered 1 to 57; Bins 5, 6, 45, and 57 are full.

2nd finger

3 Ed decided to crate 38 pieces of cedar decking from the old dock.
4 Mike, who was 38 in December, likes a piece of ice in cold cider.

3rd finger

5 Polly made 29 points on the quiz; Wex 10 points. Did they pass?
6 Sall saw Ezra pass 200 pizza pans to Sean, who fixed 20 of them.

| 1 | 2 | 3 | 4 | 5 | 6 | 7 | 8 | 9 | 10 | 11 | 12 | 13 |

SKILL BUILDING

33b Timed Writing
1. Key a 3' timed writing, working for speed.
2. Key a 3' timed writing, working for control.

all letters

	gwam	3'
So now you are operating a keyboard and don't you find it	4	38
amazing that your fingers, working with very little visual help,	8	43
move easily and quickly from one key to the next, helping you to	13	47
change words into ideas and sentences. You just decide what you	17	51
want to say and the format in which you want to say it, and your	21	56
keyboard will carry out your order exactly as you enter it. One	26	60
operator said lately that she sometimes wonders just who is most	30	64
responsible for the completed product—the person or the machine.	34	69

3' | 1 | 2 | 3 | 4 | 5 |

COMMUNICATION

33c

LETTER ADDRESSES AND SALUTATIONS

The salutation, or greeting, consists of the person's personal title (*Mr.*, *Ms.*, or *Mrs.*) or professional title (*Dr.*, *Professor*, *Senator*, *Honorable*), and the person's last name. Do not use a first name unless you have a personal relationship. The salutation should agree in number with the addressee. If the letter is addressed to more than one person, the salutation is plural.

	Receiver	Salutation
To individuals	Dr. Alexander Gray Dr. and Mrs. Thompson	Dear Dr. Gray Dear Dr. and Mrs. Thompson
To organizations	TMP Electronics, Inc.	Ladies and Gentlemen
Name unknown	Advertising Manager	Dear Advertising Manager

DRILL 1 — COMPOSE SALUTATIONS

1. In a new blank document, key the appropriate salutation for each letter recipient. (Do not key the letters *a* through *f*.)
2. Check and close. (*33-drill1*)

a. Mr. Thomas Green
b. Dr. John Watson
c. Phillips Insurance Company
d. Mr. and Mrs. Reginald Worthington
e. Senator Constance Wells
f. Smith College Board of Directors

LESSON 37 | Assessment

WARMUP 37a

Key each line, striving for control. Repeat if desired.

alphabet 1 Johnny Willcox printed five dozen banquet tickets for my meeting.

fig/symbol 2 Our check #389 for $21,460—dated 1/15/08—was sent to O'Neil & Co.

1st finger 3 It is true Greg acted bravely during the severe storm that night.

easy 4 In the land of enchantment, the fox and the lamb lie by the bush.

| 1 | 2 | 3 | 4 | 5 | 6 | 7 | 8 | 9 | 10 | 11 | 12 | 13 |

SKILL BUILDING

37b Timed Writing
Key two 3' timed writings.

LA
all letters

	gwam	3'

Many young people are quite surprised to learn that either lunch or dinner is included as part of a job interview. Most of them think of this part of the interview as a friendly gesture from the organization.

	4	48
	8	52
	13	56
	15	58

The meal is not provided just to be nice to the person. The organization expects to use that function to observe the social skills of the person and to determine if he or she might be effective doing business in that type of setting.

	18	62
	22	66
	27	71
	30	73

What does this mean to you if you are preparing for a job interview? The time spent reading about and learning to use good social skills pays off not only during the interview but also after you accept the job.

	33	77
	38	81
	42	86
	44	87

3' | 1 | 2 | 3 | 4 |

APPLICATIONS

37c

Assessment

Continue

Check

With *Keyboarding Pro DELUXE*: When you complete a document, proofread it, check the spelling, and preview for placement. When you are completely satisfied, click the Continue button to move to the next document. Click the Check button when you are ready to error-check the test. Review and/or print the document analysis results.

Without *Keyboarding Pro DELUXE*: Key the documents in sequence. When time has been called, proofread all documents again and identify errors.

NEW FUNCTIONS

33d

ENVELOPES

MAILINGS/CREATE/ENVELOPES

The Envelopes feature can insert the delivery address automatically if a letter is displayed; postage can even be added if special software is installed. The default is a size 10 envelope (4⅛" by 9½"); other sizes are available by clicking the Options button on the Envelopes tab.

To generate an envelope:

1. Display the letter you have created and select the letter address.

2. On the Mailings tab in the Create group, click Envelopes ❶. The mailing address is automatically displayed in the Delivery address box. (To create an envelope without a letter, key the address in the Delivery address box.)

3. If you are using business envelopes with a preprinted return address (assume you are), click the Return address Omit box ❷. To include a return address, do not check the Omit box; click in the Return address box and key the return address.

4. Click Print to print the envelope or click Add to Document to add the envelope to the top of the document containing the letter ❸.

DRILL 2   CREATE ENVELOPE

1. Open *32-d1*.
2. Create and attach an envelope to the letter.
3. Your instructor may have you print envelopes on plain paper.
4. Check and close. (*33-drill2*)

DRILL 3   CREATE ENVELOPE

1. In a new blank document, go to the Envelopes and Labels dialog box without keying a letter address.
2. Key the following letter address in the envelope dialog box.

   Ms. Joyce Bohn, Treasurer

   Citizens for the Environment

   1888 Hutchins Avenue

   Seattle, WA 98111-1888

3. Add the envelope to the document.
4. Check and close. (*33-drill3*).

36-d4

Block Letter/Traditional and Envelope

1. Key the letter shown below in block letter style with open punctuation. Format in the traditional format; apply the *Word 2003* style and change font to Times New Roman. Insert the current date. Supply an appropriate salutation. Remove extra spacing as necessary.

2. Center the letter vertically on the page.

3. Send a copy to **Phillip Gilbert** and **Leigh Browning**. Add an envelope.

4. Check and close. (*36-d5*)

AMASTA Company, Inc. | 902 Greenridge Drive | Reno, NV 89505-5552

We sell your digital recorders and have since you introduced them. Several of our customers now tell us they are unable to follow the directions on the coupon. They explain that there is no company log on the box to return to you as you requested.

What steps should we take? A copy of the coupon is enclosed, as is a digital recorder box. Please read the coupon, examine the box, and then let me know your plans for extricating us from this problem.

Sincerely | John J. Long | Sales Manager | Enclosures

36-d5

Move Tab

1. Open *36-d2*.

2. Select the last five lines of the memo (not including your reference initials).

3. Move the tab from position 2.5" to 3.0". This moves the last five lines to 3.0".

4. Check and close. (*36-d5*)

36-d6

E-mail

1. Compose an e-mail to your instructor using the subject line **Module 4 Quiz**. Key each question shown below and key your response to the question. Do not tap the ENTER key after the question; just space and key your answer.

   1. What are the two letter styles learned in Module 4?
   2. When formatting using the traditional format, what style is applied to the *Word 2007* document?
   3. What is the tab setting for the modified block letter style?
   4. Which letter parts are keyed at the tab you must set when keying a modified block letter?
   5. Distinguish between open punctuation and mixed punctuation.
   6. If a letter is addressed to a company, what is the appropriate salutation?
   7. What four items are included in the heading of a memo?

2. Print and send the e-mail. If you cannot send it, key it as a memo.

3. Check and close. (*36-d6*)

33-d1
Single Envelope

1. Key a single envelope to the following address. Include your address as the return address.
2. Check and close. (*33-d1*)

Mr. Jacob Gillespie
1783 West Rockhill Road
Bartlett, TN 38133-1783

33-d2
Block Letter and Envelope

1. Key the following letter in the block style with open punctuation. Begin the date at about 2". Remember to remove the extra space in the letter address.
2. Check the letter placement.
3. Add an envelope to the letter.
4. Check and close. (*33-d2*)

April 4, 2008 | Mrs. Rose Shikamuru | 55 Lawrence Street |Topeka, KS 66607-6657 | Dear Mrs. Shikamuru

Thank you for your recent letter asking about employment opportunities with our company. We are happy to inform you that Mr. Edward Ybarra, our recruiting representative, will be on your campus on April 23, 24, 25, and 26 to interview students who are interested in our company.

We suggest that you talk soon with your student placement office, as all appointments with Mr. Ybarra will be made through that office. Please bring with you the application questionnaire the office provides.

Within a few days, we will send you a company brochure with information about our salary, bonus, and retirement plans. You will want to visit our website at http://www.skylermotors.com to find facts about our company mission and accomplishments as well as learn about the beautiful community in which we are located. We believe a close study of this information will convince you, as it has many others, that our company builds futures as well as small motors.

If there is any way we can help you, please e-mail me at mbragg@skylermotors.com.

Sincerely | Myrtle K. Bragg | Human Services Director | xx

33-d3
Block Letter and Envelope

1. Key the letter at the top of the next page in block style with open punctuation. Center the letter vertically on the page.
2. Add an envelope to the letter.
3. Check and close. (*33-d3*)

36-d2

Memo with Tab

1. Key the following memo in correct format.
2. After keying the second paragraph, tap ENTER once. From the ruler bar, set a left tab at 2.5", and key the last several lines.
3. Check and close. (*36-d2*)

TO:	All Sunwood Employees
FROM:	Julie Patel, Human Resources Director
DATE:	Insert current date
SUBJECT:	Eric Kershaw Hospitalized

We were notified by Eric Kershaw's family that he was admitted into the hospital this past weekend. They expect that he will be hospitalized for another ten days. Visitations and phone calls are limited, but cards and notes are welcome.

A plant is being sent to Eric from the Sunwood staff. Stop by our office before Wednesday if you wish to sign the card. If you would like to send your own "Get Well Wishes" to Eric, send them to:

Eric Kershaw
County General Hospital
Room 401
P.O. Box 13947
Atlanta, GA 38209-4751

36-d3

Modified Block Letter and Envelope

1. Format the letter in the modified block format with mixed punctuation. Insert the current date. Position the letter attractively on the page. Remove extra spacing as necessary.
2. Supply the correct salutation and other necessary letter parts. Add an enclosure notation and a copy notation to **Laura Aimes, Sales Representative**. Set a left tab at 0.5" for keying the copy notation.
3. Create an envelope and add to the letter.
4. Preview for letter placement, check, and close. (*36-d3*)

Ms. Mukta Bhakta
9845 Buckingham Road
Annapolis, MD 21403-0314

Thank you for your recent inquiry about our wireless pet fence. The Hilton Pet Fence was developed to assist many pet owners like you who desire the safety of their pets without the barrier of a traditional fence.

Hilton Pet Fence also provides a customer support service to assist you in training your pet and a technical support team for providing technical assistance. For additional information, please call:

Customer and Technical Support
Telephone: 555-0112
9:00 a.m.-5:00 p.m., Monday-Friday, Eastern Time

Please look over the enclosed brochure. I will call you within the next two weeks to discuss any additional questions you may have.

Alexander Zampich | Marketing Manager

33-d3

Continued

Current date | Mr. Trace L. Brecken | 4487 Ingram Street | Corpus Christi, TX 78409-8907 | Dear Mr. Brecken

We have received the package you sent us in which you returned goods from a recent order you gave us. Your refund check, plus return postage, will be mailed to you in a few days.

We are sorry, of course, that you did not find this merchandise personally satisfactory. It is our goal to please all of our customers, and we are always disappointed if we fail.

Please give us an opportunity to try again. We stand behind our merchandise, and that is our guarantee of good service.

Sincerely | Margret Bredewig | Customer Service Department | xx

---

33-d4

Rough Draft Block Letter and Envelope

1. Key the following letter in block letter style with mixed punctuation. Add an appropriate salutation and other missing letter parts.
2. Center the page vertically. Create an envelope and add to the letter. Check and close. (*33-d4*)
3. Study the illustration in the Reference Guide on folding and inserting letters in an envelope. Fold the letter to insert in the envelope.

Mr. John Crane
5760 Sky Way
Seattle, WA 98108-0321

Would you like to invest in a company that will provide you with a 180% return on your investment? Consider investing in a ~~company~~ *firm* that specializes in importing and exporting with China. China's *gross* domestic product (GDP) is expected to be over a trillion dollars.

(bold & italic) Ameri-Chinois has made a significant number of business arrangements with key organizations in China to source goods and to participate in global two-way trade. Trade between China and ~~other countries~~ *the rest of the world* is expected to grow over 20% this year. China's exports are expected to rise to $244 billion in the year 2009. Imports ~~will~~ *are expected to* grow to $207 billion.

Please contact Lawrence Chen at Century Investments to learn how you can be an investor in the growing company of Ameri-Chinois. The current price *per share* is $0.52; the targeted price is $9.00. Call today! 555-0134

Sincerely

Lawrence Chen, *Agent*

LESSON 36

Correspondence Review

WARMUP 36a

Key each line, striving for control. Repeat if desired.

alphabet 1 Perhaps Max realized jet flights can quickly whisk us to Bolivia.

fig/symbol 2 Send 24 Solex Cubes, Catalog #95-0, price $6.78, before April 30.

1st finger 3 The boy of just 6 or 7 years of age ran through the mango groves.

easy 4 The auditor did sign the form and name me to chair a small panel.

| 1 | 2 | 3 | 4 | 5 | 6 | 7 | 8 | 9 | 10 | 11 | 12 | 13 |

NEW FUNCTIONS

36b

MODIFYING TABS

Tabs can be added or moved in existing documents. When adding tabs to an existing document, you must first select all portions of the document where the new tab(s) will be applied; then set the additional tab(s). When moving a tab, first select all the text that will be affected. If you fail to select all the text, then only the tab that your insertion point is on will be moved.

DRILL 1   ADDING TAB TO EXISTING DOCUMENT

1. Open *33-d4*.
2. Select the entire letter by pressing CTRL + A.

   Alternate method: Point to the left of any text until a right-pointing arrow displays; then triple-click.

3. Set a left tab at 3.25".
4. Tab the appropriate lines to format this letter in modified block letter format.
5. Check and close. (*36-drill1*)

DRILL 2   MOVING A TAB

1. Open *36-drill1*.
2 Select the entire letter.

3. Drag the tab on the ruler from 3.25" to 3.0".
4. Check and close. (*36-drill2*)

APPLICATIONS

36-d1

Edit Letter

1. Open *33-d2*, a block letter keyed in Lesson 33.
2. Set a tab at the center of the page. Make the necessary changes to change this letter to a modified block letter with mixed punctuation.
3. Edit the first sentence of paragraph 3 as follows:

   A company brochure with information about our salary, bonus, and retirement plans is enclosed.

4. Add an enclosure notation.
5. Check and close. (*36-d1*)

LESSON 34

Modified Block Letter Format

WARMUP 34a

Key each line, striving for control. Repeat if desired.

alphabet 1 Buddy Jackson is saving the door prize money for wax and lacquer.
figures 2 I have fed 47 hens, 25 geese, 10 ducks, 39 lambs, and 68 kittens.
one hand 3 You imply Jon Case exaggerated my opinion on a decrease in rates.
easy 4 I shall make hand signals to the widow with the auditory problem.

| 1 | 2 | 3 | 4 | 5 | 6 | 7 | 8 | 9 | 10 | 11 | 12 | 13 |

SKILL BUILDING

34b Textbook Keying
Key each line once, concentrating on using good keying techniques; tap ENTER twice after each 2-line group.

Balanced-hand words, phrases, and sentences

5 am an by do go he if is it me or ox or so for and big the six spa
6 but cod dot dug eye end wit vie yam make also city work gage them

7 is it|is it|is it he|is it he|for it|for it|paid for it|it is she
8 of it|pay due|pay for|paid me|paid them|also make|such as|may end

9 Sue and Bob may go to the zoo, and he or she may pay for the gas.
10 Jim was sad; Ted saw him as we sat on my bed; we saw him get gas.

| 1 | 2 | 3 | 4 | 5 | 6 | 7 | 8 | 9 | 10 | 11 | 12 | 13 |

FUNCTION REVIEW

34c

TABS

PAGE LAYOUT/PARAGRAPH

Tabs are used to indent paragraphs and to align text vertically. You will recall from Lesson 28 that default tab stops are set at every half-inch position. Take a moment to look at the Horizontal Ruler to identify the small gray lines below each half-inch position.

In Lesson 34 you will set a tab stop at the center of the page (3.25") to key the date and closing lines of a letter formatted in the modified block style. Once you have set a tab stop, all default tabs to the left of the newly set tab are automatically cleared. Therefore, if other tabs are needed, simply choose the desired tab alignment by clicking the Alignment button at the far left of the Horizontal Ruler. Then click the Horizontal Ruler where the desired tab is to be set.

DRILL 1   SET TABS

1. In a new blank document, set a left tab at 3.25". Key the date at 3.25" and tap the ENTER key twice. **Note:** All default tabs to the left of the newly set tab have been automatically cleared.

2. Set a left tab at 1". Key the following lines and tap the ENTER key once. Remove the space between the items.

    Enclosures: Promissory Note
                 Amortization Schedule

3. Set a left tab at 0.5". Key the following lines. Remove the space between the lines. Undo automatic capitalization in the first line.

    c   Ashley Nobles
             Ethan Vilella

4. Check and close. (34-drill1)

35-d1

**Block Letter in
Traditional Format**

1. Change the style set to *Word 2003* style and change the font to Times New Roman. Remember the spacing after the paragraph is now 0, the line spacing is 1.0, and the font size is 12.

2. Key the model letter on page 136 in block format with open punctuation in the traditional format.

3. Tap ENTER six times to position the date line at about 2". Insert the current date using the Automatic Date feature. Tap ENTER four times after the date and the complimentary closing. Tap ENTER twice after each paragraph.

4. Refer to the model letter for correct spacing between all letter parts. Use Show/Hide to view paragraph markers to confirm correct spacing between letter parts.

5. Check and close. (*35-d1*)

35-d2

**Modified Block Letter in
Traditional Format**

1. Key the letter below in modified block format with mixed punctuation in the traditional format using the *Word 2003* style. Change font to Times New Roman.

2. Supply appropriate letter parts. Use the Center Page command to center the letter vertically.

3. Check and close. (*35-d2*)

February 1, 2008

Mr. Thomas Prescott, President
Prescott Financial Services
3054 North Kenswick Circle
Birmingham, AL 35242-3054

Two unique and focused word processing training programs are ready for your review. Since our initial meeting with your managers, a comprehensive needs assessment of training needs was conducted, and appropriate instructional materials have been designed and piloted.

The need for two levels of users—proficient and power—necessitated the design of two focused training programs. Employees who use word processing frequently but who use only a limited numer of functions will complete the proficient-level training program. Those employees who must have an advanced level of expertise in the word processing software and troubleshoot software problems will complete the power-level training program.

We appreciate this opportunity to design these training programs and look forward to discussing them with you at our meeting on February 15.

Sincerely

Landon Maybury
Training Director

MODIFIED BLOCK FORMAT

In the modified block format, the date line and the closing lines begin at the center point of the page. All other guidelines for the block letter style are applied to the modified block letter. Remember to remove the extra spacing between the letter address and other short lines. Review the model modified block letter on the next page.

NATIONAL
ASSOCIATION OF
INFORMATION
PROCESSING
PROFESSIONALS

February 6, 2008

Mr. Justin Novarini
7490 Oregon Avenue
Arvada, CO 80002-8765

Dear Mr. Novarini: ← *Mixed punctuation*

Please consider this personal invitation to join the National Association of Information Processing Professionals (NAIPP). Membership is offered to the top 25 percent of the graduating class. NAIPP is a nonprofit organization comprised of technical professionals who are striving to stay current in their field. Member benefits include:

Career Development Opportunities—Resume preparation services, job search program, 120-day internship in many cities, and access to our online job bulletin board.

Professional Benefits—Industry standard skill testing, discounts on continuing education courses at colleges and universities, recertification programs, publications, medical insurance, financial planning programs, and free international travel services.

Sign on to our website at http://www.naipp.org to learn about many more benefits. A parking pass and discount coupons for the Multimedia Symposium on February 27 are enclosed.

Sincerely,   ← *Mixed punctuation*

Jolene Ryder, President
NAIPP Board of Directors

xx

Enclosures: Parking Pass
              Discount Coupons

c   Adam Vassel
    Bethany Corbin

**Modified Block Letter Format
with Mixed Punctuation**

Dateline:

- Position at about 2.0" or use the Center Page command.
- Begin at least 0.5" below the letterhead.
- Set a left tab at 3.25". Determine the position of the tab by subtracting the side margin from the center of the paper.

> 4.25" Center of the paper
> − 1.00" Margin
> 3.25" Tab setting

Complimentary closing: Begin keying at 3.25".

Writer's name and title: Begin keying at 3.25".

MIXED PUNCTUATION STYLE

Although most letters are formatted with open punctuation, some businesses prefer mixed punctuation. To format a letter using mixed punctuation, key a colon after the salutation and a comma after the complimentary closing.

Dear Dr. Hathorn:

Sincerely,

Mixed Punctuation

ADDITIONAL LETTER PARTS

In Lesson 32 you learned the standard letter parts. Optional parts are listed below.

Enclosure notations: If an item is included with a letter, key an enclosure notation one line below the reference initials. Tap TAB to align the enclosures at 1.0".

Left tab at 1.0" —

Enclosures: Check #831
              Order form

Enclosures: 2

Copy notation: A copy notation (c) indicates that a copy of the document has been sent to the person(s) listed. Key the copy notation one blank line below the reference initials or enclosure notation (if used). Tap TAB to align the names at 0.5". If necessary, click Undo Automatic Capitalization after keying the copy notation to lowercase the letter *c*.

Left tab at 0.5" —

c   Larry Qualls
    Wendy Mullins

E-Market, Group

10 East Rivercenter Boulevard
Covington, KY 41016-8765

About 2" ← (Tap ENTER three times or center vertically.)

Current date ↓2

Mr. Eric Seymour
Professional Office Consultants } ← Remove extra space
1782 Laurel Canyon Road
Sunnyvale, CA 94085-9087 ↓1

Dear Mr. Seymour ↓1

Have you heard your friends and colleagues talk about obtaining real-time stock quotes, real-time account balances and positions, NASDAQ Level II quotes, or extended-hours trading? If so, then they are among the many serious investors who have opened an account with E-Market Firm. ↓1

We are confident that the best decisions are informed decisions that are made in a very timely manner. E-Market Firm has an online help desk that provides information for all levels of investors, from beginners to the experienced serious trader. You can learn basic tactics for investing in the stock market, avoiding common mistakes, and picking up some advanced strategies. ↓1

To stay on top of the market and your investments, please visit our online investing website at http://www.emarketfirm.com to learn more about our banking and brokerage services and to access our online help desk. E-Market Firm is the premier site for online investing. ↓1

Sincerely ↓2

Emily Zumwalt } ——— Remove extra space
Marketing Manager ↓1

xx

Traditional Block Letter Format
(Word 2003)

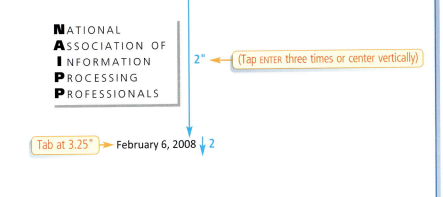

NATIONAL
ASSOCIATION OF
INFORMATION
PROCESSING
PROFESSIONALS

2" ← (Tap ENTER three times or center vertically)

Tab at 3.25" → February 6, 2008 ↓ 2

Mr. Justin Novarini
7490 Oregon Avenue
Arvada, CO 80002-8765 ↓ 1

Mixed punctuation → Dear Mr. Novarini: ↓ 1

Please consider this personal invitation to join the National Association of Information Processing Professionals (NAIPP). Membership is offered to the top 25 percent of the graduating class. NAIPP is a nonprofit organization comprised of technical professionals who are striving to stay current in their field. Member benefits include: ↓ 1

Career Development Opportunities—Resume preparation services, job search program, 120-day internship in many cities, and access to our online job bulletin board. ↓ 1

Professional Benefits—Industry standard skill testing, discounts on continuing education courses at colleges and universities, recertification programs, publications, medical insurance, financial planning programs, and free international travel services. ↓ 1

Sign on to our website at http://www.naipp.org to learn about many more benefits. A parking pass and discount coupons for the Multimedia Symposium on February 27 are enclosed. ↓ 1

Mixed punctuation → Sincerely, ↓ 2

Jolene Ryder, President
NAIPP Board of Directors ↓ 1

Tab at 1"

xx ↓ 1

Enclosures: Parking Pass
                Discount Coupons

c   Adam Vassel
       Bethany Corbin

Tab at 0.5"

Modified Block Letter Format
with Mixed Punctuation

TO CHANGE TO WORD 2003 STYLE:

HOME/STYLES/CHANGE STYLES

1. From the Home tab, click the Change Styles button **1**.
2. Click Style Set **2**.
3. Click Word 2003 **3**. The line spacing is now 1.0; the space after paragraph is 0; the font size is 12; and the side margins remain at 1.0".

DRILL 1   CHANGE STYLES

1. From the Home tab, on the Styles group, click Change Styles. Click Style Set and *Word 2003*.

2. Click on the Home tab and note the 12-point Calibri font.

3. Click on the Line Spacing button and note the 1.0 line spacing.

4. Click the Paragraph Dialog Box Launcher and note the 0 spacing after the paragraph.

5. From the Page Layout tab, click Margins and note the Normal 1" left and right margins.

6. Close the document without saving.

DOCUMENT DESIGN

35d

LETTER PARTS AND TRADITIONAL LETTER FORMAT

The traditional letter format is keyed using the defaults of *Word 2003*. To restore these defaults, apply the *Word 2003* style and change the font to Times New Roman. Because the space after the paragraph is now 0, more spacing is needed when using the *Word 2003* style. The required spacing using the traditional format is explained below and illustrated on the following page. All other formatting you have learned concerning the block and modified block format remains the same.

Changes:

Apply *Word 2003* style and change font to Times New Roman.

Date: Position at about 2" (tap ENTER six times) or use the Center Page command.

Letter address: Three blank lines below the date (tap ENTER four times).

Salutation: Double-space below the letter address (tap ENTER twice).

Body: Double-space below the salutation. Single-space paragraphs and double-space between paragraphs (tap ENTER twice).

Complimentary close: Double-space below the body.

Writer's name and title: Three blank lines below the complimentary closing (tap ENTER four times).

Reference initials: Double-space below the writer's name and title.

Enclosures: Double-space below the reference initials.

Copy notation: Double-space below the enclosure notation if included.

34-d1
Modified Block Letter

1. Open a new document and set a left tab at 3.25". Tap TAB and insert the current date at about 2.0".

2. Key the letter on page 132 in new modified block letter format with *Word 2007* defaults and use mixed punctuation. Remove extra spacing in letter address, enclosure notation, and copy notation.

3. Before keying the enclosure notation, set a left tab at 1.0". Before keying the copy notation, set a left tab at 0.5".

4. Preview the placement of the letter, check, and close. (*34-d1*)

34-d2
Modified Block Letter

1. Key the following letter in modified block letter style with mixed punctuation. Add an appropriate salutation, a complimentary closing, and any other missing letter parts. Send a copy of this letter to your instructor and a classmate. The writer is Mary Fleming-Davis, Marketing Manager.

2. Center the letter vertically.

3. Check and close. (*34-d2*)

Ms. Abbie Welborn
One Stop Printing Co.
501 Madison Road
Cincinnati, OH 45227-6398

Do you know that more and more people are opting to go on a shopping spree on the Internet rather than the mall? Businesses, ranging from small mom-and-pop stores to global multinational corporations, are setting up shop on the Web if they have not already.

Consumers expect businesses to have a website. Those companies that do not have a presence on the Web will most likely give their business to their competitors.

E-Business, Inc. has helped hundreds of businesses nationwide establish their business on the Internet. May we help integrate your online and offline sales strategies? Call us today at 555-0100 and arrange for one of our outstanding consultants to analyze your e-commerce strategies to increase your volume.

34-d3
Compose Modified Block Letter

1. Compose a letter to a businessperson in your area requesting that your keyboarding class complete a service project for that business. Format the letter as a new modified block letter with *Word 2007*; use mixed punctuation. Follow the outline below to compose your letter.

   ¶1 Introduce yourself as a keyboarding student at your college. Explain that the keyboarding course is designed to teach students various business formats. List some of the formats.

   ¶2 Explain that the class is offering keyboarding services for a three-week period so that students can learn to apply formatting skills in an authentic environment. Explain that a class office manager will accept the project assignments, and all members will format, proofread, and print the documents on company letterhead.

   ¶3 Close by asking the businessperson to call your teacher to discuss the many mutual benefits of the project. Provide a telephone number and e-mail address.

2. Check and close. (*34-d3*)

Traditional Letter Format

WARMUP 35a

Key each line, striving for control. Repeat if desired.

alphabet 1 Jacky Few's strange, quiet behavior amazed and perplexed even us.

figures 2 Dial Extension 1480 or 2760 for a copy of the 3-page 95-cent book.

double letters 3 Ann will see that Edd accepts an assignment in the school office.

easy 4 If I burn the signs, the odor of enamel may make a toxic problem.

| 1 | 2 | 3 | 4 | 5 | 6 | 7 | 8 | 9 | 10 | 11 | 12 | 13 |

SKILL BUILDING

35b Textbook Keying

1. Key each line once, concentrating on using good keying techniques; tap ENTER twice after each 2-line group.
2. Repeat the drill if time permits.

adjacent reaches 5 The people were sad as the poor relish was opened and poured out.

6 Sophia moved west with her new silk dress and poor walking shoes.

direct reaches 7 Freddy stated that hurricanes are much greater in number in June.

8 Many juniors decide to work free to add experience to the resume.

balanced hand 9 The eight ducks lay down at the end of right field for cozy naps.

10 Kala is to go to the formal town social with Henry and the girls.

NEW FUNCTIONS

35c

STYLES

The Styles feature enables you to apply a group of formats automatically to a document. A new *Word* document opens with approximately 18 styles attached to it. These styles include Normal, Heading 1, Heading 2, Heading 3, Heading 4, and Title. You will learn more about applying these styles in Module 5.

The Normal style is the default style that is automatically applied when a new *Word* document is opened. The Normal default style in *Word 2003* and *Word 2007* differ in a number of ways; however, the following differences affect formatting letters.

Word 2007 Defaults

1.15 line spacing

10-point spacing after the paragraph

11-point font size

Calibri font

1.0 left and right margins

Word 2003 Defaults

1.0 line spacing

0 spacing after the paragraph

12-point font size

Times New Roman font

1.25" left and right margins

To format a letter in the traditional format using *Word 2007* software, change to the *Word 2003* style. The key *Word 2003* style defaults are 1.0 line spacing, 0 spacing after the paragraph, and 12-point font size. Change the font to Times New Roman. Although the side margins do not change to the *Word 2003* default of 1.25", keep the 1.0" side margins.

KEYBOARDING PRO DELUXE See References/Word commands/Lesson 35

Reference Guide

1. First word of a sentence and of a direct quotation.
   We were tolerating instead of managing diversity.
   The speaker said, "We must value diversity, not merely recognize it."

2. Names of proper nouns—specific persons, places, or things.
   Common nouns: continent, river, car, street
   Proper nouns: Asia, Mississippi, Buick, State St.

3. Derivatives of proper nouns and geographical names.
   American history   English accent
   German food   Ohio Valley
   Tampa, Florida   Mount Rushmore

4. A personal or professional title when it precedes the name or a title of high distinction without a name.
   Lieutenant Kahn   Mayor Walsh
   Doctor Welby   Mr. Ty Brooks
   Dr. Frank Collins   Miss Tate
   the President of the United States

5. Days of the week, months of the year, holidays, periods of history, and historic events.
   Monday, June 8   Labor Day   Renaissance

6. Specific parts of the country but not compass points that show direction.
   Midwest   the South   northwest of town

7. Family relationships when used with a person's name.
   Aunt Helen   my dad   Uncle John

8. Noun preceding a figure except for common nouns such as *line, page,* and *sentence.*
   Unit 1   Section 2   page 2   verse 7   line 2

9. First and main words of side headings, titles of books, and works of art. Do not capitalize words of four or fewer letters that are conjunctions, prepositions, or articles.
   Computers in the News   *Raiders of the Lost Ark*

10. Names of organizations and specific departments within the writer's organization.
    Girl Scouts   our Sales Department

General guidelines

1. Use **words** for numbers *one* through *ten* unless the numbers are in a category with related larger numbers that are expressed as figures.
   He bought three acres of land. She took two acres.
   She wrote 12 stories and 2 plays in the last 13 years.

2. Use **words** for approximate numbers or large round numbers that can be expressed as one or two words. Use **numbers** for round numbers in millions or higher with their word modifier.
   We sent out about three hundred invitations.
   She contributed $3 million dollars.

3. Use **words** for numbers that begin a sentence.
   Six players were cut from the ten-member team.

4. Use **figures** for the larger of two adjacent numbers.
   We shipped six 24-ton engines.

Times and dates

5. Use **words** for numbers that precede o'clock (stated or implied).
   We shall meet from two until five o'clock.

6. Use **figures** for times with *a.m.* or *p.m.* and days when they follow the month.
   Her appointment is for 2:15 p.m. on July 26, 2009.

7. Use **ordinals** for the day when it precedes the month.
   The 10th of October is my anniversary.

Money, percentages, and fractions

8. Use **figures** for money amounts and percentages. Spell out *cents* and *percent* except in statistical copy.
   The 16% discount saved me $145. Bill, 95 cents.

9. Use **words** for fractions unless the fractions appear in combination with whole numbers.
   one-half of her lesson   5 1/2   18 3/4

Addresses

10. Use **words** for street names First through Tenth and **figures** or ordinals for streets above Tenth. (If street name is **one** number other than house number, separate it from house number with a dash.)
    One Lytle Place   Second Ave.   142—53rd St.

Use an apostrophe

1. To make most singular nouns and indefinite pronouns possessive (add **apostrophe** and **s**).

   computer + 's = computer's   Jess + 's = Jess's
   anyone's   one's   somebody's

2. To make a plural noun that does not end in s possessive (add **apostrophe** and **s**).

   women + 's = women's   men + 's = men's
   deer + 's = deer's   children + 's = children's

3. To make a plural noun that ends in s possessive. Add only the **apostrophe**.

   boys + ' = boys'   managers + ' = managers'

4. To make a compound noun possessive or to show joint possession. Add **apostrophe** and **s** to the last part of the hyphenated noun.

   son-in-law's   Rob and Gen's game

5. To form the plural of numbers and letters, add **apostrophe** and **s**. To show omission of letters or figures, add an **apostrophe** in place of the missing items.

   7's   A's   It's   add'l

Use a colon

1. To introduce a listing.

   The candidate's strengths were obvious: experience, community involvement, and forthrightness.

2. To introduce an explanatory statement.

   Then I knew we were in trouble: The item had not been scheduled.

Use a comma

1. After an introductory phrase or dependent clause.

   After much deliberation, the jury reached its decision.
   If you have good skills, you will find a job.

2. After words or phrases in a series.

   Mike is taking Greek, Latin III, and Chemistry II.

3. To set off nonessential or interrupting elements.

   Troy, the new man in MIS, will install the hard drive.
   He cannot get to the job, however, until next Friday.

4. To set off the date from the year and the city from the state.

   John, will you please reserve the center in Billings, Montana, for January 10, 2009.

5. To separate two or more parallel adjectives (adjectives could be separated by and instead of a comma).

   The loud, whining guitar could be heard above the rest.

6. Before the conjunction in a compound sentence. The comma may be omitted in a very short sentence.

   You must leave immediately, or you will miss your flight.
   We tested the software and they loved it.

7. Set off appositives and words of direct address.

   Karen, our team leader, represented us at the conference.
   Paul, have you ordered the CD-ROM drive?

Use a hyphen

1. To show end-of-line word division.

2. In many compound words—check a dictionary if unsure.
   - Two-word adjectives before a noun:
     two-car family
   - Compound numbers between twenty-one and ninety-nine.
   - Fractions and some proper nouns with prefixes/suffixes.
     two-thirds   ex-Governor   all-American

Use italic or underline

1. With titles of complete literary works.
   College Keyboarding   *Hunt for Red October*

2. To emphasize special words or phrases.
   What does *professional* mean?

Use a semicolon

1. To separate independent clauses in a compound sentence when the conjunction is omitted.

   Please review the information; give me a report by Tuesday.

2. To separate independent clauses when they are joined by conjunctive adverbs (*however, nevertheless, consequently,* etc.).

   The traffic was heavy; consequently, I was late.

3. To separate a series of elements that contain commas.

   The new officers are: Fran Pena, president; Harry Wong, treasurer; and Muriel Williams, secretary.

Use a dash

1. To show an abrupt change of thought.

   Invoice 76A—which is 10 days overdue—is for $670.

2. After a series to indicate a summarizing statement.

   Noisy fuel pump, worn rods, and failing brakes—for all these reasons I'm trading the car.

Use an exclamation point

After emphatic interjections or exclamatory sentences.

   Terrific!   Hold it!   You bet!   What a great surprise!

Proofreading Procedures

Proofread documents so that they are free of errors. Error-free documents send the message that you are detail-oriented and a person capable of doing business. Apply these procedures after you key a document.

1. Use Spelling and Grammar to check the document.
2. Proofread the document on screen to be sure that it makes sense. Check for these types of errors:
   - Words, headings, and/or amounts omitted.
   - Extra words or lines not deleted during the editing stage.
   - Incorrect sequence of numbers in a list.
3. Preview the document on screen using the Print Preview feature. Check the vertical placement, presence of headers or footers, page numbers, and overall appearance.
4. Save the document again and print.
5. Check the printed document by comparing it to the source copy (textbook). Check all figures, names, and addresses against the source copy. Check that the document style has been applied consistently throughout.
6. If errors exist on the printed copy, revise the document, save, and print.
7. Verify the corrections and placement of the second printed copy.

Proofreaders' Marks

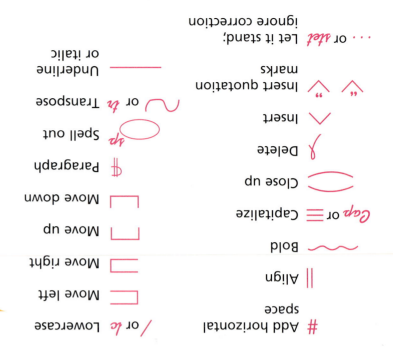

Mark	Meaning
≡ or *Cap*	Capitalize
⌣ (close up)	Close up
✗ (delete)	Delete
∧	Insert
∨∨	Insert quotation marks
⌒ or *tr*	Transpose
sp (circle)	Spell out
¶	Paragraph
⌐ Move down	Move down
⌐ Move up	Move up
⌐ Move right	Move right
⌐ Move left	Move left
/ or *lc*	Lowercase
#	Add horizontal space
‖	Align
～	Bold
—	Underline or italic
... or *stet*	Let it stand; ignore correction

Addressing Procedures

The Envelope feature inserts the delivery address automatically if a letter is displayed. Title case, used in the letter address, is acceptable in the envelope address. An alternative style for envelopes is uppercase with no punctuation.

Business letters are usually mailed in envelopes that have the return address preprinted; return addresses are printed only for personal letters or when letterhead is not available. The default size of *Word* is a size 10 envelope (4 1/8" by 9 1/2"); other sizes are available using the Options feature.

An address must contain at least three lines; addresses of more than six lines should be avoided. The last line of an address must contain three items of information: (1) the city, (2) the state, and (3) the ZIP Code, preferably a 9-digit code. Place mailing notations that affect postage (e.g., REGISTERED, CERTIFIED) below the stamp position (line 8); place other special notations (e.g., CONFIDENTIAL, PERSONAL) a DS below the return address.

IMAGE MAKERS
5131 Moss Springs Rd.
Columbia, SC 29209-4768

REGISTERED

Ms. Amy Vreede
Communications Limited
57 Santa Ynez Street
Santa Ana, CA 92708-1537

Folding and Inserting Procedures

Large envelopes (No. 10, 9, 7¾)

Step 1   Step 2   Step 3

Step 1: With document face up, fold slightly less than 1/3 of sheet up toward top.

Step 2: Fold down top of sheet to within 1/2" of bottom fold.

Step 3: Insert document into envelope with last crease toward bottom of envelope.

Formatting Decisions

Decisions regarding document formats require consideration of four elements: (1) attractiveness of the format, (2) readability of the format, (3) effective use of space on the page, and (4) efficiency in producing the format. Please note several formatting decisions made in this text regarding defaults in *Word 2007*.

Styles

Word 2007 offers a quick gallery of styles on the Home tab, and a gallery of cover pages. Using these styles results in efficient production of an attractive title page.

Default 1.15 Line Spacing

The new default line spacing of 1.15 in *Word 2007* provides readers with a more open and more readable copy.

Space after the Paragraph

The new default space after a paragraph in *Word 2007* is 10 point after the paragraph. This automatic spacing saves time and creates an attractive document.

Remove Space after the Paragraph

While enjoying the benefits of efficiency, it is also necessary to the space that is being consumed. For example, extra spacing between the lines of the letter address requires too much space and is not an attractive layout. Note the formats in this book when the extra space is removed by simply clicking on options of the Line Spacing command.

Margins

The default margins for *Word 2007* are 1" top, bottom, left side, and right side. With *Word 2003*, many people simply used the default side margins of 1.25" for both unbound and leftbound reports. With the new side margin default of 1", additional space is needed for the binding of leftbound reports.

Fonts and Document Themes

Microsoft has provided five new true type fonts in *Office 2007* and a number of new document themes that incorporate color and a variety of fonts depending on the theme selected. Color printing has become increasing popular and more cost effective. Many documents presented in the text are based on the default document theme, *Office*, and uses the default heading font, Cambria, and the default body text font, Calibri, 11 point, black text. See the illustration below of the default headings and fonts.

Title (26 pt., Cambria, Bold, Color Text 2)

Subtitle (12 pt., Cambria, Italic, Color Accent 1)

Heading 1 (14 pt., Cambria, Bold, Color Accent 1)

Heading 2 (13 pt., Cambria, Bold, Color Accent 1)

Heading 3 (11 pt., Cambria, Bold, Color Accent 1)

Heading 4 (11 pt., Cambria, Bold, Italic, Color Accent 1)

The default body text is Calibri, 11 pt. color Black.

Default Document Theme: Office:  Office

Letter Placement

Length	Dateline position	Margins
Short: 1–2 ¶s	Center page	Default
Average: 3–4 ¶s	Center page or 2"	Default
Long: 4+ ¶s	2" (default + 3 hard returns)	Default

Block Letter (Open Punctuation)

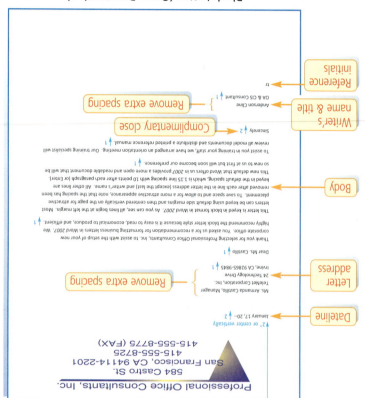

Modified Block Letter (Mixed Punctuation)

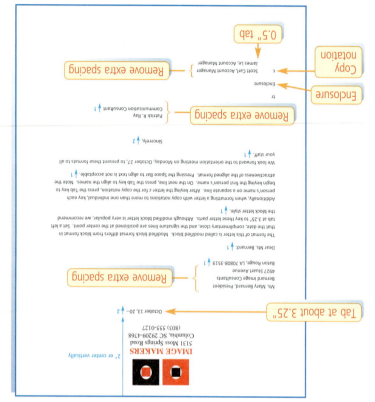

Letter Parts

Letterhead. Company name and address. May include other data.

Date. Date letter is mailed. Usually in month, day, year order. Military style is an option (day/month/year): 17/1/09).

Letter address. Address of the person who will receive the letter. Include personal title (*Mr.*, *Ms.*, *Dr.*); name; professional title, company, and address. In *Word 2007* remove the extra spacing in the letter address.

Salutation. Greeting. Corresponds to the first line of the letter address. Usually includes name and courtesy title; use *Ladies and Gentlemen* if letter is addressed to a company name.

Body. Message. Key in default 1.15 line spacing; tap ENTER once between paragraphs.

Complimentary close. Farewell, such as *Sincerely*.

Writer. Name and professional title. If the name and title are keyed on two lines, remove the extra spacing between the lines.

Initials. Identifies person who keyed the document (for example, *tr*). May include identification of writer (*ARB:tri*).

Enclosure. Copy is enclosed with the document. May specify contents. If more than one line is used, align at 1" and remove the extra spacing between the lines.

Copy notation. Indicates that a copy of the letter is being sent to person name. If more than one line is used, align at 0.5" and remove the extra spacing between the lines.

Note: To remove extra spacing between lines, click the down arrow on the Line Spacing command and select Remove Space After Paragraph.

Personal Business Letter

Janna M. Howard
587 Birch Circle
Clinton, MS 39056-0587
601-555-0001
Jhoward@cu.edu

Current date

The return address may be keyed immediately above the date, or you may create a personal letterhead as shown here.

Mrs. Linda Chandler
Financial News
32 North Critz Street
Hot Springs, AR 71913-0032

Dear Mrs. Chandler

My college degree in information technology services and my graphics design job experience in the United States and Taiwan qualify me to function well as a junior graphic designer for your newspaper.

As a result of my comprehensive four-year program, I am skilled in the most up-to-date office suite packages as well as the latest version of desktop publishing and graphics programs. In addition, I am very skilled at locating needed resources on the information highway. In fact, these skills played a very important role in the design award that I received this month.

My technical and communication skills were applied as I worked as the assistant editor and producer of the Colter Alumni News. I understand well the importance of meeting deadlines and also in producing a quality product that will increase newspaper sales.

After you have reviewed the enclosed resume, I would look forward to discussing my qualifications and career opportunities with you at *Financial News.*

Sincerely

Janna M. Howard

Enclosure

Personal Business Letter

Resume

Janna M. Howard

587 Birch Circle
Clinton, MS 39056-0587
601-555-0101

CAREER OBJECTIVE	To obtain a graphic design position with an opportunity to advance to a management position.
EDUCATION	**B.S. Information Technology Services**, Colter University, Clinton, Mississippi. May 2008. Grade point average: 3.8/4.0. Served as president of Graphic Designers' Society
SPECIAL SKILLS	Environments: Microsoft Windows and Macintosh Application software: Microsoft Office Professional, InDesign, Harvard Graphics, Fireworks, DreamWeaver Keyboarding skill: 70 words per minute Foreign language: Chinese Travel: Taiwan (two summers working as graphic design intern)
EXPERIENCE	**Colter University Alumni Office**. Clinton, Mississippi. Assistant editor and producer of the *Colter Alumni News*, 2006 to present. • Work 25 hours per week. • Design layout and production of six editions. • Meet every publishing deadline. • Received the "Colter Design Award." **Colter University Library**, Clinton, Mississippi. Student Assistant in Audiovisual Library, 2007-2008. • Worked 20 hours per week. • Created Audiovisual Catalog on computerized database. • Processed orders via computer. • Prepared monthly and yearly reports using database. • Edited and proofed various publications.
REFERENCES	Request portfolio from Colter University Placement Office

Resume

Standard Memo

2"

Tab (1" from left margin)

TO: Executive Committee ↓1

FROM: Colleen Marshall ↓1

DATE: November 8, 20-- ↓1

SUBJECT: Site Selection ↓1

Please be prepared to make a final decision on the site for next year's Leadership Training Conference. Our staff reviewed the students' suggestions and have added a few of their own. The following information may be helpful as you make your decision. ↓1

1. New York and San Francisco have been eliminated from consideration because of cost factors.
2. New Orleans is now open for consideration. New Orleans has tremendous appeal to students.
3. Charleston, San Antonio, and Tampa were suggested by students as very desirable locations for the conference. ↓1

Site selection will be the first item of business at our meeting next Wednesday. I am attaching various hotel brochures for each site. ↓1

xx ↓1

Attachments

Standard Memo

Standard Memo with Distribution List

2"

Tab (1" from left margin)

TO: Team Leaders ↓1

FROM: Form Paragraph Task Force ↓1

DATE: November 9, 20-- ↓1

SUBJECT: Initial Meetings with Task Force ↓1

The task force assigned the responsibility for developing form paragraphs to use in key departments of our company plans to work in your department beginning two weeks from today. Please assign two representatives from your department to coordinate the work with us. ↓1

The procedure that the Executive Committee asked us to follow is to collect samples of typical correspondence, meet with departmental representatives to collect additional information, and then to prepare a draft of the form paragraphs for review. After we receive your feedback on the draft copy, we will schedule a meeting to finalize the paragraphs. ↓1

Mathew Redfern has been assigned as the task force coordinator for your department. Please direct all communication about the project to him. ↓1

xx ↓1

Distribution List
Nestor Garcia, Claims
Roberta Layman, Underwriting
Rosa Romero, Agency Services
Diana Wang, Business Services

Remove extra spacing

Standard Memo with Distribution List

Standard Unbound Report

Margins: Tap ENTER three times to begin first page of report and reference page at 2"; default 1" for succeeding pages; *Side* 1"; *Bottom* 1".

Spacing: Default 1.15 line spacing; paragraphs blocked. Tap ENTER once between paragraphs.

Page numbers: Second and subsequent pages are numbered at top right of the page. One blank line follows the page number.

Titles: Title style. Main words capitalized.

Side headings: Heading 1 style. Main words capitalized.

Report Documentation

Internal citations: Provides source of information within report. Includes the author's surname, publication date, and page number (Bruce, 2008, 129).

Footnotes: References cited in a report are often indicated within the text by a superscript number (. . . story.[1]) and a corresponding footnote with full information at the bottom of the same page where the reference was cited.

Bibliography or references: Lists all references, whether quoted or not, in alphabetical order by authors' names. References may be formatted on the last page of the report if they all fit on the page; if not, list on a separate, numbered page.

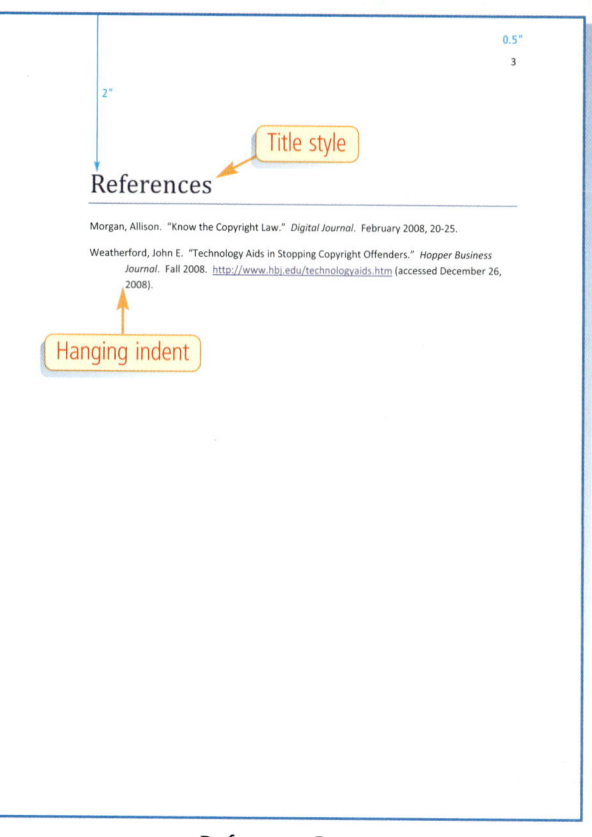

Reference Page

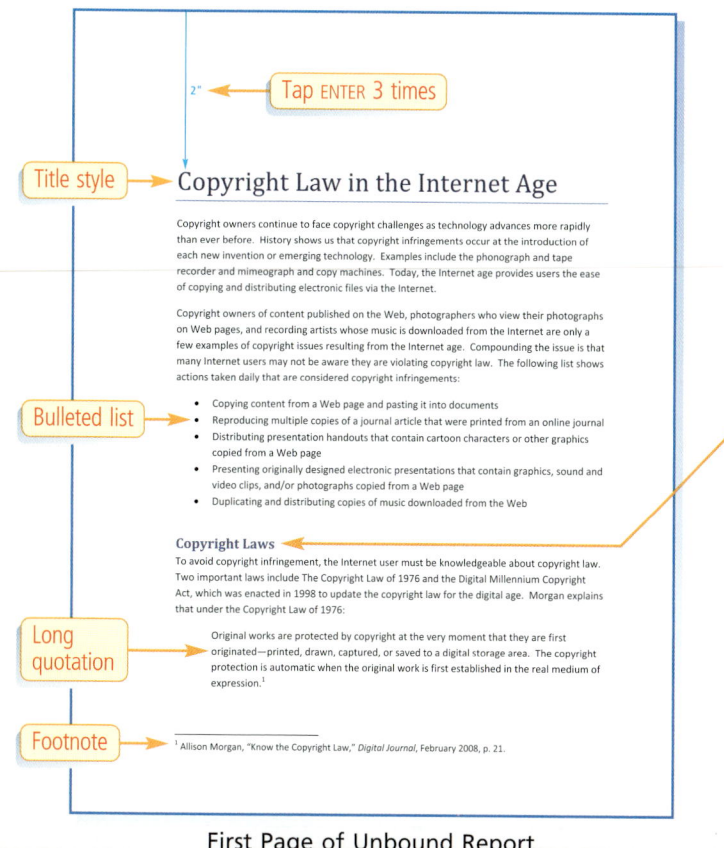

First Page of Unbound Report

Second Page of Unbound Report

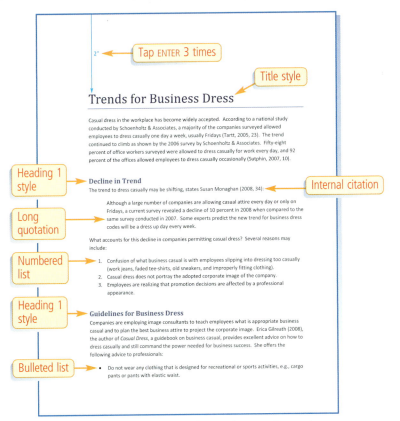

Tap ENTER 3 times

2"

Title style

Trends for Business Dress

Casual dress in the workplace has become widely accepted. According to a national study conducted by Schoenholtz & Associates, a majority of the companies surveyed allowed employees to dress casually one day a week, usually Fridays (Tartt, 2005, 23). The trend continued to climb as shown by the 2006 survey by Schoenholtz & Associates. Fifty-eight percent of office workers surveyed were allowed to dress casually for work every day, and 92 percent of the offices allowed employees to dress casually occasionally (Sutphin, 2007, 10).

Heading 1 style

Decline in Trend
The trend to dress casually may be shifting, states Susan Monaghan (2008, 34):

Internal citation

Long quotation

Although a large number of companies are allowing casual attire every day or only on Fridays, a current survey revealed a decline of 10 percent in 2008 when compared to the same survey conducted in 2007. Some experts predict the new trend for business dress codes will be a dress up day every week.

What accounts for this decline in companies permitting casual dress? Several reasons may include:

Numbered list

1. Confusion of what business casual is with employees slipping into dressing too casually (work jeans, faded tee-shirts, old sneakers, and improperly fitting clothing).
2. Casual dress does not portray the adopted corporate image of the company.
3. Employees are realizing that promotion decisions are affected by a professional appearance.

Heading 1 style

Guidelines for Business Dress
Companies are employing image consultants to teach employees what is appropriate business casual and to plan the best business attire to project the corporate image. Erica Gilreath (2008), the author of *Casual Dress*, a guidebook on business casual, provides excellent advice on how to dress casually and still command the power needed for business success. She offers the following advice to professionals:

Bulleted list

- Do not wear any clothing that is designed for recreational or sports activities, e.g., cargo pants or pants with elastic waist.

Leftbound Report with Styles and Long Quotation

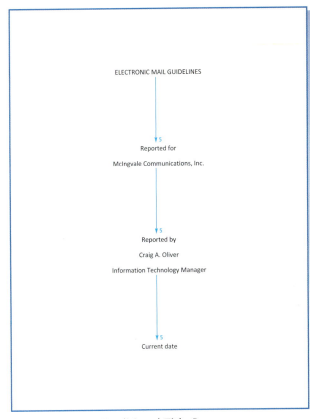

ELECTRONIC MAIL GUIDELINES

↓ 5

Reported for

McIngvale Communications, Inc.

↓ 5

Reported by

Craig A. Oliver

Information Technology Manager

↓ 5

Current date

Traditional Title Page

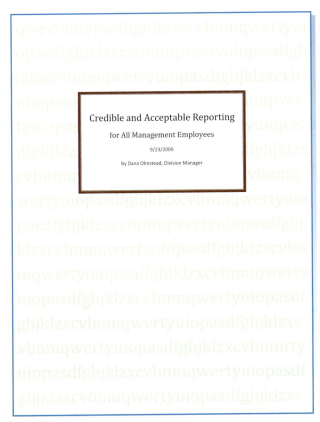

Credible and Acceptable Reporting

for All Management Employees

9/23/2009

by Dana Olmstead, Division Manager

Title Page Using Cover Feature

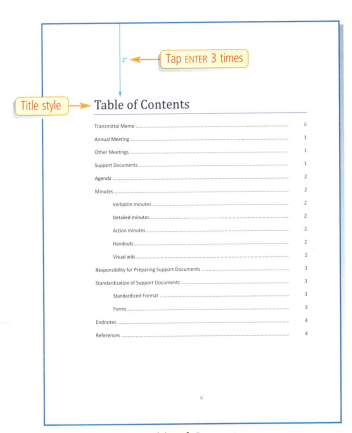

Tap ENTER 3 times

2"

Title style

Table of Contents

ii

Table of Contents

SUMMARY OF COMMANDS

Lesson	Function	Path
Module 3 Word Processing Basics		
26	Text Formats: Font, Font Size, Grow Font, Shrink Font, Bold, Italic, Underline, Text Highlight Color, and Font Color	Home/Font/Click desired text format command
	Save and Save As	Office Button/Save or Save As
	Close Document	Office Button/Close or Close button at top right of screen
	Open New Document, Open Existing Document	Office Button/New or Open; then locate the file
	Quick Print, Print, and Print Preview	Office Button/Print/Print Preview, Print, or Quick Print
	Exit Word	Office button/Exit Word
27	Paragraph Formats	Home/Paragraph/Click desired command
	Paragraph Formats: Show/Hide	Home/Paragraph/Show/Hide
	Paragraph Formats: Alignment—Align Text Left, Center, Align Text Right, and Justify	Home/Paragraph/Click desired alignment
	Bullets and Numbering	Home/Paragraph/Bullets or Numbering
	Line Spacing	Home/Paragraph/Line spacing
	Remove Space After Paragraph	Home/Paragraph/Line spacing
	Clipboard Group: Cut, Copy, and Paste	Home/Clipboard/Click Cut, Copy, or Paste
	Clipboard Group: Format Painter	Home/Clipboard/Format Painter
	Quick Access Toolbar	Upper-left corner of screen/Use down arrow to customize
	Mini Toolbar	Appears when text is selected

Lesson	Function	Path	
28	Date and Time	Insert/Text/Date and Time	Date & Time
	Margins	Page Layout/Page Setup/Margins	Margins
	Indent	Page Layout/Paragraph/Indent	Indent Left: 0.5" Right: 0.5"
	View Ruler	Click View Ruler button	View Ruler
	Tabs	View Ruler/Tab Alignment Button/ Click on Horizontal Ruler	
29	Views	Select view buttons on status bar	
	Slider: Zoom in or out	Click Slider/move left or right to zoom in or out	100%
	Spelling and Grammar	Review/Proofing/Spelling & Grammar	ABC Spelling & Grammar
	Help	Click Help button	

Module 4 Business Correspondence

Lesson	Function	Path	
31	View Ruler	Click View Ruler button	View Ruler
	Vertical Page Position	Right-click status bar/Vertical Page Position	Page: 1 of 1 At: 2"
	Remove Space After Paragraph	Home/Paragraph/Line Spacing/Remove Space After Paragraph	Line Spacing Options... Remove Space Before Paragraph Remove Space After Paragraph
32	Automatic Current Date	Key 4 characters/Enter	January (Press ENTER to Insert) Janu
	Center Page	Page Layout/Page Setup/Dialog Box Launcher/Layout tab/Vertical Alignment/Center	Page Vertical alignment: Center
33	Envelopes	Mailings/Create/Envelopes	Envelopes Labels Create
35	Normal Style (default)	Home/Styles/Normal	AaBbCcDd ¶ Normal
	Change Styles	Home/Styles/Change Styles	Change Styles

Lesson	Function	Path	
Module 5 Simple Reports			
38	Styles	Home/Styles/Quick Styles	
39	Bullets and Numbering*	Home/Paragraph/Bullets or Numbering	
	Cover Page	Insert/Pages/Cover Page	
40	Page Numbers	Insert/Header & Footer/Page Number	
	Remove Page Number on First Page	Design/Options/Different First Page	
	Line and Page Breaks	Home/Paragraph/Dialog Box Launcher/Line and Page Breaks tab	
	Insert File	Insert/Text/Object/Text from File	
41	Margins*	Page Layout/Page Setup/Margins	
	Increase Indent*	Home/Paragraph/Increase Indent	
42	Hanging Indent	Ruler/Indent Markers	
	Page Break	Insert/Pages/Page Break	
43	Footnotes	References/Footnotes/Insert Footnote	
Module 6 Create Tables			
46	Insert Table	Insert/Tables/Table	
	Table Tools	Insert/Tables/Table; click in Table/Table Tools	
	Select Portions of Table	Click in table/Table Tools/Layout/Select	

*Functions introduced earlier but taught in more depth.

Lesson	Function	Path
47	Adjust Column Width	Ruler/Column Marker/Drag to appropriate position
	Center Table Horizontally	Click in table/Layout/Table/ Properties/Center Alignment
	Table Styles	Click in table/Table Tools/Design
48	Change Table Structure	Click in table/Table Tools/Layout/Insert or delete rows or columns
	Merge and Split Cells	Click in or select cells/Table Tools/Layout/Merge or Split Cells
49	Shading in Tables	Select cells/Table Tools/Design/Shading/Theme Colors
	Change Row Height and Center Text	Click in cell/Table Tools/Layout/Cell Size/Alignment
	Remove Table Borders	Select table/TableTools/Design/Borders/No Border
	Decimal Tab in Table	Select Column/Click Tab Alignment/Decimal Tab/Click appropriate position on Ruler

Module 7 Edit Business Documents

Lesson	Function	Path
52	Symbols	Insert/Symbols/Symbol/More Symbols/Symbol
	Special Characters	Insert/Symbols/Symbol/More Symbols/Special Characters
	Clipboard	Home/Clipboard
	Paste Options Button	Home/Clipboard/Paste/Paste Options Button
	Find and Replace	Home/Editing/Find or Replace
	Customize Quick Access Toolbar	Quick Access Toolbar/Click down arrow/Click each command to be added
	Thesaurus	Review/Proofing/Thesaurus

Lesson	Function	Path	
	Module 8 Graphic Essentials		
58	Clip Art	Insert/Illustrations/Clip Art	
	Size Clip Art	Select Lower-Right or Lower-Left Handle/Drag to appropriate size	
	Move Clip Art	Picture Tools/Format/Arrange/Text Wrapping	
	Paragraph Borders and Shading	Select paragraph/Page Layout/ Page Background/Page Borders/ Borders and Shading/Borders	
	Page Borders	Page Layout/Page Background/Page Borders	
	Shapes	Insert/Illustrations/Shapes	
59	Create Columns	Page Layout/Page Setup/Columns	
	Wrap Text Around Graphic	Select graphic/Format/Arrange/Text Wrapping	
	Line Between Columns	Page Layout/Page Setup/Columns/More Columns/Line Between	

INDEX